Joel Tyler Headley

Napoleon and his Marshals

Joel Tyler Headley
Napoleon and his Marshals
ISBN/EAN: 9783743340688
Manufactured in Europe, USA, Canada, Australia, Japa
Cover: Foto ©ninafisch / pixelio.de

Manufactured and distributed by brebook publishing software (www.brebook.com)

Joel Tyler Headley

Napoleon and his Marshals

NAPOLEON

AND HIS MARSHALS

BY

J. T. HEADLEY

EMBELLISHED WITH NUMEROUS STEEL PLATE ENGRAVINGS

VOLUME I

NEW YORK
CHARLES SCRIBNER'S SONS
1888

PREFACE

For years the character and results of the great struggle of France just before and during Bonaparte's career, were wholly misconstrued by us. In the days of the old Federal party, the Federalists, still clinging in affection to the mother country, took sides with her against France, while the Jeffersonians sympathized with the latter. Bonaparte became strongly mixed up in our politics, and that, too, at a time when political animosities ran higher than they ever have since. New England was Federal, and at that time being the centre of learning and intelligence, gave tone and character to our literature. But, sharing all the hatred of England against France, and that animosity intensified by political hostility to the Jeffersonians, who hated England, the Federals filled our literature with the gross falsehoods which disgraced England, and render her records at that period utterly worthless. France was infidel, and Bonaparte an ambitious tyrant, a second Alexander, determined to conquer the world—these were established facts in the New England creed, and were rung in endless changes over the country. Some of the best and purest men of that section, accepting English history as true, wrote and spoke respecting Bonaparte and the wars in which France was engaged, with an ignorance that to-day fills us with astonishment. According to them, France was a nation without one redeeming quality, and Bonaparte guilty of every crime man is capable of committing, except cannibalism.

But the time came when the literature of this country began to shake itself clear of English trammels, and then the true character of that long and fearful struggle was revealed. The wild up-heaving of the French Revolution was seen to be the result of *our own struggle* for independence, and the succeeding wars arose from democracy throwing down the gauntlet to despotism. The sanctimonious pretence of England that she was fighting for human liberty, and to help put down the conqueror of the world, is now stamped a falsehood by every enlightened man. She, with the other Continental powers, was fighting solely to prevent the spread of our republican principles. To see marshals, dukes, and kings made out of common soldiers, offended their pride, and awoke all their hostility. Their efforts arrested, but did not extinguish this republican sentiment, and one has only to contemplate Europe before the advent of Napoleon and now, to see the wondrous change he has wrought. Let the same relative progress be made for sixty years to come, and there will hardly be a crowned head left in Europe. Such a struggle, led on by men taken from the lower classes, and mounting to power by the force of genius alone, must ever be interesting to Americans. To see kings and lords and nobles of every degree go down before men who rose from the ranks, might well astonish the world.

It has been my design, in the following work, not only to give the true character of Napoleon, and the wars he waged, but to illustrate the men who led his armies to victory—forming, as they do, a group the like of which the world has never seen. Their battles revolutionized the whole art of war, and form a gallery of pictures that has no equal in the history of any nation. Many of these renowned battle-fields I have gone over in person, and hence been able to give more accurate descriptions than I otherwise could. These will never lose their interest while great deeds are admired and true heroes honored. Napoleon's marshals can appropriately be placed side by side with our own great generals of the present war.

The portraits are copies of those in the national galleries of France, and hence must be considered accurate likenesses

CONTENTS OF VOL. I.

I.
NAPOLEON BONAPARTE.
A Defence of him against English historians—Analysis of his character—Causes of his success—His Death 11

II.
MARSHAL BERTHIER.
DUKE OF NEUFCHATEL. PRINCE OF WAGRAM.
The talents a Revolution develops—Creation of the Marshals—Berthier's character and history—Soliloquy of Napoleon—Berthier's Death 75

III.
MARSHAL AUGEREAU.
DUKE OF CASTIGLIONE.
His early Life and Character—His campaigns in Italy—Battle of Castiglione—Battle of Arcola—Revolution of the 18th Fructidor—Charge at Eylau—His traitorous conduct and disgrace 94

IV.
MARSHAL DAVOUST.
DUKE OF AUERSTADT. PRINCE OF ECKMUHL.
His Character—Battle of Auerstadt—Cavalry action at Eckmuhl—Retreat from Russia 122

V.
MARSHAL ST. CYR.
His Life—Character—Profession of a Painter—Combat at Biberach—Battle of Polotsk—Battle of Dresden 151

VI.
MARSHAL LANNES.
DUKE OF MONTEBELLO.

Principle on which Bonaparte chose his officers—Passage of Lodi—Battle of Montebello—Battle of Marengo—Siege of Saragossa—Battle of Aspern, and death of Lannes 184

VII.
MARSHAL MONCEY.
DUKE OF CORNEGLIANO.

His early life—Operations in Spain—The presentation by Napoleon of his son to him and the National Guard—His noble efforts in behalf of Ney—Reception of Napoleon's body when brought from St. Helena 228

VIII.
MARSHAL MACDONALD.
DUKE OF TARENTUM.

His early life—Quarrel with Napoleon—His passage of the Splugen—Charge at Wagram—Defence at Leipsic—His Character . . . 242

IX.
MARSHAL MORTIER.
DUKE OF TREVISO.

His early life—Character—Battle of Dirnstein—Burning of Moscow—Blowing up of the Kremlin—His bravery at Krasnoi 276

X.
MARSHAL SOULT.
DUKE OF DALMATIA.

His early career—Campaigns with Massena—His character—Battle of Austerlitz—His first Campaign in Spain—Death of Sir John Moore Storming of Oporto—Retreat from Portugal—Battle of Albuera—Second Campaign in Spain—Siege of St. Sebastiani—Soult's last struggle for the Empire 300

LIST OF ILLUSTRATIONS

		PAGE
I.	Napoleon as a General,	1
II.	Napoleon as Emperor,	17
III.	Marshal Davoust,	122
IV.	Marshal Lannes,	185
V.	Marshal Macdonald,	242
VI.	Marshal Soult,	300

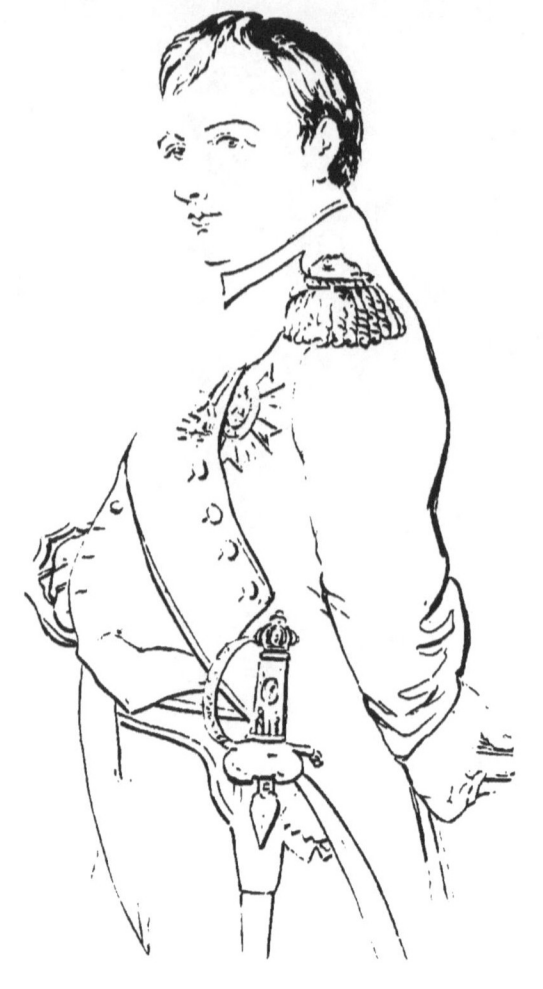

NAPOLEON BONAPARTE.

A Defence of him against English Historians—Analysis of his Character—Causes of his Success—His Death.

PERHAPS there is no greater example of the control English literature and English criticism exert over public opinion in this country, than the views they have impressed upon it respecting Bonaparte. With Wordsworth, Southey, and Byron, in poetry, and Scott, and Alison, and the English Reviews, in prose, all making him a monster in cruelty and selfishness, even though he might be an angel in genius; we have, without scruple, adopted the same sentiments, and set him down as a scourge of his race.

The few American writers that have ever attempted to give an analysis of his character, and a fair criticism on his actions, have failed, by judging him as if he had grown up on the Puritan soil of New England, instead of amid the chaos and anarchy of France, and the exciting sounds of war as Europe moved to battle. Their criticisms have in reality usually been mere essays on the horrors of war, in which Bonaparte figures as the chief illustration. There is no recognition of the peculiar trials that surrounded him, of the genius that mastered them, of the temptations to which he was exposed, and the necessity that frequently compelled him to courses that warred with his wishes.

English historians make no scruple of belying him; and while some of our American writers, by placing on him the guilt of those desolating wars that loaded Europe with the dead, have done him gross injustice; they have also committed an unpardonable error in history. That English historians should attempt to cover their most successful enemy with unmerited guilt, especially when it is necessary to do so, in order to screen their own nation against the accusations which France lays at her door, is to be expected. Still Scott has done himself more injury in his Life of Napoleon than he has the great man he slandered; and Mr. Mitchell, who has lately written three volumes to convince men that Napoleon was a fool, has succeeded only in proving himself one. Mr. Alison is almost the only one who has at all comprehended his true character; but, while he is forced to bear noble testimony to his genius, he is afraid of offending the prejudices and vanity of his countrymen, and so attempts, as an offset to his praise, to prove him destitute of conscience, and capable of great meannesses. To do this, he not only falsifies history, but drags forth, with the most ludicrous gravity, all the petulent speeches he ever made in sudden ebullitions of passion, or in the first chagrin of disappointment. The unjust and passionate remarks a man of Napoleon's temperament, however noble his character, will-always make in moments of irritation, are arrayed against his greatest acts with studied exaggeration, and declared sufficient to neutralize them all. This is like going into a man's bed-chamber to report his unguarded speeches, or making a peevish remark to a servant in a moment of irritability, offset the noblest acts of his life.

Napoleon Bonaparte, whether we think of his amazing genius—his unparalleled power of embracing vast combinations, while he lost sight of none of the details necessary to insure success—his rapidity of thought, and equally sudden execution—his tireless energy—his ceaseless activity—his ability to direct the movements of half a million of soldiers in different parts of the world, and at the same time reform the laws—restore the finances—and administer the government of his country; or whether we trace his dazzling career from the time he was a poor proud charity boy at the Military School of Brienne, to the hour when he sat down on the most brilliant throne of Europe, he is the same wonderful man—the same grand theme for human contemplation.

But before entering on his character, it is necessary that whatever unjust prejudices we entertain should be removed, and our errors in history corrected. The first great barrier in the way of rendering him justice, is the conviction every where entertained, that he alone, or chiefly, is chargeable with those desolating wars that covered the Continent with slain armies. His mounting ambition is placed at the foundation of them all, and no greatness of mind can of course compensate for the guilt of such wholesale murder.

It is impossible for one who has not travelled amid the monarchies of Europe, and witnessed their nervous fear of republican principles, and their fixed determination at whatever sacrifice of justice, human rights, and human life, to maintain their oppressive forms of government, to appreciate at all the position of France at the time of the revolution. The balance of political power had been the great object of anxiety, and all the watchfulness directed against the encroachment of one state on another; and no one can imagine the utter consternation with which Europe saw a mighty republic suddenly rise in her midst. The balance of power was forgotten in the anxiety for self-preservation. The sound of the falling throne of the Bourbons rolled like a sudden earthquake under the iron and century-bound frame-work of despotism, till every thing heaved and rocked on its ancient foundations. Our Declaration of Independence, the everlasting and immutable principles of human rights, were uttered in the ears of the astonished world, and unless that voice could be hushed, that alarming movement checked, every monarchy of Europe would soon have a revolution of its own to struggle with. That the revolution of France was justifiable, if a revolution is ever so, no one acquainted with the history of that time can for a moment doubt. The violence that marked its progress shows only, as Macauley says, the greater need of it. At all events, France, confused, chaotic, bleeding, and affrighted, stood up and declared herself, in the face of the world, a republic. She made no encroachments on other states, sought no war, for she needed all her strength and energy, to save herself from internal foes. But the powers of Europe determined to crush her at once before she had acquired strength and consistency. First, Austria and Prussia took up arms, with the avowed purpose of aiding Louis. After his death, Holland, Spain, and England came into the alliance, and moved down on that bewildered republic. Here was the commencement and origin of all the after wars that devastated Europe. Not on France, but on the allied powers, rests the guilt of setting in motion that terrible train of evils which they would fain transfer to other shoulders. It was a war of principle and a war of aggression. It was despotism invading liberty—oppression summoning human rights to lay down its arms, and because it would not, banding the world together to crush the republic that nourished them. Bonaparte was yet a boy when this infamous war was strewing the banks of the Rhine with slain armies.

After struggling bravely for years for self-defence, France at length found her saviour in the young Corsican. Quelling the revolt of the sections in Paris, he was appointed to the command of the army of Italy. He found it badly provisioned, worse paid, ragged and murmuring, yet, by his energy, skill and, more than all, by his example, restored order and confidence; and, though numbering less than forty thousand men, replenished, as it wasted away, by slender reinforcements, he with it attacked and cut to pieces several armies, the most magnificent Austria could furnish, finishing one of the most brilliant campaigns the world has ever witnessed, amid the tumultuous joy of the French. The next year he subjugated Lombardy, and forced the Austrian plenipotentiary, by his daring threats, to sign the treaty of Campo Furmio, which was most favourable to the French Republic. In the bloody battles of Millessimo, Montenotte, Lodi, Arcola, and Castiglione, and Rivoli, he certainly acted as became a general fighting under the orders of his government, carrying on a defensive war with a boldness, skill, and success, considering the superiority of the force opposed to him, deserving of the highest praise.

Returning to Paris in triumph, hailed everywhere as the saviour of France, he notwithstanding became tired of his inactive life, and still more weary of the miserable Directory to whose folly he was compelled to submit, and proposed the expedition to Egypt. This furnishes another charge against Bonaparte, and this war is denounced as aggressive and cruel, growing out of a mad ambition. That it was unjust, no one can deny; but instead of being a thing worthy of censure by the cabinets of Europe, it was simply carrying out their own systems of policy. His designs on the East, were just such as England had for years been prosecuting. The East was always to Bonaparte the scene of great enterprises, and Egypt furnished a basis to his operations, and at the same time, would serve as a check to English encroachment in the Indies.

While Russia, Austria, and Prussia, were stripping Poland; and England was extending her conquests in the Indies—cumbering its burning plains with tens of thousands of its own children, and carrying out the most iniquitous system of oppression towards Ireland ever tolerated by a civilized people—it does seem ludicrous to hear her historians complimenting the Deity on his even-handed justice, in finally arresting the cruel ambition of Bonaparte and of France.

While the expedition to Egypt was experiencing the vicissitudes that characterized it, Austria, seeing that France had got the Lion's share in Italy; joined with Naples, and again commenced hostilities. The French were driven back across the Apennines, and all the advantages gained there over Austria, were being lost, when Bonaparte returned in haste from Egypt—overthrew the imbecile Directory—was proclaimed First Consul—and immediately set about the restoration of France. The consolidation of the government—the restoration of the disordered finances—the pacification of La Vendée—the formation and adoption of a constitution, engrossed his mind, and he most ardently desired peace. He, therefore, the moment he was elected First Consul, wrote with his own hands, two letters; one to the king of England, and the other to the Emperor of Germany; hoping by this frank and friendly course to appease the two governments, and bring about a general peace. He had acquired sufficient glory as a military leader, and he now wished to resuscitate France, and become great as a civil ruler. In his letter to England, he uses the following language:—"Must the war, Sire, which for the last eight years has devastated the four quarters of the world, be eternal? Are there no means of coming to an understanding? How can two of the most enlightened nations of Europe, stronger already and more powerful than their safety or their independence requires, sacrifice to ideas of vain-glory, the well-being of commerce internal prosperity, and the peace of families? How is it they do not feel peace to be the first of necessities as the first of glories?" Similar noble, frank, and manly sentiments, he addressed to the Emperor of Germany. There were no accusations in these letters, no recriminations, and no demands. They asked simply for negotiations to commence, for the *spirit* of peace to be exhibited, leaving it to after efforts to settle the terms. Austria was inclined to listen to this appeal from the First Consul, and replied courteously to his letter. But she was trammeled by her alliance with England, and refused to enter into negotiations in which the British Empire was not represented. Pitt, on the contrary, returned an insulting letter to the French minister—heaped every accusation on Bonaparte—recapitulated individual acts of violence, and laid them at the door of the French Republic, and charged it with designing to overthrow both religion and monarchy throughout the continent. He declared that the English government must see some fruits of repentance and amendment, before it could trust the proffers of peace; and that the restoration of the Bourbon throne, was the only guarantee she should deem sufficient of the good behaviour of the French government. Bonaparte, in reply, fixed the first aggressive acts clearly on the enemies of France, and then asked what was the use of these irritating reminiscences—if the war was to be eternal, because one or the other party had been the aggressor; and then adverting to the proposal that the Bourbons should be restored, asked, "What would be thought of France, if, in her propositions, she insisted on the restoration of the dethroned Stuarts, before she would make peace?" This home-thrust disconcerted the English Minister; and in reply, he frankly acknowledged that his government did not wage war for the re-establishment of the Bourbon throne, but for the security of all governments, and that she would listen to no terms of peace until this security was obtained. This settled the question. England would have no peace while France continued to be a republic. Bonaparte had foreseen all this, and finding he could not separate Austria from her English alliance, immediately set on foot immense preparations for war. Moreau was sent with a magnificent army into Swabia, to drive back the Austrians towards their capital; Massena was appointed over the miserably provided army of Italy, while he himself fell from the heights of San Bernard, on the plains of Lombardy.

At the fierce fought battle of Marengo, he reconquered Italy, while Moreau chased the vanquished Austrians over the Danube. Victory every where perched on the French standards, and Austria was ready to agree to an armistice, in order to recover from the disasters she had suffered. The slain at Montibello, around Genoa, on the plains of Marengo, in the Black Forest, and along the Danube, are to be charged over to the British government, which refused peace in order to fight for the philanthropic purpose of giving security to governments.

Austria, though crippled, let the armistice wear away, refusing to make a treaty because she was bound for seven months longer to England. Bonaparte, in the meantime, was preparing to recommence hostilities. Finding himself unable to conclude a peace, he opened the campaign of Hohenlinden, and sent Macdonald across the Splugen. Moreau's victorious march through Austria, and the success of the operations in Italy, soon brought Austria to terms, and the celebrated peace of Luneville, of 1801, was signed.

The energy and ability, and above all, the success of the First Consul, had now forced the continental powers to regard him with respect, and in some cases with sympathy; while England, by her imperious demands, had embroiled herself with all the northern powers of Europe.

But this universal and wasting war begun at length to be tiresome to all parties, and after much negotiation and delay, a general peace was concluded at Amiens, and the world was at rest. Universal joy was spread through France and England, and the transports of the people knew no bounds.

Peace, which Bonaparte needed and wished for, being restored, he applied his vast energies to the development of the resources of France, and to the building of stupendous public works. Commerce was revived—the laws administered with energy—order restored, and the blessings of peace were fast healing up the wounds of war. Men were amazed at the untiring energy, and the amazing plans of Bonaparte. His genius gave a new birth to the nation—developed new elements of strength, and imparted an impulse to her growth that threatened to outstrip the greatness of England. His ambition was to obtain colonial possessions, like those of England; and if allowed to direct his vast energies in that direction, there was no doubt France would soon rival the British Empire in its provinces. England was at first fearful of the influence of the French Republic, but now a new cause of alarm seized her. It was evident that France was fast tending towards a monarchy. Bonaparte had been made First Consul for life, with the power to appoint his successor; and it required no seer to predict that his gigantic mind and dictatorial spirit, would not long brook any check from inferior authority. From the very superiority of his intellect, he must merge every thing into his majestic plans, and gradually acquire more and more control, till the placing of a crown on his head would be only the symbol of that supreme power which had long before passed into his hands. England, therefore, had no longer to fear the influence of a Republic, and hence fight for the security of government in general. She had, however, another cause of anxiety—the too rapid growth of her ancient rival. She became alarmed at the strides with which France advanced under the guiding genius of Napoleon, and refused to carry out the terms of the solemn treaty she had herself signed. In that treaty it was expressly stipulated that England should evacuate Egypt and Malta; while France, on her part, was to evacuate Naples, Tarento, and the Roman States. His part of the treaty, Napoleon had fulfilled within two months after its completion; but ten months had now elapsed, and the English were still in Alexandria and Malta. But Napoleon, anxious to preserve peace, did not see fit to urge matters, and made no complaint till it was suddenly announced that the English government had proclaimed her determination not to fulfil the stipulations she had herself made. The only pretext offered for this violation of a solemn contract, was her suspicions that France had designs on these places The truth was, England—with her accustomed jealousy of other nations acquiring colonial possessions, and remembering what a struggle it had just cost her to wrest Egypt and Malta from France—resolved, though in violation of her own treaty, not to give them up. Talleyrand was perfectly amazed at this decision of the British ministry, while Napoleon was thrown into a transport of rage. His keen penetration discerned at a glance the policy of England, and the dreadful conflict that must ensue. He saw that she was resolved to resist the advancement of France, and to band, while she could, the powers of Europe against her. He knew that if she would remain at peace, he could by force of arms, and diplomatic skill, compel Russia, Austria, Prussia, and Spain, to let him alone to carry out his plans for the aggrandizement of France. But with England constantly counteracting him, and throwing fire-brands in the cabinets of the Continent, he would be engaged in perpetual conflicts and wranglings. It had, therefore, come to this: England must be chastised into quietness and respect for treaties, or there was to be continual war till France should yield to the strength of superior numbers. England knew that in a protracted war France must fall; for her very victories would in the end melt away her armies, before the endless thousands all Europe could pour upon her; and this she determined to accomplish. But war at this time was the last thing Napoleon wished—it interfered with his plans, and cut short his vast projects. Besides he had won all the military renown he wished in fighting with the rotten monarchies that surrounded him, and his genius sought a wider field in which to display itself. It was, therefore, with the greatest reluctance he would entertain the idea of a rupture. He sent for Lord Whitworth, the English minister at Paris, and had a long personal conversation with him. He recapitulated the constant and unprovoked aggressions of his government on France, ever since the revolution—spoke of his ardent wish to live on terms of amity—"But," said he, "Malta must be evacuated: for although it is of no great value in a maritime point of view, it is of immense importance as connected with a sacred treaty and with the honor of France;" "For," he continued, "what would the world say, if we should allow a solemn treaty to be violated?" He asked the nation to act frankly and honestly towards him, and he would act equally so towards it. "If you doubt my sincerity," said he, "look at the power and renown to which I have attained. Do you suppose I wish to hazard it all in a desperate conflict?" The English government then endeavoured to negotiate with him to let it retain Malta. "The treaty of Amiens," he replied, "and nothing but the treaty!" Placed in this dilemma, England was compelled to do two things at once; first, violate a treaty of her own making; and second, to take upon herself in doing it, the responsibility of convulsing Europe, and bringing back all the horrors of the war that had just closed. Napoleon was right, and England was wrong, totally wrong; and if the violation of a solemn treaty is a just cause for war, then is he justifiable. From the objects of peace which had filled his mind, Bonaparte immediately strung his vast energies for the fearful encounter that was approaching. Hostilities commenced, and Napoleon resolved at once to invade England, and strike a deadly blow at the head of his perfidious enemy, or perish in the attempt. He collected an enormous flotilla at Boulogne; and the French coast, that looks towards the English isle, was alive with armies and boats, and rung with the artizan's hammer, and the roar of cannon. Nothing but unforeseen circumstances prevented his carrying out this project, which would have shaken the British throne to its foundations.

England drew Russia first into this new alliance, the basis of which was, first to reduce France to her limits before the Revolution; and second, to secure the peace and stability of the European states. Look for a moment at this perfidious policy—this mockery of virtue—this philanthropic villany. Russia, sund ered so far from France, was in peaceable possession of all her territory—had not a right to maintain, nor a wrong to redress. England, on the other hand, had no province to wrest back from the enemy—no violated treaty to defend—no encroachment to resist. Their removal from the theatre of war rendered them secure; and whose peace and stability were they to maintain? They anticipated no danger to themselves. Italy preferred the French domination to the Austrian, for it gave greater liberty and prosperity Austria did not ask to be propped up, for she had had enough of those alliances which made her own plains the field of combat; and it was with the greatest difficulty she could be brought into the confederacy, and not till her possessions in Italy, which she had ceded to France, was offered as a bribe for her co-operation. Prussia resolutely refused to enter the alliance, and at length sided with France. Russia, Austria, England, and Sweden, finally coalesced, and convulsed Europe, and deluged it in blood, to furnish security to those who had not asked their interference. From this moment Napoleon saw that either Russia or England must be humbled, or there could be no peace to Europe, no security to France. This accounts for his projected descent on England, and after desperate invasion of Russia.

In the opening of the campaign of 1805 that followed, so glorious to the French arms, the real desires of Napoleon are made apparent. Mack had surrendered Ulm, and with it thirty thousand soldiers, and as the captive army defiled before Bonaparte, he addressed them in the following remarkable language: "Gentlemen, war has its chances. Often victorious, you must expect some times to be vanquished. Your master wages against me an unjust war. *I say it candidly, I know not for what I am fighting.* I know not what he desires of me. He has wished to remind me that I was a soldier. I trust he will find that I have not forgotten my original avocation. I will, however, give one piece of advice to my brother, the Emperor of Germany. Let him hasten to make peace. This is the moment to remember that there are limits to all empires, however powerful. *I want nothing on the Continent. It is ships, colonies that I desire.*" This is the language of him who is called the desolator of Europe, in the moment of victory. It was true, he did not know for what he was fighting; he was forced into it. It was equally true, that he wished for nothing on the Continent. He emulated England in her course of greatness, and he was perfectly willing the despots of Europe should sit in quietness on their crazy thrones. For the slain left on the plains of Italy, as Massena swept the enemy from its borders—for the tens of thousands strewn on the bloody field of Austerlitz—who is chargeable? Not Napoleon—not France.—Here is a third sanguinary war waged, filling Europe with consternation and the clangour of arms—her hospitals with wounded, and her villages with mourning, and her valleys and hills with her slain children—and the guilt of the whole is charged over to Napoleon's ambition, while he never went into a war more reluctantly, or with justice more clearly on his side. Mr. Alison, who certainly will not be accused of favoring too much the French view of the matter, nor too eager to load England with crime, is nevertheless compelled to hold the following remarkable language respecting this war: "In coolly reviewing the circumstances under which this contest was renewed, it *is impossible to deny* that the British government manifested a feverish anxiety to come to a rupture, and that so far as the *two countries were concerned, they were the aggressors.*" And yet at the opening of the campaign of Austerlitz, he indulges in a long homily on the ambition of Napoleon—his thirst of glory, and the love of conquest which had seized the French nation. And these are the works we place in our libraries as *histories.*

I do not design to follow out the subsequent treaties to show who were the aggressors. Russia and England determined never to depart from the basis of their alliance till they had effected the overthrow of Napoleon; while he saw that the humiliation of one or the other of these great powers was indispensable to the preservation of his possessions and his throne. Conquests alone could produce peace; and the war became one of extermination on the one side, and of vengeance and fierce retaliation on the other. Napoleon felt that he was to be treated without mercy or faith, unless he surrendered France into the hands of the despots of Europe, to be disposed of as they should think necessary for their own security, and the stability of the feudal system, on which their thrones were based. That after this he should wage war with a desperation and violence that made Europe tremble, is not to be wondered at. But up to the peace of Tilsit, he and France are free from the guilt of the carnage that made the plains of Europe one vast Golgotha.

Some time after this assertion was written down, I had occasion to refer to Napier's Peninsular War fo some historical fact, and fell upon the following statement, which, coming as it does, from an Englishman, and one of such high authority in military matters, I am induced to quote: "Up to the peace of Tilsit," says Napier, "the wars of France were *essentially defensive;* for the bloody contest that wasted the Continent so many years, was not a struggle for preeminence between ambitious powers—not a dispute for some accession of territory—nor for the political ascendancy of one or other nation—but a *deadly conflict to determine whether aristocracy or democracy should predominate—whether equality or* PRIVILEGE *should henceforth be the principle of European governments.*"

But how much does this "up to the peace of Tilsit" embrace? First, All the first wars of the French Republic—the campaigns of 1792, '93, '94, and '95— and the carnage and woe that made up their history. Second, Eleven out of the eighteen years of Bonaparte's career—the campaigns of 1796, in Italy and Germany—the battles of Montenotte, Millesimo, Dego, Lodi, Arcola, Castiglione, and Rivoli—the campaigns of 1797, and the bloody battle fields that marked their progress. It embraces the wars in Italy and Switzerland, while Bonaparte was in Egypt; the campaign of Marengo and its carnage; the havoc around and in Genoa; the slain thousands that strewed the Black Forest and the banks of the Danube where Moreau struggled so heroically; the campaign of Hohenlinden and its losses. And yet this is but a fraction to what remains. This period takes in also the campaign of Austerlitz and its bloody battle, and the havoc the hand of war was making in Italy,—the campaign of Jena, and the fierce conflicts that accompanied it; the campaign of Eylau, and the battles of Pultusk, Golymin, Heilsberg, crowned by the dreadful slaughter of Eylau; the campaigns of Friedland and Tilsit, and the multitudes they left on the plains of Europe. All these terrible campaigns, with their immense slaughter, does an English historian declare to be the result of a defensive war on the part of France—not merely a defence of territory, *but of human rights against tyranny.* Let republicans ponder this before they adopt the sentiments of prejudiced historians, and condemn as a monster the man who was toiling over battle fields to save his country from banded oppressors.

That Bonaparte loved dominion, no one ever doubted; but that it led him to battle constantly the allied Continental powers, is untrue. On the contrary, Mr. Napier declares that he was not only defending France against aggression, but democracy against aristocracy—equal rights against privileged oppression.

Nothing can be more ludicrous than the assertion that Napoleon sought to conquer Europe, and fell in carrying out his insane project. In youth, as all young soldiers are, he was desirous of military glory. His profession was that of arms, and he bent all his young energies to the task of excelling in it, and succeeded. But when he became Emperor of France, he stood on the summit of military renown, and needed and sought no more fame as a warrior. He was then ambitious to excel as a monarch. He designed to follow in the steps of England, and finally outstrip her in her mighty progress, by extending commerce, and establishing colonies. The secret o* the whole opposition he received from her after the Republic had ceased to exist, sprung from her knowledge of his policy. The East was regarded by him as the appropriate theatre for his ambition; but the East, England determined no body should plunder of its enormous wealth but herself, and so she banded Europe together to overthrow him. The encroachments of France in the South of Europe during a time of peace are the only pretext offered by the English government for her interference and aggression. It was not that *her* territory was invaded, *her* rights assailed, or treaties with *her* violated. It was simply a philanthropic motive, if we may believe her statements, that caused her to whelm Europe in blood. The encroachments of France could not be allowed—the extension of her empire must be arrested; and yet, since she violated the treaty of Amiens—broke up a universal peace—and brought on universal war—she has solely, for the sake of *self-aggrandizement, added more to her territory in the Mysore, than France ever did to hers, put all her conquests together.* Now let France insist that England shall give up these possessions; and form an alliance with Russia, Austria, and Prussia, the basis of which shall be, war with England, till she shall retire to her original boundaries before her aggressions in the East commenced; and the conflict in which England would be plunged, and the slaughters that would follow, would be charged on her as justly as those which followed the rupture of the peace of Amiens, can be laid at the door of France. There is this difference, however. France gained her possessions in resisting aggressive power, and had them secured to her by treaty, while her domination was preferred to that which the conquered provinces must fall under should she abandon them. But England commenced an unprovoked war on a peaceful people, and reduced them to slavery from no nobler motive than the love of gold. It is time that Americans, who have suffered so much from the imperious policy of England, and seen so much on our own shores, of her grasping spirit after colonial possessions, should look on her conduct subsequent to the French Revolution, through other medium than her own literature.

I have not designed, in this defence of Napoleon, and of France, to prove that the former always acted justly, or from the most worthy motives; or that the Republic never did wrong; but to reveal the principles which lay at the bottom of that protracted war which commenced with the Revolution, and ended only with the overthrow of Napoleon. It was first a war of despotism and monarchy against republicanism, and then a war of suspicion and jealousy and rivalry.

Having thus cleared Napoleon of the crime of desolating Europe with his victorious armies, it will not be so difficult to look with justice on his character and life.

His boyish actions while a poor scholar at Brienne, have been adduced as pre-shadowings of his future career. But the truth is, with more talent than his playmates—with more pride and passion—I find nothing in him different from other boys of his age. His solitary walks, and gorgeous dreams, and brilliant hopes, at this early period, belong to every boy of ardent temperament, and a lively imagination. In ordinary times, these golden visions would have faded away with years and experience; and Napoleon Bo naparte would have figured in the world's history only as a powerful writer, or a brilliant orator. The field which the Revolution left open to adventurers, enabled him to realize his extravagant hopes. His ambition was a necessary result of his military education, while the means so unexpectedly furnished for gratifying it, fed it with a consuming flame. His abrupt, laconic style of speaking corresponded well with his impetuous temper, and evinced at an early age, the iron-like nature with which he was endowed.

His career fairly commenced with his quelling the revolt of the sections. True, his conduct at the siege of Toulon had caused him to be spoken of favorably as an under officer, but it was with unfeigned surprise that the Abbe Sieyes, Rewbel, Letourneur, Roger Ducos, and General Moulins, saw him introduced to them by Barras, as the commander the latter had chosen for the troops that were to defend the convention. Said General Moulins to him, "You are aware that it is only by the powerful recommendation of citizen Barras, that we confide to you so important a post?" "I have not asked for it," drily replied the young Lieutenant, "and if I accept it, it will be because, after a close examination, I am confident of success. I am different from other men; I never undertake any thing I can not carry through." This sally caused the members of the Convention to bite their lips, for the implied sarcasm stung each in his turn. "But do you know," said Rewbel, "that this may be a very serious affair—that the sections ——" "Very well," fiercely interrupted the young Bonaparte, "I will make a serious affair of it, and the sections shall become tranquil." He had seen Louis XVI. put on the red cap, and show himself from the palace of the

Tuilleries to the mob, and unable to restrain his indignation at the sight, exclaimed to his companion, Bourienne, "What madness! he should have blown four or five hundred of them into the air, and the rest would have taken to their heels." Deprived of his command, he had wandered around Paris during the terrible scenes of the revolution, learning every day lessons which he would yet have occasion to improve. He had gone so far as to dictate a long and written proposal to Monsieur, for the defence of the tottering throne, offering himself as commander of the troops, to be organized for the quelling of the insurgents. To the proposal of this unknown individual, no reply was deigned; and the author of it soon after saw the royal head roll on the scaffold; and retired to his bed sick from the excitement and horror of the spectacle. But the experience furnished by these scenes, rendered him a fit leader to the troops of the Convention; and when on the mighty populace, and the headlong advance of the National Guard, his artillery loaded to the muzzle with grape-shot, thundered; he announced the manner in which he would treat with a mob. After this, Barras became his patron, and introduced him to Josephine, and persuaded him to marry her, by offering as a dowry the command of the army of Italy.

It was not without misgivings that such Generals as Massena, Rampon, Augereau, and others, saw a young man of slender frame, but twenty-seven years old, assume the command of the army. But his independent manner, firm tone, and above all, the sudden activity he infused into every department by his example, soon gave them to understand that it was no ordinary leader whose orders they were to obey.

From this brilliant campaign, he went up by rapid strides to First Consul, and finally Emperor of France.

One great secret of his success, is to be found in the union of two striking qualities of mind, which are usually opposed to each other. He possessed an imagination as ardent, and a mind as impetuous, as the most rash and chivalric warrior; and yet a judgment as cool and correct as the ablest tactician. His mind moved with the rapidity of lightning, and yet with the precision and steadiness of naked reason. He rushed to his final decision as if he overleaped all the intermediate space, and yet he embraced the entire ground, and every detail in his passage. In short, he could decide quick and correctly too. He did not possess these antagonistic qualities in a moderate degree, but he was at the same time, the most rapid and the most correct of men, in the formation of his plans. He united two remarkable natures in his single person. It usually happens that the man of sage counsel and far-reaching mind, who embraces every detail and weighs every probability, is slow in coming to a decision. On the other hand, a mind of rapid decision and sudden execution, commonly lacks the power of combination, and seeing but one thing at a time, finds itself involved in plans it can neither thwart nor break through. It was the union of these two qualities that gave Bonaparte such immense power over his adversaries. His plans were more skillfully and deeply laid than theirs, and yet perfected before theirs were begun. He broke up the counsels of other men, by the execution of his own. This power of thinking quick, and of thinking right is the rarest exhibited in history. It gives the posses sor of it all the advantage that thought over has over impulse, and all the advantage, too, that impulse frequently has over thought, by the suddenness and unexpectedness of its movements.

His power of combination was unrivalled. The most extensive plans, involving the most complicated movements, were laid down with the clearness of a map, in his mind; while the certainty and precision, with which they were all brought to bear on one great point, took the ablest Generals in Europe by surprise. His mind seemed vast enough for the management of the globe, and not so much *encircled* every thing, as *contained* every thing. It was hard to tell whether he exhibited more skill in conducting a campaign, or in managing a single battle. With a power of generalization seldom equalled, his perceptive faculties, that let no detail escape him, were equally rare.

As a military leader, he has no superior in ancient or modern times. He marched his victorious troops successively into almost every capital of Europe. Meeting and overwhelming in turn the armies of Prussia, Austria, Russia, and England, he, for a long time, waged a successful war against them all combined; and exhausted at last by his very victories, rather than by their conquests, he fell before superior numbers, which in a protracted contest, must always prevail. His first campaign in Italy, and the campaign of Austerlitz, are, perhaps, the most glorious he ever conducted. The first astonished the world, and fixed his fortune. In less than a year, he overthrew four of the finest armies of Europe. With fifty-five thousand men, he had beaten more than two hundred thousand Austrians—taken prisoners nearly double the number of his whole army, and killed half as many as the entire force he had at any one time in the field. The tactics he adopted in this campaign, and which he never after departed from, correspond singularly with the character of his mind. Instead of following up what was considered the scientific mode of conducting a campaign and a battle, he fell back on his own genius, and made a system of his own, adapted to the circumstance in which he was placed. Instead of opposing wing to wing, centre to centre, and column to column, he rapidly concentrated his entire strength on separate portions in quick succession. Hurling his combined force now on one wing, and now another, and now throwing it with the weight and terror of an avalanche on the centre, he crushed each in its turn; or cutting the army in two, destroyed its communication and broke it in pieces. And this was the way his mind worked. He concentrated all his gigantic powers on one project at a time, until it stood complete before him, and then turned them unexhausted on another. He grappled with, and mastered each in turn—penetrated and dismissed it with a rapidity that astonished his most intimate friends.

He was brave as courage itself, and never scrupled to expose his life, when necessary to success. The daring he exhibited in the revolt of the sections, when, with five thousand soldiers, he boldly withstood forty thousand of the National Guard and mob of Paris, he carried with him to his fall. At the terrible passage of Lodi, where, though General-in-Chief, he was the second man across the bridge;—at Arcola, where he stood, with the standard in his hand, in the midst of a perfect tempest of balls and grape-shot;

and at Wagram, where he rode on his white steed, backward and forward, for a whole hour, before his shivering lines, to keep them steady in the dreadful fire that thinned their ranks, and swept the ground they stood upon;—he evinced the heroic courage that he possessed, and which was a part of his very nature This, with his stirring eloquence, early gave him great command over his soldiers. They loved him to the last, and stood by the republican General, and the proud Emperor, with equal affection. Bonaparte was eloquence itself. His proclamations to his soldiers evince not only his knowledge of the human heart, but his power to move it at his will. Whether causing one of the articles in Sieyes' constitution to be rejected, by his withering sarcasm; or rousing his soldiers to the loftiest pitch of enthusiasm, by his irresistible appeals; or carrying away those conversing with him, by his brilliant thoughts and forcible elocution, he exhibits the highest capacities of an orator. His appeals to the courage of his soldiers, and his distributions of honors, with so much pomp and display, perfectly bewildered and dazzled them, so that in battle it seemed to be their only thought how they should exhibit the greatest daring, and perform the most desperate deeds. Thus, soon after the battle of Castiglione, and just before the battle of Rivoli, he made an example of the 39th and 85th regiments of Vaubois Division, for having given way to a panic, and nearly lost him the battle. Arranging these two regiments in a circle, he addressed them in the following language:—"Soldiers, I am displeased with you—you have shown neither discipline, nor valour, nor firmness. You have allowed yourselves to be chased from positions, where a handful of brave men would have stopped an army. Soldiers of the 39th and 85th, you are no longer French soldiers. Chief of the Staff, let it be written on their standards, '*They are no longer of the army of Italy.*'"

Nothing could exceed the stunning effect with which these words fell on those brave men. They forgot their discipline, and the order of their ranks, and bursting into grief, filled the air with their cries,—and rushing from their ranks, crowded, with most beseeching looks and voices around their General, and begged to be saved from such a disgrace, saying, "Lead us once more into battle, and see if we are not of the army of Italy." Bonaparte wishing only to implant feelings of honour in his troops, appeared to relent, and addressing them some kind words, promised to wait to see how they should behave. In a few days he did see the brave fellows go into battle, and rush on death as if going to a banquet, and prove themselves, even in his estimation, worthy to be in the army of Italy. It was by such reproaches for ungallant behaviour, and by rewards for bravery, that he instilled a love of glory that made them irresistible in combat. Thus we see the Old Guard, dwindled to a mere handful in the fearful retreat from Russia, close round him as they marched past a battery, and amid the storm of iron that played on their exhausted ranks, sing the favourite air, "Where can a father be so well, as in the bosom of his family." So, als just before the battle of Austerlitz, in his address to the soldiers, he promised them he would keep out of danger if they behaved bravely, and burst through the enemy's ranks; but if they did not, he should himself rush into the thickest of the fight. There could not be a stronger evidence of love and confi dence between soldier and General, than was evinced by this speech, made on the commencement of one of the greatest battles of his life.

Another cause of his wonderful success was his untiring activity of both mind and body. No victory lulled him into a moment's repose—no luxuries tempted him to ease—and no successes bounded his impetuous desires. Labouring with an intensity and rapidity that accomplished the work of days in hours, he nevertheless seemed crowded to the very limit of human capacity by the vast plans and endless projects that asked and received his attention. In the cabinet he astonished every one by his striking thoughts and indefatigable industry. The forms and ceremonies of court could keep his mind, hardly for an hour, from the labour which he seemed to covet. He allowed himself usually but four or five hours rest, and during his campaigns, exhibited the same almost miraculous activity of mind. He would dictate to one set of secretaries all day, and after he had tired them out, call for a second, and keep them on the stretch all night, snatching but a brief repose during the whole time. His common practice was to rise at two in the morning, and dictate to his secretaries for two hours, then devote two hours more to thought alone, when he would take a warm bath and dress for the day. But in a pressure of business this division of labour and rest was scattered to the winds, and he would work all night. With his nightgown wrapped around him, and a silk handkerchief tied about his head, he would walk backwards and forwards in his apartment from dark till daylight, dictating to Gaulincourt, or Duroc, or D' Albe his chief secretary, in his impetuous manner, which required the highest exertion to keep pace with; while Rustan, his faithful Mameluke, whom he brought from Egypt, was up also, bringing him, from time to time, a strong cup of coffee to refresh him. Sometimes at midnight, when all was still, this restless spirit would call out "Call D'Albe: let every one arise:" and then commence working, allowing himself no intermission or repose till sunrise. He has been known to dictate to three secretaries at the same time, so rapid were the movements of his mind, and yet so perfectly under his control. He never deferred business for an hour, but did on the spot what then claimed his attention. Nothing but the most iron-like constitution could have withstood these tremendous strains upon it. And, as if Nature had determined that nothing should be wanting to the full development of this wonderful man, as well as no resources withheld from his gigantic plans, she had endowed him with a power of endurance seldom equalled. It was not till after the most intense and protracted mental and physical effort combined, that he gave intimations of being sensible to fatigue. In his first campaign in Italy, though slender and apparently weak, he rode five horses to death in a few days, and for six days and nights, never took off his boots, or retired to his couch. He toiled over the burning sands of Egypt, and through the snow drifts of Russia, with equal impunity—spurring his panting steed through the scorching sun-beams of Africa, and forcing his way on foot, with a birchen stick in his hand, over the icy path, as he fled from Moscow with the same firm presence. He would sleep in the palace of the Tuileries, or on the shore of the swollen Danube, with nought but his cloak about him, while the groans of the dying loaded the midnight air; with equal soundness. He was often on horseback eighteen hours a day, and yet wrought up to the intensest mental excitement all the while. Marching till midnight, he would array his troops by moonlight; and fighting all day, be hailed victor at night; and then, without rest, travel all the following night and day, and the next morning fight another battle, and be a second time victorious. He is often spoken of as a mere child of fortune; but whoever in this world will possess such powers of mind, and use them with equal skill and industry, and has a frame to stand it, will always be a child of fortune. He allowed nothing to escape his ubiquitous spirit; and whether two or five campaigns were going on in different kingdoms at the same time, they were equally under his control, and their result calculated with wonderful precision.

Another striking characteristic of Napoleon, and which contributed much to his success, was self-confidence. He fell back on himself in every emergency, with a faith that was sublime. Where other men sought counsel, he communed with himself alone; and where Kings and Emperors called anxiously on the statesmen and chieftains around their thrones for help, he summoned to his aid his own mighty genius. This did not result from vanity and conceit, but from the consciousness of power. He not only took the measure and capabilities of every man that approached him, but he *knew* he saw beyond their farthest vision, and hence could not but rely on himself, instead of others.

This self-confidence, which in other men would have been downright madness, in him was wisdom.

It was the first striking trait in his character he exhibited. At the siege of Toulon, a mere boy, he curled his lip at the science of the oldest Generals in the army, and offered his own plan for the reduction of the town, with an assurance that astonished them. In quelling the revolt of the sections, this sublime self-reliance utterly confounded the heads of the Convention. If it had ended here, it might have been called the rashness and ardour of youth, crowned with unexpected success. But throughout his after career; in those long protracted efforts, in which intellect and genius always triumph; we ever find him standing alone, calling none but himself to his aid. Inexperienced and young, he took command of the weak and ill-conditioned army of Italy, and instead of seeking the advice of his government and his Generals, so that he might be screened in case of defeat, where defeat seemed inevitable; he seemed to exult that he was at last alone, and almost to forget the danger that surrounded him, in his joy at having a free and open field for his daring spirit. His fame and after fortune, all rested on his success and conduct in this outset of his career; yet he voluntarily placed himself in a position where the result, however disastrous it might be, would be chargeable on him alone. He flung the military tactics of Europe to the winds, and with his little band around him, spurned both the science and the numbers arrayed against him.

With the same easy confidence he vaulted to the throne of France, and felt an empire rest on his shoulders, apparently unconscious of the weight. He looked on the revolutionary agitation, the prostration and confusion of his kingdom without alarm; and his eagle glance pierced at once the length, and breadth, and depth, and height, of the chaos that surrounded him. Yet, so natural does he seem in this position, that instead of trembling for his safety, we find ourselves inspired by the same confidence that sustained him, and expecting great and glorious results. He seems equal to any thing, and acts as if he himself was conscious he was a match for the world. Stern, decided, plain, he speaks to the King of England, the Emperor of Russia, of Austria, and to all Europe in the language of a superior, rather than of an equal. Angry, yet alarmed at the haughty tone of this plebeian King, the crowned heads of Europe gathered hastily together, to consult what they should do. In the same quiet confidence with which he saw the mob advancing on his batteries in the garden of the Tuileries, he beheld their banded armies move down on his throne. This single man—this plebeian, stood up amid the monarchies of Europe, and bending his imperial frown on the faithless kings that surrounded him, smote their royal foreheads with blow after blow, till the world stood aghast at his presumption and audacity. Their scorn of his plebeian blood gave way to consternation, as they saw him dictating terms to them in their own capitals; while the freedom with which he put his haughty foot on their sacred majesties, filled the bosoms of 'heir courtiers with horror. He wheeled his cannon around their thrones, with a coolness and inflexibility of purpose that made "the dignity which doth hedge a king," a most pitiful thing to behold. He swept, with his fierce chariot, through their ancient dynasties, crushing them out as if they had been bubbles in his path; then proudly pausing, let them gather up their crowns again. While astonished at the boldness of his irruption into Egypt, they were listening to hear again the thunder of his guns around the pyramids, they suddenly saw his mighty army hanging along the crest of the Alps; and before the astonishing vision had fairly disappeared, the sound of his cannon was heard shaking the shores of the Danube, and his victorious eagles were waving their wings over the capital of the Austrian Empire. One moment his terrible standards would be seen along the shores of the Rhine; the next, by the banks of the Borysthenes, and then again fluttering amid the flames of Moscow. Europe never had such a wild waking up before, and the name of Napoleon Bonaparte became a spell word, with which to conjure up horrible shapes of evil. Victory deserted the standards of the enemy the moment that the presence of Napoleon among his legions was announced in their camp, and when it was whispered through the ranks that his eye was sweeping the battle field, the arm of the foeman waxed weak, and he conquered as much by his name as by his armies. This boldness of movement, giving him such immense moral power, arose from his confidence in himself. Even where his plans seemed madness and folly, so confidently did he carry them on, that men believed he saw resources of which they were ignorant, and hence their course became cautious and wavering; and defeat certain.

Nothing can be more sublime than this self-reliance of Napoleon, in the midst of a world in arms against him. It is the confidence of genius and intellect, arrayed against imbecility and fear. That no hesitation should mark his course, amid the complicated affairs he was compelled to move—no vacillation of that iron will be seen, when every thing else shook about him, is indeed a marvel. The energy of a single soul, poised on its own great centre, gathering around it, as by sympathy, the mightiest spirits of the age, and crushing under it obstacles that before seemed insurmountable, has had no such exhibitions since the time of Cæsar.

But with all Napoleon's cool judgment, and self-confidence, there was not a Marshal in the army of so impetuous and impatient a temper, as he. He settled every plan in his own mind, with the precision of a mathematical problem; and if any unforeseen obstacle interposed, threatening to change the result, he became furious with excitement, acting and talking as if he thought it to be a violation of reason and justice. He planned with so much skill, and calculated results with so much precision, that if he did not succeed, he felt there must be blame, shameful neglect somewhere. From his youth up he never could brook contradiction, and drove with such headlong speed towards the object he was after, that he frequently secured it through the surprise and consternation occasioned by the desperation that marked his progress. In the cabinet and in the field, he exhibited the same restless fever of mind, and seemed really to suffer from the strong restraints his despotic judgment placed over his actions. It was impossible for him to keep still; and the most headlong speed in travelling, did not seem rapid enough for his eager spirit. Bad rider as he was, he delighted in spurring over fences and chasms, where his boldest riders had gone down; but even when sweeping over a field on a tearing gallop, he could not be quiet, but constantly jerked the reins, which he always held in his right hand. When delayed in writing despatches, behind the time appointed for his departure for the army, the moment he had finished,—the cry "to horse," acted like an electric shock on his attendants, and in a moment every man was at the top of his speed, and the next moment the entire suite were driving like a whirlwind along the road. In this way he would go all day without stopping; and if despatches met him on the way, he would read them as he rode,—throwing envelopes and unimportant letters, one after another, from the carriage window, with a rapidity that showed how quickly he devoured the contents of each. He usually opened these despatches himself, but if his secretary did it for him, he would sit and work at the window sash with his fingers,—so necessary was some outlet to the fierce action of his mind. He would drive through the army at the same furious rate; and when the outriders called out "room for the Emperor!" every one felt he could not be too quick in obeying; and before the utter confusion of clearing the way had passed, the cortège was seen flying like a cloud across the plain, beyond hearing, and almost out of sight. But through the Guards he always moved with becoming pomp and solemnity, saluting the officers as he passed.

Maps were his invariable companions in a campaign, and he always had one spread out at night in his apartment, or a tent which was always pitched amid the squares of the Old Guards,—surrounded with candles, so that he might rise at any moment and consult it; and when on the road or in the field he wanted one, so impatient was he known to be that the two officers who carried them rode down every thing between them and his horse or carriage. On such occasions he would frequently order the map he desired to be unrolled on the ground, and stretching himself full length upon it, in a moment be lost to every thing but the campaign before him. A remarkable instance of his impatience and impetuosity is exhibited in the manner he received Marie Louise on her way to meet him. As she drove up to the post town, where he expected her, he jumped into the carriage all wet with rain as he was, and embraced this daughter of the Cesars with the familiarity of an old relative; and ordering the postillions to drive at full gallop to Compeigne, insisted on having the conjugal rites before marriage, and obtained them. But perhaps there is not a more striking instance of the impetuosity of his feelings than his mad ride to Paris, when it was enveloped by the allied armies. Being himself deceived by the enemy, they had got full three days' start of him towards the capital, with a force that bore down every thing in their passage. It was then Napoleon strained every nerve to reach the city before its capitulation. He urged his exhausted army to the top of its speed, and on the 29th of March, the day before he left it, he marched with the Imperial Guard *forty miles*. Wearied out, the brave cuirassiers could no longer keep pace with his haste, and he set out alone for Paris. Despatching courier after courier to announce his approach, he drove on with furious speed; but as the disastrous news was brought him that the enemy were struggling on the heights of Montmartre, his impatience knew no bounds. He abandoned his carriage as being too slow, though it came and went with frightful velocity on the astonished peasantry, and changing it for a light Calècle, he sprung into it, and ordered the postillions to whip the horses to the top of their speed. He dashed away as if life and death hung on every step. "Fast or, faster!" he cried to the postillions, though the whip fell incessantly on the flanks of the panting steeds. "Faster, faster," he cried, as the houses and field swept past him like a vision. His throne, his crown, his empire, shook in the balance, and the flying chariot seemed to creep over the lengthened way. Nothing could satisfy him, and the cry of "faster, faster," still rung in the ears of the astonished postillions, though the carriage wheels were already on fire from their rapid evolutions. Vain speed! Paris had fallen.

This impetuosity of temper and hatred of restraint made him frequently overbearing and unjust to his officers, when they had failed in executing his plans In the first transport of passion, he would hear no defence and no apology; but after reflection made him more reasonable and just, and a generous act would repay a sudden wrong. It was this trait of character which grew stronger, as he drew towards the close of his career, that made many around him declare that he hated the truth. It was not the *truth* which aroused him, but the declaration that his plans would be or had been baffled. He was so confident that he usually knew more than all around him, that he in time became so self-opinionated that he could not brook advice which clashed with his views. With weight and velocity both, his mind had terrible momentum, and even in a wrong way often conquered by its irresistible power.

Napoleon was a great statesman as well as military leader. His conversations in his exile evince the most profound knowledge of political science, while the order he brought out of chaos, and indeed the glorious resurrection he gave to France, show that he was not great in theory alone. He was equal to Cesar as a warrior, to Bacon in political sagacity, and above all other kings in genius.

Perhaps Napoleon exhibits nowhere in his life, his amazing grasp of thought and power of accomplishment, more than in the year and a half after his arrival from Egypt. Hearing that the Republic was every where defeated, and Italy wrested from its grasp, he immediately set sail for France, and escaping the English fleet in a most miraculous manner, protected by "his star," reached France in October. By November he had overthrown the inefficient Directory, and been proclaimed First Consul with all the attributes, but none of the titles of king. He immediately commenced negotiations with the allied powers, while at the same time he brought his vast energies to bear on the internal state of France. Credit was to be restored, money raised, the army supplied, war in Vendée suppressed, and a constitution given to France. By his superhuman exertions and all pervading genius, he accomplished all this, and by next spring was ready to offer Europe peace or war. Order sprung from chaos at his touch—the tottering government stopped rocking on its base the moment his mighty hand fell upon it—wealth flowed from the lap of poverty, and vast resources were drawn from apparent nothingness. France, rising from her prone position, stood ready to give battle to the world. Europe chose war. The gigantic mind that had wrought such prodigies in seven months in France, now turned its concentrated strength and wrath on the enemy. Massena he sent to Genoa to furnish an example of heroism to latest posterity.--Moreau he despatched to Swabia to render the Black Forest immortal by the victories of Engen, Mœskirch and Biberach, and send the Austrians in consternation to their capital, while he himself, amid the confusion and wonderment of Europe at his complicated movements, precipitated his enthusiastic troops down the Alps, and by one bold and successful stroke wrested Italy from the enemy, and forced the astonished and discomfitted sovereigns of Europe to an armistice of six months. Unexhausted by his unparalleled efforts, no sooner was the truce proclaimed than he plunged with the same suddenness yet profound forethought with which he rushed into battle, into the distracted politics of Europe. By a skilful stroke of policy in offering Malta to Russia, at the moment it was certain to fall into the hands of England, he embroiled these two countries in a quarrel, while by promising Hanover to Prussia, he bribed her to reject the coalition with England, and consent to an alliance with himself. At the same time he planned the league of the neutral powers against England,—armed Denmark and Sweden, and closed all the ports of the Continent against her, and prepared succours for Egypt. While his deep sagacity was thus baffling the cabinet of England, involving her in a general war with Europe, and pressing to her lips the chalice she had just forced him to drink, he apparently devoted his entire energies to the internal state of France, and the building of public works. He created the bank of France—put the credit of government on a firm basis—began the Codes, spanned the Alps with roads—sufficient monuments in themselves of his genius—and restored the complete supremacy of the laws throughout the kingdom. All this he accomplished in six months, and at the close of the armistice was ready for war. The glorious campaign of Hohenlinden followed, and Austria, frightened for her throne, negotiated the peace of Luneville, giving the world time to recover its amazement and gaze more steadily on this mighty sphere that had shot so suddenly across the orbit of kings.

That Napoleon in all this was ambitious no one doubts, but his ambition was indissolubly connected with the welfare and glory of France. Power was the ruling star in his heaven, but he sought it in order to make France powerful. His energies developed hers, and the victories he won were for her safety and defence. He is accused of having aimed at supreme power, and nothing short of it would have satisfied him. A second Alexander, he waded through seas of blood, and strode over mountains of corpses, solely to accomplish this object, and his fall was the fall of one who aimed at universal empire. Mr. Alison takes up this piece of nonsense, and gives us pages of the merest cant about the danger of ambition and love of power, and the Providence that arrests it—declaring, in so many words, that Napoleon sought the subjugation of Europe. If this were true he might have spared the tribute he pays to Napoleon's genius, for it would rove him the sublimest fool that ever held a sceptre. To assert that he ever dreamed of being able to subjugate England, Russia, Prussia, Austria, and the northern powers of Europe, and combine them in one vast empire, of which he would be the head, is too ridiculous to receive a serious refutation. That he ever expected to make England a dependant province on France, there is not an intelligent man in the British Empire believes; yet English historians will never cease their cant about this modern Alexander, who fell because he sought to conquer the world. Napoleon, as I have said, would gladly have adopted the let-alone policy both with England and Russia, as well as with Austria and Prussia, if they would have allowed it. He was ambitious, but he knew too well that with Europe banded against him, he must sooner or later fall; and the utmost limit of his hopes was to break this coalition by crippling either Russia or England. Could he have done this, he would soon have extorted a peace from the rest of Europe that would have allowed him to prosecute his ambitious schemes in the East, where success was certain. England wished this road to wealth and to empire left open to her, so she uttered a vast deal of nonsense about unlimited power and the danger of Europe, till she induced Europe to crush Napoleon. The East, as I before remarked, with its boundless wealth and imbecile population, he always regarded as the true field where fame and empire were to be laid, and he would have been glad any moment if Europe would have left him to pursue the career he commenced in Egypt. That he would have been as unprincipled in his aggressions on peaceable states—as heartless in the means he employed—as reckless of the law of nations—as perfidious in his policy—as cruel in his slaughters—and as grasping after territory, as the British Empire has since shown herself to be, his life, character, and plans leave but little room to doubt. Perhaps it is better that he wasted his immense energies as he did, in breaking to pieces the despotisms of Europe. As it was, he rolled the Revolution over the

French borders, and sent it with its earthquake throes the length and breadth of the Continent.

I have thus spoken of Bonaparte comparatively, and not as an individual judged by the law of right. I wished to place him beside the monarchs and governments that surrounded him, and see where the balance of virtue lay. He was ambitious—so was Pitt; while the ambition of the former was far less selfish, heartless and cruel than that of the latter. One insisted on the treaty of Amiens, by which the world was bound to peace; the other broke it, and involved Europe in war solely for selfish ends. Napoleon has been blamed for robbing France of her republican form of government, and reinstating monarchy; and men are prone to compare him with Washington, and wonder why he could not have imitated his example, and, content with the peace and prosperity of his country, returned to the rank of citizen, and left a name unspotted by blood and violence. In the first place, the thing was absolutely impossible. A pure Republic France could not have been with the population the Revolution left upon her bosom. As ignorant of liberty and undisciplined, as the South American States and Mexico, she would have been rocked like them with endless revolutions, until European powers had overcome her, and replaced a Bourbon on the throne. And if her population had been prepared for complete freedom, the monarchs of Europe would not have allowed her to establish a Republic in peace. Imagine the United States in the midst of the Revolution, surrounded by despotic thrones—Canada—the West—Mexico, and Florida—all so many old monarchies, thoroughly alarmed by the sudden appearance of a free state in their midst, and in their affright banding themselves together to crush the infant Republic, and you will have some conception of the situation of France during the Revolution. Let Washington have commanded our forces, and in resisting this war of aggression have wrested from one of the powers dominions to which it had no claim, as France took Italy from Austria. Suppose this despotic feudal alliance was kept up, and no permanent peace would be made till Washington was overthrown; his career and ours would have been very different. Our plains would have all been battle fields until we had broken up the infamous coalition, or been ourselves overborne. In such a position were Bonaparte and France placed, and such a war was waged till they fell. Placing ourselves in a similar position, we shall not find it difficult to determine where the chief guilt lay, or be wanting in charity to Napoleon, for the recklessness with which he carried on a war against powers so destitute of faith and virtue, and whose aggressive policy had well nigh crushed the hopes of freedom on the Continent. But had these circumstances not existed, he never would have been a Washington, for he possessed few of his moral qualities. Washington appears in grander proportions as a moral than as an intellectual man, while Bonaparte was a moral dwarf; and I do not well see how he could be otherwise. Dedicated from childhood to the profession of arms, all his thoughts and associations were of a military character. Without moral or religious instruction, he was thrown while a youth into the vortex of the revolution; and in the triumph of infidelity, and the overthrow of all religion, and the utter chaos of principles and sentiments; it was not to be expected he would lay the foundation of a religious character. He emerged from this into the life of the camp and the battle-field, and hence became morally what most men would be in similar circumstances. Besides, his very nature was despotic. He could not brook restraint, and, conscious of knowing more than those around him, he constantly sought for power that he might carry out those stupendous plans which otherwise would have been interrupted. I have no doubt that Napoleon's highest ambition was to reign as a just and equitable monarch amid the thrones of Europe, expending his vast energies elsewhere; and that much of his violence and recklessness arose from the consciousness that he was to expect no faith or honesty, or justice, or truth, from the perfidious nations that had bound themselves together to crush him. One thing is certain, had he been *less* a monarch, France could not have withstood as long as she did, the united strength of Europe.

Bonaparte is charged with being cruel, but it is unjust. He was capable of great generosity, and exhibited pity in circumstances not to be expected from a man trained on the battle field. Hearing once of a poor English sailor, who having escaped from confinement, had constructed a frail boat of cork and branches of trees, with which he designed to put to sea, in the hopes of meeting an English vessel, and thus reaching England; he sent for him, and on learning from his lips that this bold undertaking was to get back to his aged mother, he immediately despatched him with a flag of truce on board an English ship, with a sum of money for his aged parent, saying that she must be an uncommon mother to have so affectionate a son. The guide who conducted him over the San Bernard, and who, ignorant of the mighty man that bestrode the miserable animal by his side, gave him a full account of his life and plans—of his betrothment and inability to marry for want of a piece of land,—was not forgotten by him afterwards. The land was bought and presented to the young man by order of Napoleon. Repeated acts of kindness to poor wounded soldiers, was one of the chords of iron which bound them to him. The awful spectacle which a battle-field presents after the carnage is done, frequently moved him deeply, and he wept like a child over his dying friend Lannes. His sympathies, it is true, never interfered with his plans. What his judgment approved, his heart never countermanded; and what he thought necessary to be done, he did, reckless of the suffering it occasioned. He was inflexible as law itself in the course he had decided upon as the most expedient. The murder of the Duke of Enghien is perhaps the greatest blot on his character, but he was goaded into this by the madness, and folly, and villany of the race to which this unfortunate prince belonged. In the midst of his vast preparations for a descent upon England, he was informed of a plot to assassinate him, and place a Bourbon on the throne. The two ends of this conspiracy were Paris and London, between which there was an unbroken line of communication across the channel. The secret route was discovered, and several of the conspirators arrested. The Bourbons in England were at the bottom of it, and English gold paid the expense. Pichegru had arrived in Paris, with the infamous Georges, who had so nearly succeeded in taking the life of the First Consul by the explosion of the infernal machine. Moreau had been sounded, and was found ready to aid in the assassination of his former general, but would not listen to the proposal of re-establishing the Bourbon dynasty. His envy had made him the enemy of Napoleon, and he wished to occupy his place. This jar between the conspirators caused delay and uncertainty, which enabled Napoleon to ferret it out. Georges himself, after much trouble, was taken, and he, with other inferior conspirators, confessed the plot, and acknowledged that "the prince" was expected from England to head the conspiracy. Napoleon despatched soldiers to the sea coast to arrest whoever might land at the point designated by the conspirators. They watched by the shore for days; and though a small vessel kept hovering near, as if waiting for signals to land, it was suspicious all was not right, and finally moved off altogether. Moreau was tried, found guilty, and exiled —the mildest punishment he could possibly expect. Pichegru was thrown into prison, but "the Prince," whom Napoleon was feverishly anxious to get hold of, was not to be found. This whole plot, interrupting as it did his vast plans, and exciting the feelings of the people to a state bordering on revolution, filled him with uncontrollable rage. He felt that he was not regarded as a respectable enemy; for even princes of the blood, and nobles, were endeavouring to assassinate him like a common ruffian. With his usual watchfulness he began to inquire about the exiled princes; and being told that one was at Ettenheim, near Strasbourg, he immediately despatched a spy to watch his movements, for he had not the least doubt that every Bourbon was in the conspiracy.

This spy reported that General Doumorier, another old but exiled general, was with the prince

This mistake decided Napoleon to arrest him, sacred as his person ought to have been on neutral territory. Whether he afterwards became convinced of the young Duke's innocence or not, matters very little as to his guilt. He *wished* to destroy some Bourbon prince, and he had determined to execute the first one that fell into his hands. To be waylaid and shot like a dog by Bourbon princes, enraged him so, that the voice of justice could not be heard. Seated on his proud eminence, bending his vast energies to the most stupendous plans that ever filled a human mind, he was reminded that royal blood regarded him as only a fit victim for the assassin's knife; and he determined to teach kings that he would deal by them openly as they had done by him secretly. Some idea of his feelings may be got from the language he frequently indulged in when speaking of the princes and nobles that were engaged in this conspiracy. Said he, "These Bourbons fancy that they may shed my blood like some wild animal, and yet my blood is quite as precious as theirs. I will repay them the alarm with which they seek to inspire me; I pardon Moreau the weakness and errors to which he is urged by stupid jealousy, but I will pitilessly shoot the very first of these princes who shall fall into my hands; I will teach them with what sort of a man they have to deal."* He classed the Bourbons together,—knew them to be inspired with the same feelings towards him, and whether bound by contract or not, sympathising with each other in this conspiracy. In a spirit of fierce retaliation and rage, and to stop forever the plotting of these royal assassins, he determined to make a terrible example of one, and

* Thiers' Consulate and Empire.

the young Duke d'Enghien fell. The news of his death filled the courts of Europe with horror, and was one of the causes of the general alliance against Napoleon that followed. This high-handed act of injustice cannot be condemned too emphatically, but it was not the cold-blooded act of a cruel man. It was a crime committed in passion, by a spirit inflamed with the consciousness of having been outraged by those from whom better things were to be expected. England lifted up her hands in pious horror at the act, yet had not one word to say about the *premeditated* murder of Napoleon by the Bourbons. If *he*, instead of one of their number, had fallen, we should have heard no such outcry, from the crowned heads of Europe. He had only made a Bourbon drink the cup they had prepared for his lips. The horror of the crime consisted not in its *injustice*, but that he had dared to lay his hands on the sacred head of royalty. And yet this act, as unjust and wicked as it is conceded to have been, was no more so than that of England, in banishing Napoleon, when he had thrown himself on her generosity, to a lonely and barren isle, where she could safely vent her august spleen in those petty annoyances she should have disdained to inflict; or that of the allies, in allowing Marshal Ney to be shot, in direct violation of a treaty they had themselves made.

The sum of the matter is, Napoleon's moral character was indifferent enough; yet as a friend of human liberty, and eager to promote the advancement of the race, by opening the field to talent and genius, however low their birth, he was infinitely superior to all the sovereigns who endeavoured to crush him. He loved not only France as a nation, and sought her glory; but he secured the liberty of the meanest of her subjects. There was something noble in his very ambition, for it sought to establish great public works, found useful institutions, and send the principles of liberty over the world. As a just and noble monarch, he was superior to nine-tenths of all the kings that ever reigned in Europe, and as an intellectual man, head and shoulders above them all.

The attempt has also been made to fix the charge of cruelty and oppression on him, from the joy manifested in France at his overthrow, and the cursings and obloquy that followed his exile. But the first exultation that follows a new peace, is not to be considered the sober feeling of the people. His return from Elba is overwhelming evidence against such accusations. Without any plotting beforehand, any conspiracy to make a diversion in his favour, he boldly cast himself on the affections of the people. An established throne, a strong government, and a powerful army, were on one side—the love of the people on the other, and yet, soldier as he was, he believed the latter stronger than all the former put together. What a sublime trust in the strength of affection does his stepping ashore with his handful of followers exhibit? Where is the Bourbon, or European monarch, that would have dared to do this;—or felt he had, by his efforts for the common welfare, laid the people under sufficient obligations, to expect a universal rush to his arms? It was not the soldiers, but the common people who first surrounded him. As he pitched his tent without Cannes, the inhabitants flocked to him with their complaints, and gathered around him as the redresser of their wrongs. As he advanced towards Grenoble, the fields were alive with peasants

as they came leaping like deer from every hill, crying
"*Vive l' Empereur!*" Thronging around him, they
followed him with shouts to the very gates of the town.
The commandant refused him admittance, yet the
soldiers within stretched their arms through the
wickets, and shook hands with his followers without.
At length a confused murmur arose over the walls,
and Napoleon did not know but it was the gathering
for a fierce assault on his little band. The tumult
grew wilder every moment; six thousand inhabitants
from one of the fauxburgs had risen *en masse*, and
with timbers and beams came pouring against the
gates. They tremble before the resistless shocks—
reel and fall with a crash to the ground, and the excited multitude stream forth. Rushing on Napoleon,
they drag him from his horse, kiss his hands and
garments, and bear him with deafening shouts, on
their shoulders, into the town. He next advances on
Lyons, the gates of which are also closed against him,
and bayonets gleam along the walls. Trusting to
the power of affection, rather than to arms, he gallops
boldly up to the city. The soldiers within, instead of
firing on him, break over all discipline, and bursting
open the gates, rush in frantic joy around him,
shouting "*Vive l' Empereur!*" He is not compelled
to plant his cannon against a single town: power
returns to him not through terror, but through love.
He is not received with the cringing of slaves, but
with the open arms of friends, and thus his course
towards the capital becomes one triumphal march.
The power of the Bourbons disappears before the
returning tide of affection, like towers of sand before
the waves; and without firing a gun, Napoleon again
sits down on his recovered throne, amid the acclama-

tions of the people. Who ever saw a tyrant and an oppressor received thus? Where is the monarch in Europe, that dare fling himself in such faith on the affections of his subjects? Where was ever the Bourbon that could show such a title to the throne he occupied? An! the people do not thus receive the man who forges fetters for their limbs; and Napoleon at this day, holds a firmer place in the affections of the inhabitants of France, than any monarch that ever filled its throne.

The two greatest errors of Napoleon, were the conquest of Spain, and the invasion of Russia. The former was not only an impolitic act, but one of great injustice and cruelty. The invasion of Russia might have terminated differently, and been recorded by historians, as the crowning monument of his genius, but for the burning of Moscow by the inhabitants; an event certainly not to be anticipated. He lost the flower of his army there, and instead of striking the heart of his enemy, he pierced his own.

It is useless, however, to speak of the mistakes that Napoleon made, and show how he should have acted here, and planned there, to have succeeded; or attempt to trace the separate steps, in the latter part of his career, to his downfall, and pretend to say how they might have been avoided. After taking into the calculation all the chances and changes that did or would come—all the losses that might have been prevented, and all the successes that might have been gained, and pointing out great errors here and there in his movements, it is plain that nothing less than a miracle could have saved the tottering throne of the Empire. After the disaster of Leipsic, and the losses sustained by different divisions of the army in that campaign, and the mortality which thinned so dreadfully the French armies on the Rhine, France felt herself exhausted and weak. In this depressed state, the civilized world was preparing its last united onset upon her. From the Baltic to the Bosphorus—from the Archangel to the Mediterranean, Europe had banded itself against Napoleon. Denmark and Sweden struck hands with Austria, and Russia, and Prussia, and England; while, to crown all, the Princes of the confederation of the Rhine, put their signature to the league, and *one million and twenty-eight thousand men* stood up in battle array on the plains of Europe, to overthrow this mighty spirit that had shaken so terribly their thrones.

France, which had before been drained to meet the losses of the Russian campaign, could not, with her utmost efforts, raise more than a third of the number of this immense host.

Her provinces were invaded, and this resistless array were pointing their bayonets towards Paris. In this dreadful emergency, though none saw better than he, the awful abyss that was opening before him, Napoleon evinced no discouragement and no hesitation. Assembling the conscripts from every quarter of France, and hurrying them on to head quarters, he at length, after presenting his fair haired boy to the National Guards, as their future sovereign, amid tears and exclamations of enthusiasm, and embracing his wife for the last time, set out for the army. His energy, his wisdom and incessant activity, soon changed the face of affairs. He had struggled against as great odds in his first Italian campaign; and if nothing else could be done, he at least could fall with honour on the soil of his country. Never did his genius shine forth with greater splendour than in the almost superhuman exertions he put forth in this his last great struggle for his empire. No danger could daunt him—no reverses subdue him —no toil exhaust him—and no difficulties shake his iron will. In the dead of winter, struggling with new and untried troops, he fought an army outnumbering his own two to one—beat them back at every point, and sent dismay into the hearts of the allied sovereigns, as they again saw the shadow of his mighty spirit over their thrones. He was everywhere cheering and steadying his men, and on one occasion worked a cannon himself as he did when a youth in the artillery; and though the balls whistled around him till the soldiers besought him to retire, he exclaimed, "Courage! the bullet that is to kill me is not yet cast." At length the whole allied army was forced to retreat, and offered peace if he would consent to have his empire dismembered, and France restored to its limits before the revolution. This he indignantly refused; preferring rather to bury himself amid the ruins of his empire. But with his comparatively handful of raw recruits, what could he do against the world in arms? His rapid victories began to grow less decisive; the glory with which he had anew covered the army, waxed dim; and his star that had once more blazed forth in its ancient splendour in the heavens, was seen sinking to the horizon.

The allies entered the capital, and Napoleon was compelled to abdicate. On the day after the signature of the treaty, by which he was divested of power, and sent an exile from the country he had saved—deserted by all his soldiers, his marshals, his army—even by his wife and family, he said to Caulincourt at night, after a long and sad revery, "My resolution is taken, we must end: I feel it." At midnight the fallen Emperor was in convulsions; he had swallowed poison. As his faithful Caulincourt came in, he opened his eyes, and said, "Caulincourt, I am about to die. I recommend to you my wife and son;—defend my memory. I could no longer endure life. The desertion of my old companions in arms had broken my heart." Violent vomiting, however, gave him relief; and his life was saved.

His farewell to his faithful Old Guard, before he departed from Fontainbleau for Elba, was noble and touching. He passed into their midst as he had been wont to do when he pitched his tent for the night in their protecting squares, and addressed them in words of great tenderness. "For twenty years," said he, "I have ever found you in the path of honour and of glory. Adieu, my children; I would I were able to press you all to my heart,—but I will at least press your eagle." With overpowering emotion, he clasped the General in his arms, and kissed the eagle. Again bidding his old companions adieu, he drove away, while cries and sobs of sorrow burst from those brave hearts that had turned from him the tide of so many battles. They besought the privilege of following him in his fallen fortunes; but were refused their prayer.

But Elba could not long hold that daring, restless spirit. The next year he again unrolled his standard in the capital of France, and the army opened its arms to receive him. After an exhibition of his wonted energy and genius during the hundred days' preparation, he at length staked all on the field of Waterloo. There the star of his destiny again rose over the horizon, and struggled with its ancient strength to mount the heavens of fame. The battle-cloud rolled over it; and when it again was swept away, that star had gone down—sunk in blood and carnage, to rise no more forever.

Volumes have been written on this campaign and last battle; but every impartial mind must come to the same conclusion,—that Napoleon's plans never promised more complete success than at this last effort. Wellington was entrapped; and with the same co-operation on both sides, he was lost beyond redemption. Had Blucher stayed away as Grouchy did, or had Grouchy come up as did Blucher, victory would once more have soared with the French eagles. It is vain to talk of Grouchy's having obeyed orders. It was plainly his duty, and his only duty, to detain Blucher, or follow him.

Bonaparte has also been blamed for risking all on the last desperate charge of the Old Guard; but he well knew that nothing but a decided victory could save him. He wanted the moral effect of one; and without it he was lost;—and he wisely risked all to win it. He is also blamed, both in poetry and prose, for not throwing away his life when the battle was lost. If personal daring and personal exposure had been called for in the disorder, and success could have been possible, by flinging himself into the very jaws of death, he would not have hesitated a moment. But the route was utter; and though he did wish to die, and would have done so but for his friends, had he succeeded in his purpose, it would have been simply an act of suicide, for which his enemies would have been devoutly thankful.

His last hope was gone, and he threw himself into the hands of England, expecting generous, but receiving the basest treatment. She banished him to an inhospitable rock in the midst of the ocean; and having caged the lion, performed the honourable task of watching at the door of the prison, while her parasites kept a faithful record of the complaints and irritations of the noble sufferer, whose misfortunes they had not the magnanimity to respect. But not all this could dim the splendour of that genius whose great work was done. The thoughts that here emanated from him, and the maxims he laid down, both in political and military life, show that he could have written one of the most extraordinary books of his age, as easily as he had become one of its greatest military leaders and rulers.

But at length that wonderful mind was to be quenched in the night of the grave; and Nature, as if determined to assert the greatness of her work to the last, trumpeted him out of the world with one of her fiercest storms. Amid the roar of the blast, and the shock of the billows, as they broke where a wave had not struck for twenty years—and amid the darkness, and gloom, and uproar of one of the most tempestuous nights that ever rocked that lonely isle, Napoleon's troubled spirit was passing to that unseen world, where the sound of battle never comes, and the tread of armies is never heard. Yet even in this solemn hour; his delirious soul, caught perhaps, by the battle-like roar of the storm without, was once more in the midst of the fight, struggling by the Pyramids, or Danube, or on the plains of Italy. It was the thunder of cannon that smote his ear; and amid the wavering fight, and covering smoke, and tumult of the scene, his glazing eye caught the heads of his mighty columns, as torn yet steady, they bore his victorious eagles on, and "*Tête d'Armée*," broke from his dying lips. Awestruck and still, his few remaining friends stood in tears about his couch; gazing steadfastly on that awful kingly brow, but it gave no farther token, and the haughty lips moved no more. Napoleon lay silent and motionless in his last sleep.

When the prejudice and falsehood and hatred of his enemies shall disappear, and the world can gaze impartially on this plebeian soldier rising to the throne of an empire—measuring his single intellect with the proudest kings of Europe, and coming off victorious from the encounter—rising above the prejudices and follies of his age, "making kings of plebeians and plebeians of kings"—grasping, as by intuition, all military and political science—expending with equal facility his vast energies on war or peace—turning with the same profound thought from fierce battles to commerce, and trade, and finances;—I say when the world can calmly thus contemplate him, his amazing genius will receive that homage which envy, and ignorance, and hatred, now withhold.

And when the intelligent philanthropist shall understand the political and civil history of Europe, and see how Napoleon broke up its systems of oppression and feudalism—proclaiming human rights in the ears of the world, till the Continent shook with the rising murmurs of oppressed man—study well the changes he introduced, without which human progress must have ceased—see the great public works he established—the institutions he founded—the laws he proclaimed, and the civil liberty he restored—and then, remembering that the bloody wars that offset all these, were waged by him in self-defence, and were equal rights struggling against exclusive despotism;—he will regret that he has adopted the slanders of his foemen, and the falsehoods of monarchists.

II.

MARSHAL BERTHIER.

The Talents a Revolution developes—Creation of the Marshals—Berthier's Character and History—Soliloquy of Napoleon—Berthier's Death.

NOTHING is more unfortunate for a great man, than to be born beside a greater, and walk, during life-time, in his shadow. It is equally unfortunate to be great only in one department that is still better filled by another. Had Shakspere not lived, Massinger might have stood at the head of English dramatists; and had Alfiery kept silent, a host of writers, now almost unknown, would have occupied the Italian stage. Had it not been for Cæsar, Brutus might have ruled the world; and were it not for Bonaparte, many a French general would occupy a separate place in that history of which they are now only transient figures. Great men, like birds, seem to come in flocks; and yet but *one* stands as the representative of his age. The peak which first catches the sunlight is crowned monarch of the hills, and the rest, however lofty, are but his bodyguard. Much injustice has been done to Bonaparte's generals by not allowing for the influence of this principle. There is scarcely a historian that will concede to such men as Lannes, Davoust, Murat, and Ney, any dominant quality, except bravery. Under the guiding intellect of Napoleon, they fought nobly; but when left to their own resources, miserably failed. Yet the simple truth is: being compelled, by their relative position, to let another plan for them, they could do little else than execute orders. A mind dependent is cramped and confined, and can exhibit its power only by the force and vigor.r with which it *executes* rather than *forms* plans.

But if it be a misfortune for a *great* man to live and move in the shadow of a still greater, it is directly the reverse with a weak man. The shadow of the genius in which he walks, mantles his stupidity, and by the dim glory it casts over him, magnifies his proportions. Such was the position of Boswell to Johnson, and this is the secret of Berthier's fame. Being selected by Napoleon as the chief of his staff, and his most intimate companion; he has linked himself indissolubly with immortality.

The times in which Bonaparte lived, were well calculated to produce such men as he gathered around him. A revolution, by its upturnings, brings to the surface materials, of the existence of which, no man ever dreamed before. Circumstances make men, who then usually return the compliment, and make circumstances. In ordinary times, as a general rule, the souls of men exhibit what force and fire they may contain, in those channels where birth has placed them. This is more especially true in all monarchical and aristocratical governments. The iron framework they stretch over the human race, effectually presses down every throb that would otherwise send an undulation over the mass. No head can lift itself except in the legitimate way, while very *small* heads that happen to hit the aperture aristocracy has kindly left open, may reach a high elevation. Revolution rends this frame-work as if it were a cobweb, and lets the struggling, panting mass beneath, suddenly erect themselves to their full height and fling abroad their arms in their full strength. The surface, which before kept its even plane, except where a star or decoration told the right of the wearer to overlook his fellow, becomes all at once a wild waste of rolling billows. Then man is known by the force within him, and not by the pomp about him. There is also a prejudice and bigotry always attached to rank, which prevents it from seeing the worth below it, while it will not measure by a just standard, because that would depreciate its own excellence. Those, on the contrary, who obtain influence through the soul and force they carry within them, appreciate these things alone in others, and hence judge them by a true criterion.

Thus Bonaparte—himself sprung from the middle class of society—selected men to lead his armies from their personal qualities alone. This is one great secret of his astonishing victories. Dukes and princes led the allied armies, while *men* headed the battalions of France. Bonaparte judged men by what they could *do*, and not by their genealogy. He looked not at the decorations that adorned the breast, but at the deeds that stamped the warrior—not at the learning that made the perfect tactician, but the real practical force that wrought out great achievements. Victorious battle-fields were to him the birth-place of titles, and the commencement of genealogies; and stars were hung on scarred and war-battered, rather than on noble breasts. He had learned the truth taught in every physical or moral revolution, that the great effective moulding characters of our race always spring from the middle and lower classes. All reformers also start there, and they always must, for not only is their sight clearer and their judgment more just, but their earnest language is adapted to the thoughts and sympathies of the many. Those men also who rise to power through themselves alone, feel it is by themselves alone they must stand; hence the impelling motive is not so much greatness to be won as the choice between it and their original nothingness. Bonaparte was aware of this, and of all his generals who have gone down to immortality with him, how few were taken from the upper classes. Augereau was the son of a grocer, Bernadotte of an attorney, and both commenced their career as private soldiers. Bessières, St. Cyr, Jourdan, and the fiery Junot, all entered the army as privates. Kleber was an architect; the impetuous Lannes the son of a poor mechanic; Lefevre, Loison, and the bold Scotchman Macdonald, were all of humble parentage. The victorious Massena was an orphan sailor boy, and the reckless, chivalric Murat, the son of a country landlord. Victor, Suchet, Oudinot, and the stern and steady Soult, were each and all of humble origin, and commenced their ascent from the lowest step of Fame's ladder. And last of all, NEY, the "bravest of the brave," was the son of a poor tradesman of Sarre Louis.

Immediately on the assumption of supreme power, Napoleon created eighteen Marshals, leaving two vacancies to be filled afterwards. Four of these were honorary appointments, given to those who had distinguished themselves in previous battles, and were now reposing on their laurels as members of the Senate. The other fourteen were conferred on Gen erals destined for active service, but in reward of their former deeds. The first four were Kellerman, Lefevre, Periguin, and Serruier. The fourteen active Marshals were Jourdan, Berthier, Massena, Lannes, Ney, Augereau, Brune, Murat, Bessières, Moncey, Mortier, Soult, Davoust, and Bernadotte. Kleber and Desaix, were dead, both killed on the same day, one in Egypt, and the other at Marengo, or they would have been first on this immortal list.

All these had been active Generals, and had distinguished themselves by great deeds, and won their renown by hard fighting, except Berthier. Their honours were the reward of prodigies of valour, and exhibitions of heroism seldom surpassed. Berthier alone obtained his appointment for his services in the staff, and partly, I am inclined to believe, for his personal attachment to Napoleon. Without any merit as a military leader, he still deserves a place among the distinguished Marshals of the Empire, for his intimate relationship with Napoleon.

Alexander Berthier was born at Versailles, on the 20th of November, 1753. His father was coast surveyor to Louis XVI., and acquired great reputation for his skill in this department. Young Berthier naturally became proficient in mathematical studies—was a capital surveyor and excelled in drawing. Though filling the situation in his father's office with a faithfulness and ability that promised complete success in his profession, he nevertheless preferred the army. By his father's connection with government, he was enabled to obtain a commission at the outset in the dragoons, and as Lieutenant in Rochambeau's staff, came to the United States; and served during the war of the American Revolution. I know of no act of his, during this time, worthy of note. He had none of the daring and intrepidity so necessary to form a good commander. At the time of the French Revolution, he was an officer in the National Guards, and stood firm to the royal cause till the Guards themselves went over, when he himself became a fiery republican. He was Chief of the Staff in the first campaigns of the Republic, on the Rhine and Northern Frontier, and though faithful and efficient in the discharge of his duties, received no promotion. Not having sufficient energy and force to distinguish himself by any brilliant exploit, he obtained merely the reputation of being a faithful officer. In the first campaign in Italy, he was quarter-master to Kellerman; but when Bonaparte took command of the army, he made him Chief of his Staff, and promoted him to the rank of Major-General.

From that time on, for eighteen years, he scarce ever left the side of Bonaparte. We find him with him on the sands of Egypt, and amid the snows of Russia: by the Po, the Rhine, the Danube, and the Niemen, and admitted to an intimacy that few were allowed to enjoy. It seems natural for a strong, powerful mind to attach itself to a weak one; for its desire is not so much for sympathy and support, as for the privilege of relaxing and unbending itself without impairing its dignity, or exposing its weaknesses. Berthier seemed to place no restraint on him. He had such a thorough contempt for his intellect, and knew in what awe and reverence he held him, that his presence relieved his solitude without destroying it. It is true, Berthier's topographical knowledge, and his skill in drawing maps and charts, and in explaining them, made him indispensable to Bonaparte who relied so much on these things in projecting his campaigns. Especially as the channel through which all his orders passed, he became more necessary to him, than any other single officer in the army.— Yet, Berthier was admitted into privacies to which none of these relations gave him a claim. When it was necessary for Bonaparte to be in the open air for a long time, early in the morning, or late at evening, a huge fire was always built by the Chasseurs, to which he allowed no one to approach, unless to feed it with fuel, except Berthier. Backwards and forwards, with his hands behind his back, he would walk—his grave and thoughtful face bent on the ground—until the signals were made of which he was in expectation, when he would throw off his reserve, and call out to Berthier, " To horse."

Bonaparte's travelling carriage, a curiosity in itself, was arranged as much for Berthier, as for himself.— Notwithstanding the drawers for his despatches, and his portable library, he had a part of it partitioned off for the latter. True, he did not give him half, nor allow him the *dormeuse*, on which he himself could recline and refresh himself. But Berthier was content even with the privilege allowed him, though it furnished him anything but repose, for Bonaparte made use of the time, in which his cortège was sweeping like a whirlwind along the road, to examine despatches, and the reports of the positions, &c. As he read he dictated his directions, which Berthier jotted down, and, at the next stopping place, filled out, with a precision that satisfied even his rigorous master. Methodical in all he did—doing nothing in confusion— the rapid hints thrown out by Napoleon, assumed a symmetry and order under his pen, that required on explanation, and scarce ever needed an alteration. In this department he was almost as tireless as Napoleon himself. He would write all night, with a clearness of comprehension, and an accuracy of detail, that was perfectly surprising. Apparently without the mental grasp and vigour necessary to comprehend the gigantic plans he filled out with such admirable precision; he nevertheless mapped them down as if they had been his own. A hint from Napoleon was sufficient for him; for so accustomed had he become to the action of his mind, that he could almost anticipate his orders. He had lived, and moved, and breathed so long in the atmosphere of that intellect, that he became a perfect reflector to it. He knew the meaning of every look and gesture of the Emperor, and a single glance would arrest him, as if it had the power to blast. At the battle of Eylau, when Augereau's shattered ranks came flying past him, pursued by the enemy, Napoleon suddenly found himself, with only his staff about him, in presence of a column of four thousand Russians. His capture seemed inevitable, for he was on foot, and almost breast to breast with the column. Berthier immediately, in great trepidation, called out for the horses. Napoleon gave him a single look, which pinned him as silent in his place, as if he had been turned into stone. Instead of mounting his horse, he ordered a battalion of his guard to charge. The audacious column paused, and before it could recover its surprise, six battalions of the Old Guard, and Murat's Cavalry, were upon it, rending it to pieces. So perfectly mechanical was his mind, that it was impossible to confuse him by the rapid accumulation of business on his hands. He was among papers, what Bonaparte was on a battle field—always himself; clear-headed and correct, bringing order out of confusion, in a manner that delighted his exacting master. Bonaparte appreciated this quality in his Major-General, and tasked it to the utmost. He once said that this was the great merit of Berthier, and of "inestimable importance" to him. "No other could possibly have replaced him.' The services he performed, were amply rewarded by making him Marshal of the Empire, grand huntsman, Prince of Neufchatel, and Prince of Wagram. Yet, such a low opinion did Napoleon have of this Prince's and Marshal's character, that he once said, " Nature has evidently designated many for a subordinate situation ; and among them is Berthier. As Chief of the Staff, he had no superior; but he was not fit to command five hundred men." From this intimate relationship with Napoleon, however, and all the orders coming through his hands, many began to think that he was the light of Napoleon's genius. "Napoleon and Berthier" were coupled so constantly in men's mouths, that they began to be joined in praise by those who knew neither personally, and there might, to this day, have been a great difference of opinion respecting his merit, if he had never attempted anything more than to obey orders.

Still Berthier showed at times ability, which brought on him the commendations of the Commander-in-Chief. At Lodi, Arcola, and indeed throughout the first campaign of the young Bonaparte, he behaved with so much bravery, and brought such aid to the army, that he was most honourably mentioned in the reports to the Directory.

On Bonaparte's return to Paris, after his victorious campaign in Italy, Berthier was left in command of the army. Not long after, in an *emeute* in Rome, the French Legation was assailed, and the young General Duphet killed, which brought an order from the Directory to Berthier to march on the city. Arrived at the gates of the home of the Cæsars, the soldiers were transported with enthusiasm; and they, with the republican citizens, conducted Berthier through the Porta di Popolo, in triumph to the capital, as the victorious generals of old were wont to be borne. The intoxicated multitude, thinking the days of ancient glory, when Rome was a republic, had returned, sung the following memorable hymn as they carried him towards the capital:

> Romain leve les yeux : là fut le Capitole ;
> Ce pont est le pont du Coclès
> Ces chàdons sont couverts des cendres de Scèvole,
> Lucrèce dort sous ces cyprès
> Mà Brutus immola là race ;
> Ici s'engloutit Curtius ;
> Et Cesar à cette autre place
> Fut poignardè par Cassius.
> Rome, là libertè t'appele !
> Romp tes fers, ose t'affranchir ;
> Un Romain dort libre pour elle,
> Pour elle un Romain dort Mourir.

Te Deum was chanted in St. Peter's by fourteen cardinals, and the old Roman form of government proclaimed in the ancient forum.

But he was no sooner installed in his place, than he began to practice such extortion and pillage, that even his own officers broke out in open complaints against him; and he had to leave the army, and set out for Paris.

He was one of those selected by Bonaparte to accompany him to Egypt. Berthier could not bear to leave his "beloved General's" side : but, though forty three years of age, he had conceived such a violent passion for one Madame Visconti, that it quite upset his weak intellect, and drove him into paroxysms of grief, when he thought also of leaving the object of his passion. He hastened to Toulon, and told Bonaparte that he was sick, and could not go; and requested to be left behind. But his prayers and tears fell on a heart that had no sympathy with such nonsense, and he was forced to set sail. The long, tedious voyage— the separation of so many thousand miles—the new and glorious field to honour and fame which Egypt spread out before him, could not drive the image of his dear Visconti from his mind. He had a tent placed beside his own fitted up in the most elegant style, in which was suspended the portrait of this lady. Here, "the chief of the staff of the army of Egypt" would retire alone, and prostrating himself before it, indulge in the most passionate expressions of love and grief, and went so far at times even as to burn incense to it, as if it were a goddess, and he an ignorant devotee. At Alexandria, his grief became so intense that he besought Bonaparte to allow him to return. Finding it impossible to drive this absurd passion from the turned head of his Major-General, he at length granted his request. Poor Berthier bade his commander a solemn farewell, and departed. In a few hours, however, he returned, his eyes swimming in tears, saying, after all, he could not leave his "beloved General."

He accompanied Bonaparte in his return to France and with Lannes and Murat, was his chief reliance and confidant in his plans to overturn the Directory. After the establishment of the Consular system, and his own appointment as First Consul, Napoleon did not forget the services of Berthier, but gave to him the Portfolio of War. He bestowed on him also, at different times, large sums of money, which might as well have been thrown in the Seine, as to all good they did this imbecile spendthrift. On one occasion, he presented him with a magnificent diamond worth nearly twenty thousand dollars, saying, "Take this; we frequently play high: lay it up against a time of need." In a few hours it was sparkling on the head of his lady-love.

This mad passion, outliving separation, change, and all the excitements of the camp and battle-field, was doomed to a most bitter disappointment. At the urgent request of Napoleon, he finally married a princess of Bavaria. But scarcely was the marriage consummated, when, as if on purpose to complete his despair, the husband of Madame Visconti died. This was too much for Berthier. Cursing his miserable fate, he hastened to Napoleon, overcome with grief, exclaiming, "What a miserable man I am! had I been only a little more constant, Madame Visconti would have been my wife."

I remarked before that Berthier might possibly have passed for a good general, had he not gratuitously revealed his own weakness to the eyes of Europe.— At the opening of the campaigns of Abensberg, Landshut, and Echmuhl, Napoleon despatched him to the head quarters of the army, with definite directions—the sum of which was, to concentrate all the forces around Ratisbon, unless the enemy made an attack before the 15th, in which case he was to concentrate them on the Lech, around Donauwerth. Berthier seized with some wonderful idea of his own, instead of carrying out the Emperor's orders to the very letter, as he had ever before done, acted directly contrary to them. Instead of concentrating the army, he scattered it. The Austrians were advancing, and the notion instantly seized him of executing a prodigious feat, and of stopping the enemy at all points.

Massena and Davoust, commanding the two principal corps of the army, he separated a hundred miles from each other, while at the same time he placed Lefebvre, Wrede, and Oudinot in so absurd a position, that these experienced generals were utterly amazed. Davoust became furious at the folly of Berthier —told him he was dooming the army to utter destruction, while Massena urged his strong remonstrance against this suicidal measure. As he was acting under Napoleon's orders, however, they were compelled to obey him, though some of the Marshals declared that he was a traitor, and had been bribed to deliver up the army. Nothing but the slowness of the Archduke's advance saved them. His army of a hundred and twenty thousand men could, at this juncture, have crushed them almost at a blow, if it had possessed one quarter the activity Napoleon soon after evinced. While affairs were in this deplorable state, and Berthier was in an agony at his own folly, and utterly at loss what to do, Napoleon arrived at head-quarters. He was astounded at the perilous position in which his army was placed.

His hasty interrogations of every one around him, soon placed the condition of the two armies clearly before him; and his thoughts and actions, rapid as lightning, quickly showed that another spirit was at the head of affairs. Officers were despatched hither and thither on the fleetest horses—Berthier's orders were all countermanded, and the concentration of the army was effected barely in time to save it. Immediately on his arrival at Donauwerth, he despatched a note to Berthier, saying, "What you have done appears so strange, that if I was not aware of your friendship, I should think you were betraying me. Davoust is at this moment more completely at the Archduke's disposal, than my own." Davoust was also perfectly aware of this, but thought only of fulfilling his orders like a brave man. In speaking of this afterward, Napoleon said—"You cannot imagine in what a condition I found the army on my arrival, and to what dreadful reverses it was exposed if we had to deal with an enterprising enemy. I shall take care that I am not surprised again in such a manner." The chief of the staff was never after suspected of being anything more than a mere instrument in the hands of the Emperor.

The change that passed over the French army was instantaneous, and the power of intellect and genius working with lightning-like rapidity, was never more clearly seen than in the different aspect Napoleon put on affairs in a single day. Under his all-pervading, all-embracing spirit, order rose out of confusion, and strength out of weakness. Had an Austrian General committed such a blunder in his presence, as Berthier did in the face of the Archduke Charles, he would have utterly annihilated him.

It it useless to follow Berthier through the long campaigns, in which he never quitted the Emperor's side, as he only now and then appears above the surface, and then merely as a good chief of the staff, and a valuable aid in the cabinet with his topographical knowledge. He was with him in his last efforts to save Paris and his throne. He, with Caulincourt was by his side in that gloomy night when, in his haste to get to his capital, he could not wait for his carriage, but walked on foot for a mile, chafing like a fettered lion. They were the only auditors of that terrible soliloquy that broke from his lips as he strode on through the darkness. Just before, when news was brought that Paris had capitulated, the expression of his face as he turned to Caulincourt and exclaimed—"*Do you hear that?*" was enough to freeze one with horror; but now his sufferings melted the heart with pity. Paris was illuminated by the innumerable watch-fires that covered the heights, and around it the allied troops were shouting in unbounded exultation over the glorious victory that compensated them for all their former losses; while but fifteen miles distant, on foot, walked its king and emperor through the deep midnight—his mighty spirit wrung with such agony that the sweat stood in large drops on his forehead, and his lips worked in the most painful excitement. Neither Berthier nor Caulincourt dared to interrupt the rapid soliloquy of the fallen Emperor, as he muttered in fierce accents, "I burned the pavement—my horses were swift as the wind, but still I felt oppressed with an intolerable weight; something extraordinary was passing within me. I asked them to hold out only twenty-four hours. Miserable wretches that they are! Marmont, too, who had sworn that he would be hewn in pieces, rather than surrender! And Joseph ran off, too—my very brother! To surrender the capital to the enemy—what poltroons! They had my orders; they knew that, on the 2d of April, I would be here at the head of seventy thousand men! My brave scholars, my National Guard, who had promised to defend my son all men with a heart in their bosoms, would have joined to combat at my side! And so they have capitulated, betrayed their brother, their country, their sovereign—degraded France in the sight of Europe! Entered into a capital of eight hundred thousand souls, without firing a shot! It is too dreadful! That comes of trusting cowards and fools. When I am not there, they do nothing but heap blunder on blunder. What has been done with the artillery? They should have had two hundred pieces, and ammunition for a month. Every one has lost his head; and yet Joseph imagines that he can lead an army, and Clarke is vain enough to think himself a minister; but I begin to think Savary is right, and that he is a traitor;" then suddenly rousing himself, as if from a troubled dream, and as if unable to believe so great a disaster, he turned fiercely on Caulincourt and Berthier and exclaimed, "Set off, Caulincourt; fly to the allied lines; penetrate to head quarters; you have full powers; FLY! FLY!"* It was with difficulty that Berthier and Caulincourt could persuade him that the capitulation had been concluded. Yielding at length to the irreversible stroke of fate, he turned back, joined his carriages, and hastened to Fontainbleau, where he arrived a little after sunrise.

That was a gloomy day for him; and while he was pondering on his perilous position, endeavouring to pierce the night of misfortune that now enveloped him, Paris was shaking to the acclamations of the multitude, as the allied armies defiled through the streets. Caulincourt had been sent off to make terms with the victors, but nothing would do but Napoleon's abdication—and he was forced to resign. Then commenced

* Vide Caulincourt and Alison.

the shameful desertion of his followers, which broke his great heart, and drove him in his anguish to attempt the destruction of his life. Among these feeble and false-hearted men, was Berthier. Napoleon was a crownless, throneless man, without an army—without favour, or the gifts they bring—and Berthier had no longer any motive for attaching himself to him, except that of honour and noble affection—both of which he was entirely destitute of. Afraid to turn traitor before his benefactor's face, he asked permission to go to Paris on business, promising to return the next day. When he had left, Napoleon turned to the Duke of Bassano, and said, "He will not return." "What!" replied the Duke, "can Berthier take such a farewell?" "He will not return," calmly replied Napoleon. "He was born a courtier. In a few days you will see my Vice Constable begging an appointment from the Bourbons. It mortifies me to see men I have raised so high in the eyes of Europe, sink so low. What have they done with that halo of glory, through which men have been wont to contemplate them?" He was right; Berthier returned no more. Too mean to entertain or even *act* a noble sentiment—and yet with sufficient conscience to feel the glaring ingratitude and baseness of his treachery, and fearing to confront the man who had elevated him to honour, and heaped countless benefits on his head; he shrunk away like a thief, to kiss the foot of a Bourbon. A few days after, he presented himself at the head of the Marshals before Louis XVIII., saying —"France having groaned for the last twenty-five years under the weight of the misfortunes which oppressed her, had looked forward to the happy day which now shines upon her." This infamous falsehood, crowning his base treason, ingratitude, and blasphemy; was uttered within one week after he had sworn to Bonaparte he would never desert him, whatever adversity might befal him. When the Bourbon king made his public entry into Paris, Berthier was seen riding in front of the carriage in all the pomp of his new situation. But even the common people could not witness the disgrace this companion and private friend of Napoleon put on human nature, in silence. As he rode along, reproachful voices met his ear, saying, "Go to the island of Elba, Berthier! go to Elba!" There was his place. Honour, gratitude, affection, manhood—all called him there, but called in vain. A seat in the Chamber of Peers, and a command in the king's body guard, were the price he received for covering himself with infamy in the sight of the world.

But his baseness was doomed to receive another reward, for the next year Napoleon was again in France. As Louis withdrew to Ghent, Berthier wished to accompany him; but the king had sufficient penetration to see that one who had deserted his greatest friend and benefactor in the hour of adversity, would not be slow to betray *him;* and hence intimated that he could dispense with his company. Trusted by no one, he retired to Bomberg, in his father-in-law's dominions. Here, on the 19th of May, 1815, he was seen leaning out of the window of his hotel, as the allies were defiling past, in their retreat from France. A moment after, his mangled body was lifted from the pavement, where it lay crushed and lifeless at the very feet of the Russian soldiers. Some say he was thrown out by the soldiers themselves; others, that he leaped purposely from the window to destroy himself. His death is shrouded in mystery; but the common belief is, that, Judas-like, stung with remorse and shame for his treachery, and finding himself deserted by his new master, and fearing the vengeance of his old one; he took this method of ending a life which had become burdensome, and added to all his other crimes, that of suicide.

But he need not have feared Bonaparte—the latter held him in too great contempt to make him an object of vengeance, and was heard to say, on his march to Paris, "The only revenge I wish on this poor Berthier, would be to see him in his costume of Captain of the body-guard of Louis." He knew that he would writhe under his smile of contempt, more than under the stroke of a lance.

Berthier wrote a history of the expedition into Egypt, and if he had survived Napoleon, would probably have given an account of his private life, which would have added much to the facts already collected.

III.

MARSHAL AUGEREAU.

His Early Life and Character—His Campaigns in Italy—Battle of Castiglione—Battle of Arcola—Revolution of the 18th Fructidor—Charge at Eylau—His traitorous Conduct and Disgrace.

THERE is very little pleasure in contemplating a character like that of Augereau, especially when one is led, from his rank and titles, to expect great qualities. Augereau had simple bravery, nothing more to render him worthy of a place amid the Marshals of the Empire. He was not even a second-rate man in anything, but courage; and there he had no superior. As a fierce fighter—one whose charge was like a thunderbolt, and whose tenacity in the midst of carnage and ruin, nothing seemed able to shake—he was worthy to command beside Massena, Ney, Lannes, Davoust, and Murat—but there the equality ended. He owed his Marshal's baton not so much to his Generalship as to his having served in Bonaparte's first campaigns in Italy, and helped, by his bravery, to lay the foundation-stone of the young Corsican's fame. Napoleon, in the height of his power, did not forget the young chiefs, with whom he won his first laurels, and to whose unsurpassed valour he owed the wondrous success of his first campaigns. It was with such men as Murat, Massena, Lannes, Victor, and Augereau, that he conquered four armies, each large as his own. With all his genius, he could have accomplished so much with no other men. In those rapid and forced marches—those resistless onsets, and in that tireless activity, without which he was ruined—these men were equal to his wishes and his wants. Massena and Augereau were among the first of these fiery leaders, and astonished Europe by the brilliancy of their exploits. Bonaparte, in his letter to the Directory, calls him "the brave Augereau." At Lodi, Castiglione, and Arcola, he won his Ducal title, and his Marshal's staff.

Born, November 14th, 1757, in the Fauxbourg St. Marceau, of Paris, the son of a grocer, Pierre-Francois-Charles Augereau always retained the marks of his origin. Living in a democratic quarter of the city, and sprung from a democratic stock, he was as thorough a Jacobin as ever outraged humanity.

Of an adventurous, ardent spirit, he left Paris when a mere youth, and entered the army of the King of Naples as a common soldier. Finding nothing to do, and apparently nothing to gain in the service; he left it in mingled disappointment and disgust. Poor and without friends, he taught fencing in Naples, as a means of support, and remained there till he was thirty-five years of age. But the all-powerful Revolution, which dragged into its vortex every stern and fierce spirit France possessed, soon hurried him into scenes more congenial to his tastes. Being compelled to leave Naples, in 1792, by the edict of the King, which forced all Frenchmen of Revolutionary principles out of the kingdom; he returned to Paris, and enlisted as a volunteer in the army of the Pyrenees. Here he had a clear field for his daring, and soon won himself a reputation that secured his rapid promotion. When he entered the army as a volunteer, he was thirty-five years of age—at thirty-eight he found himself Brigadier-General, and in two years more General of Division. Foremost in the place of danger—resistless in the onset, he had acquired a reputation for daring, that made him a fit companion for Napoleon in his Italian campaigns. Though so much older than the Commander-in-Chief, he soon learned to bow to his superior genius; and followed him with a courage and fidelity that did not go unrewarded.

I have often imagined the first interview between the young Bonaparte and the veteran Generals of the army of Italy. There were Rampon, Massena, and Augereau, crowned with laurels they had won on many a hard-fought field. Here was a young man, sent to them as their Commander-in-Chief, only twenty-seven years of age. Pale, thin, with a stoop in his shoulders, his personal appearance indicated anything but the warrior. And what else had he to recommend him? He had directed some artillery successfully against Toulon, and quelled a mob in Paris, and that was all. He had no rank in civil matters—indeed, had scarcely been heard of—and now, a mere stripling, without experience, never having conducted an army in his life; he appears before the two scarred Generals, Massena and Augereau, both nearly forty years of age, as their Commander-in-Chief. When called to pay their first visit to him, on his arrival, they were utterly amazed at the folly of the Directory The war promised to be a mere farce. Young Bonaparte, whose quick eye detected the impression he had made on them, soon, by the firmness of his manner, and his vigour of thought, modified their feelings. At the Council of War, called to discuss the proper mode of commencing hostilities, Rampon volunteered a great deal of sage advice—recommended circumspection and prudence, and spoke of the experienced Generals that were opposed to them. Bonaparte istened, full of impatience, till he was through; and then replied, in his impetuous manner, "Permit me, gentlemen, with all due deference to your excellent observations, to suggest some new ideas. The art of war, rest assured, is yet in its infancy. For many ages men have made war in a theatrical and effeminate manner. Now is not the time for enemies mutually to appoint a place of combat, and advancing, with their hats in hand, say, " *Gentlemen, will you have the goodness to fire.*" We must cut the enemy in pieces—precipitate ourselves like a torrent on their battalions, and grind them to powder; that is, bring back war to its primitive state—fight as Alexander and Cæsar did. Experienced Generals conduct the troops opposed to us !—So much the better, so much the better! It is not their experience that will avail them against me. Mark my words, they will soon burn their books on tactics, and know not what to do. * * * * The system I adopt, is favourable to the profession of arms; every soldier becomes a hero; for when men are launched forward with impetuosity, there is no time for reflection, and they will do wonders. Yes, gentlemen, the first onset of the Italian army will give birth to a new epoch in military affairs. *As for us, we must hurl ourselves on the foe like a thunderbolt, and smite like it. Disconcerted by our tactics, and not daring to put them in execution, they will fly before us as the shades of night before the uprising sun.*" The manner and tone, in which this was said, and that eloquence, too, which afterwards so frequently electrified the soldiers; took the old Generals by surprise, and Augereau and Massena turned to each other with significant looks; and Rampon, after he had gone out, remarked, "Here is a man that will yet cut out work for government."

Such feelings and bold projects, suited well the impetuous and daring Augereau, and Bonaparte could not have had a better General in the kind of war he was to wage. Where it was to be marching all night, and fighting all day, for days in succession—and one must be equal to three, by the rapidity of his movements, and the force of his onsets—Augereau was just the man. There was little room for the exhibition of military tactics, on the part of the several Commanders. The whole theatre of war was under the immediate inspection of Bonaparte. He planned and directed every thing, without going through even the form of calling a Council of War. His officers had simply to obey orders—and to a man, like Augereau, who could never reason, but was great in action—this was the very field for him to win fame in. There was little room for mistakes, except on the field of battle, and he made few there. Tell him to storm such a battery—cross such a river, in the midst of a murderous fire, or force such a wing of the army, and he would do it, if it was to be done. His soldiers loved him with devotion, and would follow him into any danger. His activity and rapidity of motion, together with his tireless energy, also rendered him a powerful ally to Bonaparte. In campaigns where such velocity of movement was necessary, in order to compensate for numbers, that the army seemed endowed with wings, flying from point to point, to the utter astonishment of the enemy; and an endurance was demanded that could cope with that of Bonaparte, who seemed made of iron; Augereau was at home. In the first battle of Montenotte, we find him fighting beside the young Corsican, and at the close of the battle, left in command, with instructions to renew the attack in the night. But not yet fully understanding the spirit that headed the army, he neglected to obey the order, and hence lost a great advantage. A few days after he assailed the Piedmontese, at Millessimo, and won that bloody battle. With such fury did he charge them, and so terrible was the shock, that every pass leading into Piedmont was forced; and in the hurry and tumult of the overthrow, their General was driven, for self-preservation, with ten thousand men, into an old and impregnable castle. Around this structure, Augereau formed his columns, and marched boldly up, to carry it by assault. Then commenced one of those struggles of knightly days. The assailants rained down stones and rocks, and missiles of every description, which bore away whole companies at a time. Amid the cries and shouts of the assailants, and the falling of the stones, the combat raged, till night closed the scene. In the morning, Provera, the Piedmontese commander, was compelled to surrender.

Piedmont was humbled, and entered into a treaty with Bonaparte. In the two engagements at Castiglione, he fought one alone, and one with Bonaparte; and earned the title of Duke of Castiglione, which the Emperor afterwards bestowed on him. Bonaparte advanced with Massena on Lonato, and sent Augereau to drive the Austrians from the heights of Castiglione. The latter had driven General Valette from them the day before; and Augereau was sent to retake them. Valette, though he fought with an obstinacy that would have honoured an Austrian, had not resisted with the courage that must animate the army of Italy, if it would not be lost. It was no common firmness that could resist the successive shocks to which it was exposed. While one was compelled to fight two, and as he beat them, ever fight other two—a courage and tenacity were needed that no ordinary assault could overcome. Bonaparte, in his fierce rides to and fro to different parts of the army, had killed five horses in a few days. He himself had planned the campaigns—fought at the head of the columns—marched all night, and battled all next day—bivouacked with the common soldier, and ate his coarse bread—passed sleepless nights and anxious days—and to have an important post yielded because assailed by superior force, was an example, which, if followed, would insure his overthrow—and he made an example of Valette to the whole army. He broke him in presence of his own troops and all the officers; thus stamping him with everlasting disgrace. He wished to impress on his officers and men, that he expected desperate deeds of them, and nothing else would satisfy him. No sooner was this done, than he sent Augereau to retake the lost heights. Burning with rage at the disgrace Valette had brought on the French arms, he departed with exultation on his dangerous mission. Never would *he* be broke in the presence of his soldiers for want of courage. Bonaparte might break his sword above his grave—but never fix the stain of cowardice on his name. He reached Castiglione as Bonaparte arrived at Lonato. Burning with impatience, he formed his men into columns, and rushed to the assault. Then commenced one of the most terrible days of Augereau's life. Placing himself at the head of his troops, he moved up the slope, and entered the storm of grape shot that swept the hill-side. His smitten columns staggered before it — then closed up their rent ranks, and marched, with a shout of defiance, forward. But when they came within range of the musketry also, the double storm was too severe to withstand; and they recoiled before it. Augereau rallied them again to the attack, and the brave fellows joyfully entered the destructive fire over the dead bodies of their companions; but the overwhelming force of such superior numbers, and such commanding and powerful batteries were too much for human energy; and again the army slowly and reluctantly swung back its bleeding, mangled form down the hill. Augereau, begrimed with powder and smoke, and enraged at the defeats he endured, seemed to court death. Where the balls fell thickest, there was he fighting in front of his men; and where the storm raged fiercest he was seen sternly breasting it. Again and again did he lead his exhausted and diminished army to the perilous assault; and there in the midst of whole companies that fell at every discharge, cheer on the soldiers. Amid the dead and the dying, he moved that day like a spirit of the infernal world. He seemimpervious to bullets; while the fierce purpose of his heart, to carry those heights or leave his crushed army, and his own body upon them, imparted to his aspect and his movements, a desperation that told his men that victory or annihilation was before them. For the last time he lead them to the assault — the heights were carried, amid deafening cheers — and the French standards waved from the summit. Auge reau's brow cleared up; and, as he looked off from the spot of victory, he saw Bonaparte hastening to his relief. The heart of this veteran swelled with pride as he received the commendations of the young commander-in-chief. Bonaparte never forgot this battle; and years after, when a captive on the isle of St. Helena, he said, "Ah! *that was the most brilliant day of Augereau's life.*"

BATTLE OF CASTIGLIONE.

A few days after, the second battle of Castiglione was fought, and Italy again put up as the mighty stake. The two armies stood perpendicular to a range of hills that crossed the plain on Bonaparte's left. On these heights the left wing of the French and the right of the Austrians rested, while the two armies stretched in parallel lines out into the plain All night long had Bonaparte been riding among his troops to arrange them for the coming conflict, and when daylight first broke over the eastern hills, he saw Serruerier's division approaching the field of battle. The action then commenced on the heights where Massena commanded. The two armies, inactive on the plain below, turned their eyes upon the hillside where volumes of smoke were rising in the morning air; and the incessant roll of musketry amid strains of martial music, told where their companions were struggling in the encounter of death. Augereau commanded the centre in the plain, and as he watched the firing along the heights, his impatient spirit could scarcely brook the inaction to which he was doomed. At length he received the welcome orders to charge. The onset was tremendous, and though the Austrians —being superior in numbers by one-third—resisted bravely, they were at length forced to yield to the shock. The whole line along the heights and through the plain bent backward in the struggle, and finally turned in full retreat. The victory was in the hands of the French, but the soldiers were too weary to urge the pursuit. The sun was stooping to the western horizon when the combat was done, and the exhausted army slept on the field of battle. For days they had marched and combated without cessation, and human endurance could go no further. Even Bonaparte was worn out, for his slender frame had been tasked to the utmost, and his thin features looked haggard and wan. He had galloped from division to division over the country, superintending every movement and directing every advance; for he would trust nobody with his orders, since the slightest mistake would ruin him. Nothing but lofty genius, combined with ceaseless energy and the most tireless activity, could have saved his army. It is said, that during these six days he never took off his boots, or even lay down. A week of such mental and physical excitement, without one moment's interval of repose, was enough to shatter the most iron constitution; and it is no wonder he is found writing to the Directory that his strength is gone, and all is gone but his courage. With thirty thousand men he had, in these six days, defeated sixty thousand—killed and taken prisoners two-thirds the number of his own army, and astonished the world by his achievements.

The next day Augereau was pressing after the flying enemy, and entered Verona in triumph. A few weeks after, he and Massena fought their way into Bassano together, through the fire of the enemy, leaving the ground without, covered with the dead. Be naparte arrived at night on the field of battle, and as he was spurring his horse through the corpses that strewed the ground, a dog leaped out from under the cloak of his dead master, and barked furiously at him. He would now lick his unconscious master, then stop to bark at Napoleon, and again return to his caresses. The silence of the mournful scene, broken so abruptly by this faithful dog—the strength of his attachment outliving that of all other friends, and showing himself here on the field of the dead—and the picture of that affectionate creature lavishing its unheeded caresses on the hand that should feed it no more—produced an impression on his heart that he never forgot, and affected him more than that of any other battle scene of his life. But perhaps Augereau never appeared to greater advantage than at the

BATTLE OF ARCOLA.

Bonaparte, wearied by continual fighting—exhausted by his very victories—was with his army of fifteen thousand men at Verona, when a fresh Austrian army of more than thirty thousand suddenly appeared before the town. His position was desperate, and his ruin apparently inevitable. The soldiers murmured, saying, "After destroying two armies, we are expected to destroy also those from the Rhine." Complaints and discouragements were on every side; but in this crisis, Napoleon, without consulting any one, took one of those sudden resolutions that seem the result of inspiration. In the rear of the Austrians was a large marsh, crossed by two long causeways, and on these he determined to place his army. Crossing the Adige twice during the night, the morning saw his army in two divisions,—one under Massena, and the other under Augereau,—stretched in two massive columns on these two dykes, while on every side of them was a deep marsh. This daring and consummate stroke, none but the genius of Bonaparte would ever have conceived, or dared to have adopted, if proposed. Along these narrow causeways numbers gave no advantage; everything depended on the courage and firmness of the heads of the columns. With Augereau and Massena to lead on his own, he had no doubt of success. Augereau, leading his column along the causeway on which he was posted, came up to the Adige and bridge of Arcola—on the opposite side of which was the town of Arcola—and attempted to force it. But the tremendous fire that swept it, almost annihilated the head of the column, and it fell back. It was then he performed the daring deed, which Bonaparte on his arrival imitated. Seeing his men recoil before the fire, he seized a stand of colours, and bidding his men follow after, rushed on the bridge and planted them in the midst of the iron storm. With a loud and cheering shout, the brave troops again rushed to the charge; but nothing could withstand that murderous fire. The head of the column sunk on the bridge, and Augereau himself, overthrown, was borne back in the refluent tide of his followers.

Soon after, the Austrians, under Mitrouski, attacked him in turn upon the dyke; but after a fierce struggle he repulsed them, and chasing them over the bridge, again attempted to pass it. But though the column advanced with the utmost intrepidity into the volcano that blazed at the farthest extremity, the fire was too severe to withstand, and it again recoiled, and the soldiers threw themselves down behind the dyke to escape the balls. At this critical juncture, Bonaparte, who deemed the possession of Arcola of vital importance, came up on a furious gallop. Springing from his horse, he hastened to the soldiers lying along the dyke, and asking them if they were the conquerers of Lodi, seized a standard, as Augereau had done, and exclaiming, "Follow your General!" advanced through the hurricane of grape-shot to the centre of the bridge, and planted it there. The brave grenadiers pressed with level bayonets close after their intrepid leader; but unable to endure the tempest of fire which the hotly-worked battery hurled in their faces, they seized Bonaparte in their arms, and trampling over the dead and dying, came rushing back through the smoke of battle. But the Austrians pressed close after the disordered column, and drove it into the marsh in the rear, where Bonaparte was left up to his arms in water. But the next moment, finding their beloved chief was gone, the soldiers cried out, over the roar of battle, " Forward, to save your General! Pausing in their flight, they wheeled and charged the advancing enemy, and driving them back over the morass, bore off in triumph the helpless Napoleon. In this deadly encounter of the heads of columns, and successive advances and repulses, the day wore away and the shades of a November night parted the combatants. The Austrians occupied Arcola, while the French retired to Ronco, or sunk to rest in the middle of the causeways they had held with such firmness during the day. The smoke of the guns spread itself like a mist over the marsh, amid which the dead and the dying lay together. In the morning the strife again commenced on this strange field of battle—two causeways in the midst of a march. The Austrians advanced in two columns along them, till they reached the centre, when the French charged with the bayonet, and routed them with prodigious slaughter—hurling them in the shock by crowds, from the dyke, into the marsh The second day passed as the first, and when night returned, the roar of artillery ceased, and Bonaparte slept again on the field of battle. The third morning broke over this dreadful scene, and the diminished, wearied armies, roused themselves for a last great effort. Massena charging on the run, cleared his dyke; while the left hand one, after a desperate encounter, was also swept of the enemy, and Arcola evacuated. Bonaparte now thinking the enemy sufficiently disheartened and reduced, to allow him to hazard an engagement in the open field, deployed his army into the plain across the Alpon, where the two armies drew up in order of battle. Before the signal for the onset, he resorted to a stratagem, in order to give force to his attack. He sent twenty-five trumpeters through a marsh of reeds that reached to the left wing of the Austrians, with orders to sound the charge the moment the combat became general. He then directed Massena and Augereau to advance. With an intrepid step they moved to the attack, but were met with a firm resistance, when all at once the Austrians heard a loud blast of trumpets on their flank, as if a whole division of cavalry was rushing to the charge. Terror-stricken at the sudden appearance of this new foe, they gave way and fled. At the same time the French garrison of Legnagno, in the rear, issuing forth, by order of Napoleon, and opening their fire upon the retiring ranks, completed the disorder, and the bloody battle of Arcola was won. Augereau and Massena were the two heroes of this hard-fought field.

This was in November—the next January the battle of Rivoli took place, and while Napoleon and Massena were struggling on the heights, Augereau was pressing the rear guard of the Austrians, who had come between him and the blockading force of Mantua. He had taken 1500 prisoners, and fourteen cannon, and was still straining every effort to arrest the danger that was threatening the troops around the town, when Bonaparte arrived from the field of victory with reinforcements; and Mantua fell.

In these astounding victories, Augereau appears as one of the chief actors. When all the other Generals were wounded, he and Massena stood, the two pillars of Napoleon's fortune. To carry out successfully his system of tactics—requiring such great activity, firmness, and heroism—Augereau was all he could wish. Beloved by his soldiers, he could hurl them into any danger, and hold them firm against the most overwhelming numbers.

After the fall of Mantua, he was sent to Paris to present to the Directory sixty stands of colours, the fruits of the recent victories. His heroic conduct had paved the way for a cordial reception; and the Directory had already honoured him, by presenting to him and Bonaparte the colours each had carried at Arcola, at the head of his grenadiers, and planted on the centre of the bridge in the midst of the fire.

The presentation of the colours was a magnificent sight. They were carried by sixty old veterans, who bore them along with the pride and martial bearing of youthful heroes. Augereau placed his father and mother beside him, notwithstanding their low origin while one of his brothers acted as his aid-de-camp. The son had returned covered with glory, and they were called in to share it.

The next June he was again sent to Paris for a double purpose; first, and chiefly to get him out of the army, where his violent republican principles were fomenting disorder. With peace and idleness, came the discussion of political subjects among the soldiers, and Augereau showed himself a thorough Jacobin. The second object, was to sustain the Directory, which was threatened with overthrow. Augereau was delighted with this mission; for he loved the strife of faction as much as he did the combat of the field, though much less fitted for it. He made himself ridiculous at once. To be in Paris, which he first left a poor boy, as a victorious general—flattered on every side by eulogies and public entertainments—turned his head, and he went about bragging of his exploits, and boasting that he had taught Bonaparte the art of war—indeed originated those brilliant plans to which the latter owed his victories. He frightened his best friends, all but Barras, who liked to see him among the Jacobins, uttering his ultra-revolutionary principles. There was no taming him by reason, for Augereau was incapable of serious thought, and so they approached him through his vanity. At length he became a little more circumspect, and was appointed to the command of the 17th Military Division, of Paris. As Commander-in-chief he soon played an important part in the political affairs of the Capital. The Revolution of the 18th Fructidor, was effected by him. All had been prepared on the evening of the 17th, and at midnight the inhabitants of Paris were alarmed, by seeing twelve thousand soldiers. with Augereau at their head, marching towards the palace of the Tuileries. There was no commotion, no apparent cause for this extraordinary military display; yet all night long was heard the steady tramp of soldiers, and the heavy rumbling of artillery, over the pavements. At length a solitary cannon, the signal gun, sent its roar over the breathless city, calling to mind the nights when the loud peal of the tocsin, and the beat of the alarm drum, roused up the multitude to scenes of violence and blood. Immediately the troops approached the gates of the palace of the Tuileries, and ordered them to be opened. The guards refused, and there was preparation for resistance, when Augereau appeared with his staff.

Ramel, the commandant, notwithstanding the defection among his troops, still showed a disposition to resist, when Augereau thus addressed him : " Commandant Ramel, do you recognize me Chief of the 17th Military Division?" " Yes," replied Ramel. " Well, then, as your superior officer, I command you to place yourself under arrest." He immediately obeyed. At six o'clock in the morning, the deputies were prisoners, and the revolution effected.

For the management of this affair, which Augereau attributed to his own cleverness, he expected and sought a seat in the Directory. He expostulated and threatened, but the Directors had used him all they wished, and they would not call him to sit among them. He had no other resource left, but to get a majority of the vote of the Councils in his favour. Failing in this also, he became turbulent, and violent; and finally, as a last resort, the Directory, to get rid of him, appointed him to the command of the army of Germany, a post left vacant by the death of General Hache. Enacting the fool here in his style of living, and the outward pretensions he exhibited, he finally alarmed the Directory, by the Jacobinical principles he was disseminating in the army, and the discontent he spread among the inhabitants; and was deprived of his command, under the pretext of sending him to Perpignan, to collect an army that was destined for Portugal. This appointment was a mere farce, and Augereau was to all intents disgraced. In 1799, he was elected by the department of the Upper Garonne, as a member of the council of Five Hundred.

When Bonaparte returned from Italy, Augereau withdrew from him, and during the revolution of the 18th of Brumaire, by which the Directory was overthrown, and the power of France passed into the hands of the First Consul; he stood ready to take advantage of any favorable movements to place himself at the head of the troops; and overwhelm the hero of Egypt and his friends. As things began to grow dark around Napoleon, in that most critical day of his life, he determined to go to the two Councils with his staff. He met Augereau on the way. The latter said to him sarcastically, " There, you have got yourself into a pretty plight." " It was worse at Arcola," was the brief reply of Bonaparte.

The establishment of the Consular government and the subsequent brilliant campaign of Marengo, wrought a wonderful change in Augereau's republican principles, and he was glad to pay court to Napoleon; and, for his timely conversion, was restored to favour. In 1805, '6, in Austria and Prussia, he exhibited his old valour. At Jena, especially, he showed himself

worthy to combat beside his former comrades in Italy
Afterwards at Golymin, Lechocqzin, and Landsberg
though fifty years of age, he evinced the impetuosity
and firmness of his early days. His political ambition
had been given to the winds, as he once more found
himself on the field where glory was to be won.

The next year, at the battle of Eylau, he commenced
the action, and exhibited there one of those heroic
deeds which belong to the age of chivalry, rather than
to our more practical times.

CHARGE AT EYLAU.

The night previous to the battle, he had lain tossing
on his uneasy couch—burned with fever, and tortured
by rheumatic pains, that deprived him almost of
consciousness. But at daylight, the thunder of cannon shook the field on which he lay. The tremendous
batteries on both sides, had commenced their fire,
making the earth tremble under their explosions as if a
volcano had suddenly opened on the plain. Augereau
lay and listened for a while to the stern music his soul
had so often beat time to—then hastily springing from
his feverish bed, called for his horse. His attendants,
amazed at this sudden energy, stood stupified at the
strange order; but the fierce glance of the chieftain
told them that he was not to be disobeyed. His battle steed was brought, and the sick and staggering
warrior with difficulty vaulted to the saddle. Feeling his strength giving way, and that he was unable
to keep his seat, he ordered his servants to bring
straps and bind him on. They obeyed, and strapped
him firmly in his place, when, plunging his spurs into
his steed, he flew, in a headlong gallop, to the head of
his corps. His sudden appearance among his sol

diers animated every heart. The two armies were in battle array—the trumpets sounded, and amid the furious beat of drums, and roar of cannon, Soult poured his mighty columns on the centre, while Augereau, at the head of sixteen thousand men, charged, like fire, on the left. Two hundred Russian cannon swept the field where they passed, in one incessant shower of fire. Whole ranks went down at every discharge; for the heavy shot tore through Augereau's dense masses with frightful effect. Still the columns closed over the huge gaps made in them and pressed forward to the assault. But suddenly, while Augereau was cheering on his men, and straining every nerve to make headway against the desolating batteries, a snow squall darkened the air, and swept with the rush of a whirlwind over the two armies, blotting out the very heavens. So thick and fierce was the driving storm, that Augereau could not see two rods ahead of him. Both armies were snatched from his sight in an instant, and even of his own men none but those directly about him could be seen. In a moment the ground was white with snow, which it sifted over the columns as if silently weaving their funeral shroud. Baffled and confused, not knowing which way to move, they staggered blindly over the field. Still the Russian cannon, previously trained on the spot, played furiously through the storm. Unable to see even the blaze of the discharge, these brave soldiers would hear the muffled explosions in the impenetrable gloom, and then behold their ranks mowed through, and mangled, as it a falling rock had crushed among them. In the midst of this awful carnage—enveloped by the blinding, driving snow, they were suddenly assailed or both sides by infantry and cavalry. In the midst of the uproar of nearly a thousand cannon, Augereau could not hear either the tread of the infantry, or the tramp of the cavalry, and was wholly unaware of their approach. The Russians had marked the course of the columns before the snow squall wrapped them from sight, and now advanced on both sides to crush them to pieces. Without warning or preparation, the French soldiers suddenly saw the long lances of the Cossacks emerge from the thick storm, in a serried line, in their very faces; and in the twinkling of an eye, those wild horsemen were trampling through their ranks. Before this terrible tide of cavalry and infantry the columns sunk as if engulphed in the earth. The hurried commands and shouts of Augereau, were never heard, or heard in vain. Still bound to his steed, he spurred among the disordered troops—striving by his voice and gestures, and more than all, by his daring example, to restore the battle. But wounded and bleeding, he only galloped over a field of fugitives flying in every direction, while the Cossacks and Russian cavalry, sabred them down without mercy. *Of the sixteen thousand, only fifteen hundred found their ranks again.* Trampling down the dead and dying, the victorious enemy burst with loud hurrahs into Eylau, and even into the presence of Napoleon himself, and nearly made him prisoner. It was to arrest this sudden disorder, that Murat, with his fourteen thousand cavalry, backed by the Imperial Guard, was ordered to charge.

The wounded Augereau was left without a corps to command, and sent back to Paris, in order to recover his health—the author of the "Camp and Court of Napoleon" says—"in disgrace to gratify a fit of spleen." Says that author, "Enraged at the indecisive result of the day, Napoleon wrecked his spleen on the Marshal, and sent him home in disgrace." Whatever might be the disgrace, the cause here assigned is a gratuitous falsehood. In Napoleon's bulletin home—giving an account of the battle of Eylau—he speaks of Augereau three times;—first, to describe the sudden snow squall that blinded his army, causing it to lose its direction, and grope about for half an hour in uncertainty; second, to make mention of his wound; and finally, to say, "the wound of Marshal Augereau was a very unfavorable accident, as it left his corps, in the very heat of the battle, without a leader to direct it." In a bulletin dated nineteen days after, Augereau is again mentioned in the following terms: "A la battaille d'Eylau le Maréchal Augereau, couvert de rheumatismes, etait malade et avait à peine connoisance; mais le cannon reveille les braves: il vole au galop à la tête de son corps, apres s'etre fait attaches sur son cheval. Il a étè constantement exposè au plus grand feu, et a meme étè lègèrement blessè. L'Empereur vient de l'autoriser a rentrer en France pour 'y soigner sa santè."* This is an unique mode of venting one's spleen on a man.

Two years after he was appointed to supercede St. Cyr in Spain; then besieging Gerona. Taken sick in his route, it was some time before he assumed the command of the army, and he even delayed it after

* At the battle of Eylau, Marshal Augereau, covered with rheumatism, lay sick, and almost without consciousness; but the sound of cannon awakens the brave. He flew on a gallop to the head of his corps, after having caused himself to be bound to his horse. He has been constantly exposed to the severest fire, and has been lightly wounded The Emperor grants him permission to return to France to attend to his health.

he was recovered. He saw that the service was to be a harassing one; requiring great efforts, without yielding much glory. At length, however, he took the command of the seige, and humanely offered an armistice of a month, provided the inhabitants would surrender at the termination of it, should no army come to their relief. They refusing this proposal, he pressed the siege, and reduced the town. His whole management, however, in the Peninsula; his foolish proclamations, and useless cruelties, and failures—show the little real strength of character he possessed. He was soon recalled. While Napoleon was engaged in the Russian expedition, Augereau remained stationed at Berlin. Although he was an admirable leader of a division, and brave in the hour of battle; Napoleon found him unfit to direct an army, or to be entrusted with weighty matters in a great campaign. The truth is, Augereau's rank as Marshal entitled him to a command he was not able to fill—a good general, he made a bad marshal. Nevertheless in the last struggle to save the tottering empire of France, he fought with his accustomed valour. Especially at Leipzic he appears in his former strength and daring. Hastening by forced marches to the city, scattering the enemy from his path as he came, he arrived in time to strike once more for Napoleon and his throne. The next year the Emperor entrusted him with the defence of Lyons, with the order to hold it to the last extremity. Arriving at the city, he found there only seven hundred regular troops, and a thousand National Guards, while twenty thousand Austrians were marching towards it. Knowing he could not defend the city with this feeble force, he hastened to Valence in the south, to bring up reinforcements. For a while, though fifty seven years old, he exhibited the vigour of his early campaigns. He wrote to Napoleon, demanding help, while at the same time he strained every nerve to strengthen himself. He sen a thousand men in post carriages from Valence in a single day. This was the last spark, however, of the old fire; for though reinforced by Napoleon till his army numbered twenty thousand men, he did not follow up his successes as he ought, and contributed nothing in the desperate struggle the Emperor was making for his throne. The latter wished Augereau to hover on the rear of the allied army, while he dashed against it in front; but all his orders to that effect were powerless to remove the torpor that had seized his energies. He said he was afraid to trust his troops, as they were inexperienced soldiers, &c. Napoleon, in reply, told him to forget his age, and think of the days of glory when he fought at Castiglione. He urged him to move his troops together into one column, and march into Switzerland. Said Clarke, writing in the name of the Emperor, in reply to his complaint of the meagre equipments of his soldiers, "He desires me to tell you that the corps of Gerard, which has done such great things under his eyes, is composed entirely of conscripts half naked. He has at this moment, four thousand National Guards in his army with round hats, with peasants' coats and waistcoats, and without knapsacks, armed with all sorts of muskets, on whom he puts the greatest value;—he only wishes he had thirty thousand of them." But the appeal was all in vain; and while the knell of the empire was tolling, Augereau remained inactive and useless. At length, however, he seemed to rouse himself for a moment, and obeying Napoleon's orders, marched on Geneva, and defeated the Austrians before the town. Compelled, however to retire, he retreated towards Lyons, and at Limonet fought his last battle. It was brave and worthy of his character; but though he left nearly three thousand of the enemy dead on the field, while he lost but two thousand, he was compelled to retire, and evacuate Lyons, retreating towards Valence.

At the latter place, a proclamation was issued by the inhabitants on Napoleon's abdication, loading the fallen Emperor with the most opprobrious epithets, and extolling Louis XVIII. as the idol of his country. To this atrocious proclamation Augereau's signature was affixed. On his way to Elba, Napoleon met Augereau unexpectedly near Valence, and an interview took place, which from the different versions given of it furnishes a curious illustration of the historical contradictions connected with this period.

Says the "Court and Camp of Napoleon," "Soon after this the 'Fructidor General' and the ex-emperor met at a short distance from Valence, as the latter was on his way to Elba. "I have thy proclamation," said Napoleon, "thou hast betrayed me."—"Sire," replied the Marshal, "it is you who have betrayed France and the army, by sacrificing both to a frantic spirit of ambition." "Thou hast chosen thyself a new master," said Napoleon—"I have no account to render thee on that score," replied the General—"Thou hast no courage," replied Bonaparte—"'T'is thou hast none," responded the General, and turned his back without any respect on his late master." This precious bit of dialogue is detailed with so much minuteness, that one would incline to believe it, ever against counter statements, were it not for the falsehood it bears on its own face. The whole scene is unnatural; and to wind up with a charge of cowardice on the part of each, is supremely ridiculous. For two men who had fought side by side at Lodi, Arcola, and Castiglione, and stormed together ever so many battle-fields, to accuse each other of cowardice at that late hour, would be a child's play that Augereau might stoop to—but Napoleon never.

Here is another account of this interview by Mr. Alison : " At noon on the following day, he accidentally met Augereau on the road, near Valence, both alighted from their carriages, and *ignorant of the atrocious* proclamation, in which that Marshal had so recently announced his conversion to the Bourbons, the Emperor embraced him, and they walked together on the road for a quarter of an hour in the most *amicable manner*. It was observed, however, that Augereau kept his helmet on his head as he walked along. A few minutes after, the Emperor entered Valence, and beheld the proclamation placarded on the walls." It need not be remarked, that the latter is the most reliable account of the two. A great many of the incidents of Napoleon's life, which have been gathered up by English writers, are as fabulous as the first account of this interview between him and Augereau.

Louis XVIII. rewarded him by making him Peer of France, and bestowed on him the Cross of St. Louis, and the command of the 14th Division in Normandy.

On Napoleon's landing from Elba, Augereau was struck with astonishment to find himself proclaimed by the Emperor as a traitor. He, however, made no reply hoping by a seasonable conversion, to extricate himself from the difficulties that surrounded him. Republican as he was, he never allowed his principles to interfere with his self-interest, nor his conscience with his safety. No sooner had Napoleon entered Paris in triumph, than Augereau issued a proclamation to his soldiers, urging them once more to "march under the victorious wings of those immortal eagles, which had so often conducted them to glory." Napoleon, who had never respected him, and after his infamous proclamation at Valence, thoroughly despised him, paid no attention to this delicate compliment of his flexible Marshal. Knowing him too thoroughly to trust him, and disdaining to molest him, he let the betrayer of two masters pass into silent neglect. Poor Augereau, robbed of his plumes, retired to his country estate, where he remained till the second restoration, when he again sent in his protestations of devotion to the king. But there is a limit, even to a Bourbon's vanity; and Louis, turning a deaf ear to his solicitations and flattery, he again retired to his estate, where he died in June, 1816, of a dropsy in the chest.

Augereau was essentially a mean man, though a brave one. He was a weak-headed, avaricious, selfish, boasting soldier; yet possessing courage that would not have disgraced the days of chivalry. His soldiers loved him, for he kept strict order and discipline among them, and exposed himself like the meanest of their number in the hour of danger. Without sufficient grasp of thought to form a plan requiring any depth of combination, or even intellect enough to comprehend one already furnished to his hand; he nevertheless surveyed a field of battle with imperturbable coolness, and his charge was like a falling thunderbolt.

His want of education, and the early habits and associations he formed, were enough to spoil a man of even more strength of character than he possessed. He came under the influence of Napoleon's genius at too late an age to receive those impressions which so effectually remoulded some of the younger lieutenants.

IV.

MARSHAL DAVOUST.

His Character—Battle of Auerstadt—Cavalry Action at Echmuhl—Retreat from Russia.

It is hard to form a correct opinion of such a man as Davoust. The obloquy that is thrown upon him especially by English historians, has a tendency to destroy our sympathy for him at the outset, and distorts the medium through which we ever after contemplate him. Positive in all his acts, and naturally of a stern and fierce temperament, he did things in a way, and with a directness, and an abruptness, that indicated a harsh and unfeeling nature. But if we judge of men by their actions, and not also by the motives which prompted them, we shall be compelled to regard the Duke of Wellington as one of the most cruel of men. His whole political course in England—his steady opposition to all reform—his harsh treatment of the petitions of the poor and helpless, and heartless indifference to the cries of famishing thousands, argue the most callous and unpitying nature. But his actions—though causing so much suffering, and awakening so much indignation, that even his house was mobbed by his own countrymen, and his gray hairs narrowly escaped being trampled in the dust by an indignant populace—have all sprung from his education as a military man. Every

thing must bend to the established order of things, and the suffering of individuals is not to be taken into the account. The same is true of Davoust Trained from his youth to the profession of arms—accustomed, even in his boyhood, to scenes of revolutionary violence—with all his moral feelings educated amid the uproar of battle, or the corruptions of a camp—the life of the warrior was to him the true life of man. Success, victory, were the only objects he contemplated; making up his mind beforehand, that suffering and death would attend the means employed. Hence his fearful ferocity in battle—the headlong fury with which he tore through the ranks of the enemy, and the unscrupulous manner in which he made war support war. These were the natural results of his firm resolution to conquer, and of his military creed, that "to the victors belong the spoils." He did nothing by halves, nor had he anything of the "suaviter in modo," which glosses over so many rough deeds, and conveys the impression they were done from necessity, rather than desire.

Louis-Nicholas Davoust was born at Annaux, in Burgundy, 10th of May, 1770, one year after Bonaparte. His family could lay claim to the title of noble, though, like many Italian *cavaliers*, who are too poor to own a horse; it was destitute of lands or houses. Young Davoust being destined for the army, was sent to the military school of Brienne, where was also the charity-boy, Bonaparte. At the age of fifteen, he obtained a commission; but his fiery, impetuous nature, soon involved him in difficulty with his superior officers, and it was taken from him. In the revolution, he became a fierce republican, and after the death of Louis, was appointed over a bat talion of volunteers, and was sent to join Doumourier then commanding the army of the Republic, on the Rhine. When Doumourier—disgusted with the increasing horrors of the revolution—endeavoured to win the army over, to march against the Terrorists, the young Davoust used his utmost endeavours to steady the shaking fidelity of the troops Doumourier was finally compelled to flee to the Austrians, almost alone; and Davoust, for his efforts and faithfulness, was promoted to the rank of Brigadier-General, and during five years, fought bravely on the banks of the Rhine and Moselle. When Bonaparte returned from Italy, where he had covered himself and the army with glory, Davoust sought to unite his fortunes with those of the young Corsican. He was consequently joined to the expedition to Egypt, and under the walls of Samanhout and Aboukir, fought with a bravery, that showed he was worthy of the place he had sought. He was not included with those selected by Bonaparte to accompany him to France, and did not return till the latter was proclaimed First Consul.

Attaching himself still more closely to one whose fortunes were rising so rapidly, he was placed at the head of the grenadiers of the Consular Guard, and soon after, through the influence of Bonaparte, obtained the hand of the sister of General Le Clerc—a lady of captivating manners, and rare beauty.

The road to fame was now fairly open to the young soldier, and he pursued it with a boldness and energy that deserved success. In 1804, he was made Marshal of the Empire, and the next year found him at the head of a corps of the Grand Army. Around Ulm, at Austerlitz, chief of all at Auerstadt, he per formed prodigies of valour, and fixed forever his great reputation. At Eylau and Friedland he proved that honours were never more worthily bestowed, than when placed on his head. For his bravery and success at Echmuhl, he received the title of Prince of Echmuhl, and soon after, at Wagram, showed that Bonaparte neved relied on him in vain.

The three following years he spent in Poland, as Governor of the country, and commander of the French army there, and gave great offence to the inhabitants by the heavy contributions he laid upon them, and the unfeeling manner in which they were collected.

In 1812, we find him at the head of the first corps of the Grand Army—the first to cross the Niemen and commence the splendid pageant of that memorable day. He crossed at one o'clock in the morning, and took possession of Kowno. Napoleon had his tent pitched on an eminence, a few rods from the bank, and there watched the movements of his magnificent legions. Two hundred thousand men, on that day, and forty thousand horses, in splendid array and full equipment, and most perfect order, slowly descended to the bridges, and to the stirring strains of martial music, and under the folds of a thousand fluttering banners, moved past the imperial station, rending the heavens with their shouts, while the saluting trumpets breathed forth their most triumphant strains. Throughout this disastrous campaign he fought with the heroism and firmness of Ney himself.

The next year after the Russian campaign, he made his head-quarters in Hamburgh, and defended the city, heroically, against the Russians, Prussians, and Swedes combined. He held out long after Napoleon's abdication, resolutely refusing to surrender the place, until General Gerard arrived on the part of Louis XVIII. He then gave in his adhesion to the Bourbons, but was among the first to declare for the Emperor, on his return from Elba. After the overthrow at Waterloo, he took command of that portion of the army which still remained faithful to Napoleon, and retreated to Orleans, and did not give in his adhesion to the Bourbons, until the Russians were marching against him.

This brief outline of Davoust's career, embraces the whole active life of Napoleon, and was filled up with the most stirring scenes, and marked by changes that amazed and shook the world. The role that he played in this mighty Napoleonic drama, shows him to have been an extraordinary man, and furnishes another evidence of the penetration that characterised Bonaparte in the selection of his Generals.

The three striking characteristics of Davoust, were great personal intrepidity and daring—perfect self-possession and coolness in the hour of peril, and almost invincible tenacity. With all these rare gifts, he was also a great General. In the skill with which he chose his ground, arranged his army, and determined on the point and moment of attack, he had few superiors in Europe. Rash in an onset, he was perfectly cool in repelling one. This combination of two such opposite qualities, so prominent in Napoleon, seemed to be characteristic of most of his Generals and was one great cause of their success.

His personal daring became proverbial in the army, and whenever he was seen to direct a blow, it was known that it would be the fiercest, heaviest one that could be given. His susceptibility of intense excitement, carried him in the hour of battle, above the thought of danger or death.

BATTLE OF AUERSTADT.

One of the most successful battles he ever fought, was that of Auerstadt, where he earned his title of Duke. The year before, at Austerlitz, he had exhibited that coolness in sudden peril, and that unconquerable tenacity, which made him so strong an ally on a battle field. The night before the battle of Jena, Napoleon slept on the heights of Landgrafenberg, whither he had led his army with incredible toil, and at four in the morning—it was an October morning—rode along the lines and addressed his soldiers in that stirring eloquence, which he knew so well how to use. The dense fog that curtained in the dark and chilly morning, lifted, and rent before the fierce acclamations that answered him, and with the first dawn his columns were upon the enemy. When the unclouded sun, at nine o'clock, broke through, and scattered the fog, it shone down on a wild battlefield, on which were heard the incessant thunder of artillery, and rattle of musketry; interrupted, now and then, by the heavy shocks of cavalry, and the shouts of maddened men. Napoleon was again victorious, and at six o'clock in the evening, rode over the cumbered ground, while the setting sun shone on a different scene from that which its rising beams had gilded. But not at Jena was the great battle of the 14th of October fought, nor was Napoleon the hero of the day. Less than thirty miles distant—within hearing of his cannon, could he have paused to listen—Davoust was winning the victory for him, by prodigies of valour, to which the hard fought battle of Jena was an easy affair. Napoleon imagined he had the King of Prussia, with his whole army, on the heights of Landgrafenberg—and they *were* behind them, two days previous. With ninety thousand men, he supposed he was marching on over a hundred thousand, instead of on forty thousand, as the result proved. After several hours of hard fighting, the Prussians, it is true, were reinforced by twenty thousand, under Ruchel, making sixty thousand against ninety thousand, with Napoleon at their head, and Murat's splendid cavalry in reserve. At Auerstadt, matters were reversed. The King of Prussia, with nearly two-thirds of his army, had marched thither, and with sixty thousand men threatened to crush Davoust, with only thirty thousand. Napoleon, ignorant of this, sent a dispatch to him, which he received at six o'clock in the morning, to march rapidly on Apolda, in the rear of the army he was about to engage and defeat. If Bernadotte was with him, they were to march together; but as the former had received his orders before, and this seemed a permission rather than an order, he refused to accede to Davoust's request to join their armies. He took his own route, and but for the heroism and unconquerable firmness of the latter, this act would have cost him his head.

Davoust, with his thirty thousand troops, of which only four thousand were cavalry, pushed forward, not expecting to meet the enemy till towards evening. But a short distance in front of him, on the plateau of Auerstadt, that spread away from the steep ascent up which his army, fresh from their bivouacs, was toiling —lay the King of Prussia, with fifty thousand infan try, and ten thousand splendid cavalry—the whole commanded by the Duke of Brunswick. The fog that enveloped Napoleon on the heights of Landgrafenberg and covered the battle-field of Jena with darkness, curtained in, also, the heights of the Sonnenberg, and the army of the King of Prussia. At eight in the morning, the vanguard of Davoust came unexpectedly upon the enemy, also advancing. The dense and motionless fog so concealed everything, that their bayonets almost crossed, before they discovered each other. Even then, both supposing they had come on a single detachment only, sent forward a small force to clear the way—the Prussians to open the defile up which Davoust was struggling, and the French to do the same thing, so that they could continue their march.

The upper end of this defile opened, as I remarked, on to the elevated plain of Auerstadt, far up the Sonnenberg mountains. Davoust sent on the brave and heroic Gudin, with his division, to clear it, and occupy the level space on the top, at all hazards. In a few minutes Gudin stood, in battle array, on the plateau, though entirely shut out from the enemy by the dense fog. Blucher, with nearly three thousand hussars, was ordered to ride over the plateau and sweep it of the enemy. The former part of the order he obeyed, and came dashing through the mist, with his body of cavalry, when, suddenly they found themselves on the bayonets' point, and the next moment shattered and rolled back by a murderous fire, that seemed to open from the bowels of the earth Rallying his men, however, to the charge, Blucher came galloping up to the French, now thrown into squares, and dashed, with his reckless valour, on their steady ranks. Finding, from the incessant roll of musketry, that Blucher was meeting with an obstinate resistance, the King of Prussia sent forward three divisions to sustain him. These, with Blucher's hussars, now came sweeping down on Gudin's single division, threatening to crush it with a single blow. One division against three, supported by twenty-five hundred cavalry, was fearful odds; but Gudin knowing his defeat would ruin the army, now packed in the defile below and making desperate efforts to reach the plateau; presented a firm front to the enemy, and proved, by his heroic resistance, worthy to be under the illustrious Chief that commanded him. Hitherto the combat had been carried on amid the thick fog, that stubbornly clung to the heights, involving everything in obscurity, and only now and then, lifted, like the folds of a huge curtain, as the artillery and musketry exploded in its bosom. At this dreadful crisis, however, it suddenly rolled over the mountain, and parting in fragments, rode away on the morning breeze, while the unclouded sun flashed down on the immense Prussian host, drawn up in battle array. It was at this same hour the fog parted on the plains of Jena, and revealed to the astonished Prussians their overwhelming enemy rushing to the charge. *There* the sun shone on ninety thousand Frenchmen, moving down, with resistless power, on forty thousand Prussians; but *here* on sixty thousand Prussians, enveloping thirty thousand Frenchmen. Nothing could be more startling, than the sudden revelation which that morning sun made to Davoust—he expected to find only a few detachments before him, and lo! there stood a mighty army with the imposing front of battle. As his eye fell on the glittering ranks of infantry, and flashing helmets of the superb cavalry, it embraced at once the full peril of his position. It was enough to daunt the boldest heart, but fear and Davoust were utter strangers. He was not to reach Apolda that day, that was certain, and fortunate he might consider himself if he reached it at all in any other way than as a prisoner of war. The struggle before him was to be against desperate odds, one against two, while ten thousand cavalry stood in battle array—their formidable masses alone sufficient, apparently, to sweep his army from the field. Of Gudin's brave division, of seven thousand men, which had fought, one against three, to maintain the plateau till his arrival, half had already fallen. The tremendous onsets of cavalry and infantry together on him could not be much longer withstood; but at this juncture the other divisions of the army appeared on the field, and with rapid step, and in admirable order, moved into the line of battle. The two armies were now fairly engaged. The mist had rolled away, as if hasting in affright from the scene of carnage, and under the unclouded sun there was no longer any room for deception. Davoust was fairly taken by surprise, and had on his hand an army double of his own, while a retreat without a rout was impossible. With that coolness and self-possession which rendered him so remarkable in the midst of the conflict, he gave all his orders, and performed his evolutions and conducted the charges; thus inspiring, by his very voice and bearing, the soldiers with confidence and courage. He rode through the lines; his brow knit with his stern resolve, and with the weight that lay on his brave heart, and his clear, stern voice, expressing by its very calmness the intensity of the excitement that mastered him. The next moment the plain trembled under the headlong charge of the Prussian cavalry, as they came pouring on the French infantry. The shock was terrific; but that splendid body of horse recoiled from the blow, as if it had fallen against the face of a rock instead of living men. The French threw themselves into squares, and the front rank kneeling, fringed with their glittering bayonets the entire formations, while the ranks behind poured an incessant volley on the charging squadrons. These would recoil, turn, and charge again, with unparalleled, but vain bravery. Prince William, who led them on, disdaining to abandon the contest, again and again hurried them forward with an impetuosity and strength, that threatened to bear down every thing before them. Sometimes a square would bend and waver a moment, like a wave of flame when it meets the blast, but the next moment spring to its place again, presenting the same girdle of steel in front, and the same line of fire behind. Goaded to desperation and madness by the resistance he met with, and confident still of the power of his cavalry to break the infantry, he rallied his diminished troops for the last time, and led them to the charge. These brave men rode steadily forward through the storm of grapeshot and bullets that swept their path, till they came to the very muzzles of the guns; but not a square broke, not a battalion yielded. Furious with disappointment, they then rode round the squares, firing their pistols in the soldiers' faces, and spurring their steeds in wherever a man fell. But all this time a most murderous fire wasted them; for while they swept in rapid circles round each square a girdle of light followed, rolling round the living wall, enveloping it in smoke and strewing its base with the dead. At length Prince William himself was stretched on the field where half his followers already lay bleeding, and the remainder withdrew.

Davoust, feeling how every thing wavered in the balance, multiplied himself with the perils that environed him. With no cavalry able to contend with that of the enemy, he was compelled to rely entirely on his infantry. The rapidity, coolness, and precision with which they performed their evolutions, saved him from a ruinous defeat. Now he would suddenly throw a division into squares, as the splendid Prussian cavalry came thundering upon it; and repelling the shock, unroll them into line to receive a charge of infantry, or throw them into close columns to charge in turn. The battle rested on his life; yet his personal presence at the points of danger was equally necessary to victory, and he seemed to forget he had a life to lose. He never appeared better than on this day. The intense action of his mind neutralized the strong excitement of his feelings which usually bore him into battle; and he rode through the driving storm with the stern purpose, never to yield, written on his calm marble-like countenance, in lines that could not be mistaken. He had imparted the same feelings to his followers, and the tenacity with which they disputed every inch of ground, and held firm their position against the united onsets of cavalry and infantry astonished even their enemies.

The heights of Sonnenberg never witnessed such a scene before, and the morning sun never looked down on a braver fought battle. The mist of the morning had given place to the smoke of cannon and musketry that curtained in the armies; and the whole plateau was one blaze of light streaming through clouds of dust, with which the fierce cavalry had filled the air. Old Sonnenberg quivered on his base under the shock, and its rugged sides were streaked with wreaths of smoke that seemed rent by violence from the tortured war-cloud below. Amid this wild storm Davoust moved unscathed—his uniform riddled with balls—and his guard incessantly falling around him. At length a shot struck his chapeau, and bore it from his head among his followers. Prince William was down—the Duke of Brunswick had been borne mortally wounded from the fight, while scores of his own brave officers lay stretched on the field of their fame—yet still Davoust towered unhurt amid his ranks. At length Morand was ordered to carry the heights of Sonnenberg, and plant the artillery there, so as to sweep the plateau below. This brave General put himself at the head of his columns, and with a firm step, began to ascend the slope. The King of Prussia, perceiving at a glance how disastrous to him the conquest of this position would be, charged in person at the head of his troops. For a moment the battle wavered; but the next moment the heroic Morand was seen to move upward, and in a few minutes his artillery opened on the plain, carrying death and havoc through the Prussian ranks.

The plateau was won, and Davoust master of the field. But not satisfied with his success, he determined to complete the victory by carrying the heights of Eckartsberg, which protected the retreat of the enemy. The trumpets immediately sounded the charge, and the wearied Gudin pressed forward. But the King had already rallied his shattered troops behind a reserve of fifteen thousand men, which had not yet been engaged. There, too, in security the iron-souled Blucher rallied the remnants of his splendid cavalry. It was in this crisis Davoust showed himself the great commander, and fixed forever his military fame. This reserve, only a third less than his entire force, would have wrung the victory from almost any other hand than his. I do not believe there were three Generals in the French army, that would not have been defeated at this point—there was not *one* in the allied armies. Here was an army of some twenty-four thousand men, wearied with a morning's march, and a half-day's severe fighting, dragging its bleeding columns up to a perilous assault; while fifteen thousand fresh troops, sustained by the now reformed cavalry and infantry, fell with the energy of despair upon it. Blucher stood eyeing the ranks, ready, the moment a column shook, to dash on it with his cavalry. The day so nobly battled for and won, seemed at last about to be lost. Wearied troops against fresh ones—a division against a corps—such was the relative strength of the armies. But Davoust gathered his energies for a last effort, and poured his wearied but resolute troops in such strength and terror on the enemy, that they swept down every thing in their passage—charged the artillery-men at their pieces, and wrenched their guns from their grasp—turned the cavalry in affright over the field, and carried the heights with shouts of victory that were echoed back from old Sonnenberg, as Morand, driving back the enemy that had just attacked him in his position, came driving down the slope, scattering like a whirlwind every thing before him.

The Prussians were utterly defeated, and the tired Davoust paused amid the wreck of his army, and surveyed the bloody field that should stand as an everlasting monument of his deeds.

That was a gloomy night for the Prussian king Fleeing from the disastrous field, with his disheartened troops; he was soon crossed in his track, by the fugitives from the equally disastrous plains of Jena. The wreck of Jena came driving on the wreck of Auerstadt, and the news of one overthrow was added to that of another, sending indescribable confusion and terror through the already broken ranks. Whole divisions disbanded at once. The artillery-men left their guns—the infantry their ammunition and baggage wagons—all order was lost, and nothing but a cloud of fugitives of all that magnificent army that moved in such pomp to battle, was seen driving through the darkness. The King himself, well nigh captured, struggling no longer for his army, but for his life.

Such was the battle of Auerstadt, fought on the same day with that of Jena. For his heroic conduct, Davoust was created Duke of Auerstadt, and to honor him still more, Napoleon appointed him to enter first the Prussian capital—thus showing to the whole army his right to the precedence. Not satisfied with having done this, and also with mentioning him in terms of unqualified praise in his bulletin home; he two weeks after, in reviewing his corps, on the road to Frankfort, extolled the valour of the soldiers; and calling the officers in a circle around him, addressed them in terms of respect and admiration, and expressed his sympathy for the losses they had sustained. Davoust stepped forward and replied

"Sire, the soldiers of the third corps, will always be to you what the tenth Legion was to Cæsar."* Brave words, which his after conduct, and that of his corps, on many a hard-fought field, verified. This battle cost Davoust about eight thousand killed and wounded, among which were two hundred and seventy officers. The brave Gudin lost more than half of his whole division.

In the campaign of Eylau, the same year, Davoust sustained the high reputation he had gained at Auerstadt. He commanded the advance guard on the route to Warsaw, and at the passage of the Ukra, at Pultusk and Golymin, fought with his accustomed bravery. But it was at the bloody combat of Eylau, he performed the greatest service for Napoleon, for he

* Mr. Alison, in giving an account of this battle, with his accustomed readiness to accuse Napoleon of falsehood and meanness, and equal readiness himself to falsify, says, "Napoleon's official account of the battle of Jena, in the fourth bulletin of the campaign, (it was the *fifth* Bulletin) is characterised by that extraordinary intermixture of truth and falsehood, and unceasing jealousy of any General who appeared to interfere with his reputation, which, in one who could so well afford to be generous in that particular, is a meanness in an especial manner reprehensible." And further on he quotes the bulletin itself, commencing thus: "On our right the corps of Marshal Davoust performed prodigies. Not only *did he keep in check, but maintain a running fight for three leagues with* the bulk of the enemy's troops," &c., &c. Now, if Napoleon said this, he uttered a downright falsehood, as great as the one Mr. Alison has himself uttered. But by what authority he presumes to translate " *Mais mena battant pendant plus de trois lieues*," " Maintained a running fight," one would be puzzled to determine ; and the French scholar will transfer to him the charges he prefers against Napoleon. And instead of treating him with neglect, he, in this hasty, short bulletin places Davoust far before all his other Marshals in the praise he bestows, while he *practically* goes still farther, making him Duke of Auerstadt—conferring on him the honour of leading his brave corps first into Berlin, and afterwards selecting him and his officers out to receive his special approbation in sight of the army. Davoust did not complain, and this heaping of honour upon honour did not look like "jealousy and meanness."

8*

saved him from utter defeat. Twice that day, was Napoleon rescued from ruin—first, in the morning, by Murat's splendid charge of cavalry on the Russian centre, after the destruction of Augereau's corps, and the repulse of Soult; and last, by the victory Davoust won over the left wing of the army, just before night closed over the scene of slaughter. The French left and centre had been driven back—the Russians were far in advance of their position in the morning, and they only waited the approach of Lestocq on the right, to complete the victory. But the heroic corps that had won the battle of Auerstadt, was there. Davoust had struggled since morning with invincible bravery; and Friant and Morand, who had covered themselves with glory at Auerstadt, here enacted over again their great deeds. The victory swung to and fro, from side to side, till at length the two lines approached within pistol shot of each other, when the Russians gave way. The artillery-men were bayonetted at their guns, and though reinforced and partially successful in turn, the mighty columns of Davoust poured over that part of the field like a resistless torrent. Huge columns of smoke rising from burning Serpallen, which he had set on fire in his passage, came riding the gale that swept along the Russian lines—heralded by the triumphant shouts of his conquering legions as they thundered over the field and carried dismay to the astonished Russians. The left wing was forced back till it stood at right angles with the centre; when the reserve was brought up, and the victorious Davoust, who had so suddenly brightened the threatening sky of Napoleon, was arrested in his career. At this critical moment, Lestocq arrived on the field. He had but one hour before dark, in which to recover these heavy losses. Instantly forming his men into three columns, he advanced on the nearest hamlet, Kuschnitten, which St. Hiliare had just carried, and where he had established himself, threatening seriously the Russian lines. Under a tremendous cannonade, Lestocq stormed and retook it; and immediately forming his men into line, advanced on Anklappen, where Davoust, with the other divisions of his corps, lay, right in rear of the Russian centre, and which formed the limit of his onward movement. He had fought for eight dreadful hours, and at last wrung victory almost from defeat itself; and now wearied and exhausted, could poorly withstand the assault of these fresh troops. He roused himself, however, for the last time, and that little hamlet, and the wood adjoining, became the theatre of a most deadly combat. It was fighting over again the Prussian reserve at Auerstadt, save that now he was exhausted by eight, instead of four hours' fighting. Still he put forth almost superhuman efforts to keep the advantage he had gained. He rushed into the thickest of the fight in person, cheered and rallied on his wearied troops for the twentieth time, calling on them by their former renown to brave resistance. "Here," said he, "is the spot where the brave should find a glorious death, the coward will perish in the deserts of Siberia." The brave fellows needed no fiery words to stimulate their courage. They joyfully followed their leaders to the charge, but in vain. Napoleon, in the distance, through the dim twilight, saw this little hamlet enveloped in a blaze of light as the army rushed upon it, and for a whole hour watched his brave Marshal, wrapped in the fire of the enemy, struggling to win for him the victory. With grief he saw him at length forced out of the blazing ruins, and slowly retire with his bleeding army, over the field. And now the night drew her curtain round the scene—darkness fell on the mighty hosts—the flash of musketry grew less and less frequent—the sullen cannon ceased their roar, and the bloody battle of Eylau was over. At midnight the Russians began to retreat, and Bonaparte remained master of the field—thanks to the brave and fiery-hearted Davoust.

CAVALRY ACTION AT ECKMUHL.

The battle of Eckmuhl, where he earned the title of Prince, was distinguished by one of the fiercest cavalry actions on record; and as described by Stuttenheim, Pelet, and others, must have been a magnificent spectacle.

Lannes, who had recently arrived from Spain, took command of two of his divisions, and with two such leaders, that renowned corps could not well fail of victory. Coming from Landshut, where he had been victorious the day before, Davoust and his brave troops ascended the slope whose summit looked down on the villages of Eckmuhl and Laichling. It was a spring noon, and that green valley lay smiling before them, as if fresh from the hand of its Creator. Embosomed in trees, and gardens, and winding streams, it seemed too sacred to be trampled by the hoof of war. But though no clangour of trumpets broke its repose, and the trees shook their green tops in the passing breeze, and the meadows spread away like carpets from the banks of the streams, and here and there the quiet herds were cropping the fresh herbage, or reclining under the cool shade; yet there was an ominous stillness in the fields. No husbandman was driving his plough, and no groups of peasants were seen going to their toil; but that bright valley seemed holding its breath in expectation of some fearful catastrophe. Banners were silently fluttering in the breeze; and in the openings of the woods, glittered bayonets and helmets, for the Archduke Charles was there with his army, waiting the approach of the enemy. Napoleon gazed long and anxiously on the scene, and then issued his orders for the attack. Davoust came fiercely down on the left, while Lannes, with two divisions of the corps, assailed the village in front. In a moment all was uproar and confusion. The roar of artillery, the rolling fire of the infantry, and the heavy shock of cavalry, made that village tremble as if on the breast of a volcano. In a few minutes the shouts of Davoust's columns were heard over the noise of battle, as they drove the enemy before them. His success and that of Lannes together, had so completely turned the 'Archduke's' left, that he was compelled to order a retreat. The streets of Eckmuhl were piled with the dead, and the green meadows ploughed up by the artillery, were red with flowing blood.

Napoleon then directed an advance of the whole line. The Archduke retired behind Eglofsheim, where he planted powerful batteries, curtained in front by twelve squadrons of heavy armed cuirassiers and a cloud of hussars. The French infantry, in hot pursuit, paused as they saw this living wall rise before them. Napoleon then ordered up his own cavalry to fall upon them. The hussars on both sides charged first, while the cuirassiers looked on. After witnessing charge after charge, leaving the victory in the hands of neither party, the Austrian cuirassiers put themselves in motion. The trumpets sounded the charge—thousands of helmets rose and fell at the blast—the plain shook with the muffled tread of the advancing host, and the next moment they burst with the sound of thunder on the French hussars—scattering them like pebbles from their feet;—and sweeping in one broad, resistless wave over the field, bore down with their terrible front on the French infantry. But there was a counter blast of trumpets, and before the startling echoes had died away, Napoleon's resistless cuirassiers emerged into view. Spurring their steeds into a trot, and then into a headlong gallop, with their plumes and banners floating back in the breeze, they swept forward to the shock. The spectacle was sublime, and each army held its breath in awe as these warlike hosts went rushing on each other. Their dark masses looked like two thunder-clouds riding opposite hurricanes, and meeting in mid-heaven. The clouds of dust rolling around their horses' feet—the long lines of flashing helmets above—and the forest of shaking sabres over all, gave them a most terrible aspect as they swept onward. The shock in the centre shook the field; and the two armies ceased their firing to witness the issue. The cannonier leaned on his gun, and the soldier stooped over his musket, absorbed in the spectacle; while in the first rude meeting horses and riders, by scores and hundreds, rolled on the plain. Then commenced one of those fierce hand-to-hand fights so seldom witnessed between cavalry. In the first heavy shock one body or the other gives way, and a few minutes decide which is the success ful charge. But here it was like two waves of equal strength, and volume, and velocity, meeting in full career, and cresting and foaming over each other as they struggle for the mastery. The sudden silence that fell over the field as the two armies ceased firing, added to the terror of the scene. The sight was new, even to those veteran troops. They were accustomed to the tumult and uproar of battle, where the thunder of cannon, and rattle of musketry, and shock of cavalry, are mingled in wild confusion. But here there was nothing heard but the clear ringing of steel, save when the trumpets gave their blast.

It was not the noise of a battle-field, but that of ten thousand anvils ringing under the fierce strokes of the hammer. The sun went down on the struggle, and his farewell rays glanced over swaying helmets and countless sabres crossing each other like lightning in the air. Twilight deepened over the field, and then it was one broad gleam of light above the struggling hosts, as the fire flew beneath their rapid strokes. The stars came out upon the sky, but their rays were dimmed by the dazzling sparks as sword crossed sword or glanced from steel armour—and at length the quiet moon came sailing in beauty up the heavens and shed her reproving light on the strife. But nothing could arrest the enraged combatants. Fighting in the light of their own flashing steel, they saw neither moon nor stars.

At length the ringing strokes grew fainter and fainter, and that dark mass canopied with fire of ts own making, seemed to waver to and fro in he gloom; and then the heavy tramp of rushing steeds was heard. The Austrians after leaving two-thirds of their entire number stretched on the plain, broke and fled, and horses and riders lay piled together in heaps on the rent and trodden plain.

The next day the victorious army was at the gates of Ratisbon.

The three following years Davoust spent in Poland, as commander-in-chief of the forces, and governor of the country. His conduct here, and after the campaign of Russia, at Hamburgh, has given rise to severe accusations against him. It has been characterized as "ruthless and oppressive." The Abbé de Pradt declared that "he filled all Poland with dread and brought much disgrace on the French name." To acquire such a reputation from an ally like Poland, goes far to prove that his character as a General was sullied by his conduct as a governor. But the character an enemy may give of their conqueror, especially if he is forced to levy heavy contributions, and create distress among the inhabitants in order to support his army, must be taken with many grains of allowance. Thus, the title of the "Hamburgh Robespierre," which the citizens of Hamburgh gave him, while he held the city against the combined attacks of the allies, may or may not be just. Their assertion is of no consequence, one way or the other. If many poor families were turned out to starve, and the hospitals seized for his own sick and wounded, and women were forced to work at the fortifications, and ruinous contributions were levied, and much distress produced, as is asserted; they do not prove the epithet given him to be merited. The whole question turns on the fact, whether these things were necessary for the defence of the place, and the salvation of the army. The famine and pestilence and death which a besieged army usually brings on the inhabitants, would by this mode of reasoning stamp every commander of a city as a monster, unless he surrendered without resistance. There is no proof that Davoust did anything that his perilous position did not render necessary. He defended himself against a united army; and exhibited that tenacity of purpose and power of will over the most discouraging obstacles, which rendered him illustrious.

His exactions in Poland were not for his personal benefit, but for the maintainance of his troops, and it is unjust to stamp a commander as cruel because his situation calls for severe measures. Contributions levied for personal aggrandizement, and suffering inflicted from personal revenge or hatred, leave the author of them without excuse; but the same results caused by an effort to save the army may be justifiable on the strictest rules of war. Napoleon, both in his memoirs, and at St. Helena, does not corroborate the statements of English historians respecting Davoust. In speaking of the defence of Hamburgh, he says that Davoust was a name abhorred by the inhabitants, but adds, "when a general receives the defence of the city, with orders to maintain it all hazards, it is not easy for him to receive the approbation of the inhabitants;" and at St. Helena, where he had no motive to disguise the truth, he said, "I do not think him a bad character. He never plundered for himself. He certainly levied contributions, but they were for the army. It is necessary for an army, especially when besieged, to provide for itself."

In the campaign of Russia, Davoust distinguished himself and his corps in almost every great battle. He fought bravely at Valentina, and his corps suffered severely. But, alas! Guidin at the head of his im mortal division, with which he commenced the battle of Auerstadt, was here, while heading a charge, struck by a cannon ball, and borne dead from the field. The next morning this division showed the marks of the fierce encounter they had sustained. As Napoleon rode past it, he saw nothing but skeletons of regiments left in it. The wearied soldiers, black with the smoke of battle, stood looking on their bent bayonets, twisted in the fierce shock of the day before; while the field around them exhibited a perfect wreck of overthrown trees, shattered wagons, dead horses, and mangled men. He was so deeply impressed with the scene, that he remarked, "*with such men you could conquer the world.*"

Davoust opened the "battle of the giants" at Borodino. As he moved over the field with his dense masses towards the flame of the batteries, his horse mortally wounded, fell under him, and he himself received a blow, which, for awhile, rendered him unable to command his troops. Recovering, however, he rushed in the thickest of the fight; just as Ney hurled his corps on the centre. These two illustrious chiefs united their armies and fought side by side, in that desperate, unparalleled struggle for the heights of Semonowskie.

Previous to this, Davoust and Murat had a quarrel, which well nigh ended in a fight. Commanding the advance guard together, they could not agree on the measures to be adopted. The headlong rashness of Murat, seemed downright madness to the methodical mind of Davoust, and the latter became insubordinate under the command of the former. Thus in approaching Wiasma, the cavalry of the two armies became engaged, and Murat, wishing to support his own with the infantry, put himself at the head of one of Davoust's divisions, and was about to make a charge, when the latter stepped forth and forbade his men to march—declaring that the movement was rash and perilous. Murat appealed to the gallantry of the soldiers, and endeavored to lead them on, but the authority of Davoust prevailed. After the battle was over, the "*preux chevalier*" shut himself up in his tent and gave way to a violent fit of rage, declaring that Davoust had insulted him, and he would wipe out the affront with his sword. He was just starting to go and attack him, when Belliard prevented him by pointing out the consequence to his friends and the army. He was persuaded to pocket the insult, though in the effort to do it, tears started to his eyes, and the fearless warrior wept that he could not avenge himself.

But through all this campaign Davoust was a host in himself. When the retreat from Moscow commenced he was appointed to command the rear guard, which post he held till his corps was almost annihilated, and then he joined the Emperor.

In the battle of Krasnoi, which Napoleon fought in order to save Davoust, whom the Russians threatened to cut off; the Marshal was so hard pressed, that he lost his baton and a great part of his corps. Napoleon was at Krasnoi, and Davoust struggling up from Smolensko, enveloped in the enemy. Hearing of his Marshal's peril, he drew his sword, saying, "I have long enough acted the Emperor; now is the moment to become the General again," and marched on foot towards Smolensko. He soon descried Davoust coming up, but it was a sight enough to appal the stoutest heart. He was moving slowly forward, perfectly enveloped in Cossacks that formed a dense moving mass, of which he and his devoted followers were the centre. Added to this, the French Marshal in his great efforts to join Napoleon, was marching straight on a superior force of the Russians. He saved but the skeleton of his corps.

But, though no longer commanding the rear guard, he still kept halting resolutely in every defile, and giving battle to the enemy—disputing with his accustomed bravery, every spot of ground on which a defence could be made. It was there he showed the advantage of that stern military discipline, which had so often brought on him the charge of cruelty. He and Ney alone, of all the Marshals, were able to preserve order among their troops. Through the dreary wilderness, plunging on amid the untrodden snow, without provision or fuel, stumbling over the fallen ranks of their comrades, and pressed by a victorious enemy; the French soldiers gave way to despair, and flung away their arms and lay down to die. Amid these trying circumstances, Davoust exhibited his great qualities. Giving way to no discouragement—disheartened by no reverses, he moved amid the wreck around him, like one above the strokes of misfortune. To arrest this disorder among his troops, he caused every soldier that flung away his arms to be stripped by his companions and insulted; and thus made despair fight despair. He arrived at Orcha, with only four thousand, out of the seventy thousand, with which he started. He had lost every thing belonging to himself—endured cold, hunger, and fatigue, without a murmur, and entered Orcha with the fragments of his army, on foot, pale, haggard, and wasted with famine. He had not even a shirt to put on his back, and a handkerchief was given him to wipe his face, which was covered with frost. A loaf of bread was offered him which he devoured with the eagerness of a starving man, and then sat down exclaiming, "None but men of iron frames can support such hardships; it is physically impossible to resist them and there are limits to human strength, the farthest of which have been endured."

Segur relates an anecdote of him when called from the wreck of the army to Paris, which was worthy of Murat. Passing through a small town with only two others, where the Russians were daily expected, their appearance enraged the already exasperated populace, and they began to press with murmurs and execrations, around his carriage. At length some of the most violent, attempted to unharness the horses, when Davoust rushed among them, seized the ringleader, and dragging him along, bade his servants fasten him behind his carriage. The boldness of the action perfectly stunned the mob, and without a show of resistance, they immediately opened a passage for the carriage, and let it move untouched through their midst, with its prisoner lashed on behind.

Of his after career, I have already spoken. When Bonaparte returned from Elba, Davoust, among the first to welcome him, was made Minister of War. He is accused of having treated the fallen Napoleon, after his second overthrow, like a man destitute alike of honour or shame. But there is no proof he ever uttered the language put into his mouth, and he held on firmly to the last. He finally gave in his adherence though not in the most manly or heroic style, and returned to his country seat. The next year, however, he obtained permission to reside in Paris, and three years after, 1819, he was given a seat in the chamber of Peers. He lived but four years after this, and died in June, 1823, of a pulmonary affection. His son ucceeded to his wealth, and his peerage.

V.

MARSHAL ST. CYR.

His Life—Character—Profession of a Painter—Combat at Biberach—Battle of Polotsk—Battle of Dresden.

Louis Gouvion St. Cyr was a different man from many of the other marshals. His character was more firm and complete—settled on a broader basis, and capable of greater development. Though he seems not to have run his career with the same uninterrupted success as the others, and he is sometimes called unfortunate; yet the cause is to be found in himself. Less impulsive and more methodical than those daring spirits which cast light around the mighty genius they followed—his devotion less warm and his admiration less enthusiastic—his complaints and recriminations meant more in the ears of Bonaparte than those of such men as Murat, and Junot, and Lannes. The penetrating mind of the Emperor, which fathomed at a glance every character that came under his observation, saw less to love and more to fear in St. Cyr, than in them. The anger of the latter was not a sudden spark that kindled and went out; and when once estranged he was not easily won over. Even his hatred was not impulsive, but rooted itself in his judgment and thoughts rather than in his passing feelings. Power was not likely to be conferred on a man whose stern independence diminished the value of the gift. Still he had no cause to complain of fortune, nor of the neglect of Napoleon, if we except the long delay of his marshal's baton.

He was born at Toul, of humble parentage, in April, 1764. His parents designed him for a painter, and in his youth he went to Rome to study the great masters, before entering on his career. There his mind became filled with those wonderful creations of art, and his youthful ambition pointed to a field as unlike the one he was to tread as it well could be. In ordinary times he might have been a respectable painter, perhaps a distinguished one. But his life was to be one of action rather than of imagination—his hand was to wield a sword instead of a pencil, and to enact great scenes on a battle-field rather than trace them on canvass. The breaking out of the Revolution summoned him, with thousands of others, to a field of great exploits, and overturning all at once his schemes as an artist, sent him forth into the world a soldier of fortune. He enlisted as a private in a company of volunteers and marched to the Rhine, where the Republic was making its first struggle for existence. He rose rapidly from one grade to another till, at the age of thirty-one, he found himself general of division. His promotion was not owing so much to his personal bravery and deeds of daring, as to his knowledge of military tactics.

In 1798 he combated under Massena in Italy; and after that commander was compelled to withdraw from Rome, on account of the insurrection of his troops, was appointed in his place and by his reputation as a just man and his wise management, restored subordination and discipline. When Bona parte returned from Egypt, St. Cyr was sent to the Rhine to take part in that victorious campaign.

The theatre on which Moreau was to act, was the angle made by the Rhine, where it bends at Basle from its western direction, and flows north along the shores of Germany and France. The famous Black Forest is enclosed in this bend of the river. Here the Austrian General, M. de Kray, was posted, with his lines reaching almost from Constance to Strasburg—ready to dispute the passage of the Rhine with the French. St. Cyr had served under Moreau a long time, and on this very ground, and the latter placed great confidence in his judgment. The third corps, composed of twenty-five thousand men, was placed under his command, and formed the centre of the army. But at the outset an unhappy cause of division arose between the two generals, which never healed, and ended finally in an open rupture. Not satisfied with dividing the army into four corps, each complete in itself, with cavalry, artillery, &c., thus leaving much discretionary power to each general, Moreau insisted on taking the separate command of one corps himself. This St. Cyr opposed on the ground that his attention would be too much taken up with the affairs of this single corps, and the general movements of the army neglected. The end proved that he was right; but Moreau, persisting in his arrangements, as he most certainly had a right to do, the co-operation of the former was not so hearty and generous as it ought to have been. Thus, at the battle of Engen, and afterwards at Maeskirch, where Moreau was hard pushed, and came near losing the day, St. Cyr did not arrive on the field till the fight was over. The officers around Moreau accused St

Cyr of treachery, and of keeping back on purpose to allow the army to be cut to pieces. But the truth is, the latter, offended at Moreau's procedure, ceased to concern himself about his movements and confined himself to his own corps. He would not stir without orders, and seemed determined to make Moreau feel the necessity of changing his conduct by acting the part of a mere machine; moving or stopping as he was bidden, and doing nothing more. Such independent dilatoriness would have cost him his place at once under Bonaparte. His tardiness during the battle of Maeskirch, saved the Austrians from a total route. His excuse for not coming up was that he had received no orders, though Moreau insisted he had sent them. It made no difference, however; he was in hearing of the heavy cannonading in front, and knew that a tremendous struggle was going on, and the fate of the army, perhaps, sealing. Had Desaix acted thus at Marengo, Bonaparte would have lost Italy. Not only did *he* have no orders to march on Marengo, but counter ones to proceed to Novi—yet no sooner did he hear the distant roll of cannon towards the former place than he put his army in motion, and marching it at the top of its speed, arrived just in time to turn a ruinous defeat into a victory.

The next day, however, St. Cyr would have wiped out the remembrance of this negligence, by crushing the Austrian army to pieces, had Moreau not been full of suspicions and averse to everything but the most mathematical regularity. The Austrians, in their retreat, were crowded on the shores of the Danube, in a sort of half circle, made by the bend of the river; so that there was no room to manœuvre, while consternation was visible in their ranks. St.

Cyr, though cool and steady, saw at once that by a firm and impetuous charge, he could roll the whole unwieldy mass into the river, and waited anxiously the order to advance. In the meantime he brought forward some of his guns, and trained them on the close packed troops of the enemy. Finding, however, that his cannonading failed to draw the attention of Moreau to the spot, he sent an officer to him requesting permission to charge. But the former refused, either from too great prudence, or, as it is more probable, from want of confidence in the good faith of his general. The opportunity slipped by, and the Austrians made good their passage over the Danube.

COMBAT AT BIBERACH.

A few days after, however, St. Cyr performed one of those brilliant actions which stamp the man of genius. The Austrians had retreated, and Moreau did not expect to overtake them for another day. In the mean time, St. Cyr had received orders to push on beyond Biberach, a little town which lay on the line of the enemy's retreat. But to his surprise on coming up to this village, he found that the Austrians had recrossed the Danube and marched back to Biberach to defend it on account of the magazines it contained. The entrance to it by the road St. Cyr was marching, was through a narrow defile which opened right in front of the village. The Austrian general thinking it would be unsafe to put the defile in his rear left ten thousand men to guard it while he posted his army behind the town on an eminence forming an excellent position. As St. Cyr came up he saw at once the ad vantage it gave the enemy. But, thinking the route of the ten thousand guarding the pass would shake the courage of the whole army in rear, he wished to order an attack immediately, and would have done so had his whole corps of twenty-five thousand men been with him. But his best division under Ney, had been sent to observe the Danube, and though orders were immediately despatched to hasten him up, he could nowhere be found. At this lucky moment, however, he heard the firing of Richenpanse's division, which had come up by a cross road. Thus strengthened, he no longer hesitated, and without waiting for the whole to form in order, he hurled his own battalions on the enemy. The order to charge was given, and his brave troops advanced at double quick time to the onset. Overthrown and routed, the enemy swept in a confused mass through the defile and through the village, hurrying onwards to the heights on which the army was posted. Following close on their heels, St. Cyr entered Biberach in hot pursuit.

Here, however, he arrested and re-formed his men, and began to reconnoitre the enemy's position. The river Riess—crossed by a single bridge—and a marsh, lay between the village and those heights on which nearly sixty thousand men were drawn up in order of battle. It was a bold attempt to attack with a little over twenty thousand men sixty thousand occupying so formidable a position; and for a moment he hesitated in his course. Pushing forward his men, however, he crossed the Riess, and the marsh, and drew up in front of the enemy. At this moment he saw the Austrians he had routed at the defile approach the army on the heights. The ranks opened to let them pass to the rear, and in this movement his clear and practised eye saw evidences of alarm and irresolution, which convinced him at once that the firmness of the enemy's troops was shaken. He immediately sent forward some skirmishers to fire on them. The general discharge which this mere insult drew forth made it still clearer that the whole *moral* power, which is ever greater than physical strength, was on his side; and though the enemy outnumbered him three to one, and occupied a splendid position, his resolution was immediately taken. Forming his three divisions into three solid columns, he began to ascend with a firm step the slopes of the Wittemberg.

Nothing can be more sublime than this faith in the moral over the physical. This was not the headlong rashness of Murat, reckless alike of numbers or position, but the clear calculations of reason. St. Cyr, who was one of the ablest tacticians in the French army, perceived at a glance that on one side were numbers and irresolution, on the other confidence and courage. When the Austrians saw those columns scaling the mountain side with such an intrepid step and bold presence, they were seized with a panic, and turned and fled, leaving thousands of prisoners in the hands of St. Cyr. He carried out here successfully the very plan he proposed to Moreau when the enemy lay packed in a curve of the Danube.

The Austrians retreated to Ulm, which was strongly fortified, and St. Cyr, who had tried the metal of their soldiers; and who, from a convent that overlooked the enemy, saw and comprehended their position, begged permission to carry it by assault. In this, he was joined by Ney and Richenpanse, who offered to answer for the success of it on their own heads. But Moreau did everything by manœuvres, and preferring a less certain good to a probable greater one; refused his consent. A man never storms through mathematics, and to Moreau, war was a mathematical science. A short time after, however, one of his grand manœuvres came very near destroying his left wing. Pretending he was about to march to Munich, he extended his line over the space of sixty miles, leaving St. Suzanne with 15,000 men alone on the left bank of the Danube. If the Austrian General had possessed any genius, or even common sense, he would have crushed this division at a blow, by falling with his entire force upon it. As it was, however, he sent a large body of cavalry to assail it, which enveloped it like a cloud, threatened to sweep it from the field. In the meantime, masses of Austrian infantry came pouring out of Ulm to second the attack, until these fifteen thousand brave French were compelled to resist the onset of twenty-four thousand Austrian infantry, and twelve thousand cavalry. Retreating in squares, they mowed down their assailants with their rolling fire, steadily pursuing their way over the field. Hour after hour did the combat rage, and though the ground was strewed with the dead, not a square broke, not a battalion fled. St. Cyr, posted on the other side on the river, at some distance from the scene—where the Iller joins the Danube—hearing the cannonading, hastened forward to the spot It was not Moreau in danger, but St. Suzanne, and he waited for no orders. Coming up opposite the field of battle, he found all the bridges broken down, and immediately planting his artillery so as to cover a ford, across which he was beginning to pour his intrepid columns; he opened a fierce fire on the enemy. Hearing this cannonading, and fearing for their re treat, the Austrians immediately began to retire towards Ulm.

After this engagement, from the movements of Moreau, the whole army expected an assault on the city, but after various manœuvres, this cautious leader established his army and determined to remain inactive till he heard from Bonaparte, who was descending into Italy. The Generals complained—St. Cyr openly remonstrated, and had many fierce altercations with him. The unequal distribution of provisions, was another cause of dissension, and bitter recriminations. General Grenier, arriving at this time, St. Cyr wished to resign his command to him, but Moreau, refusing his consent, he retired altogether from the army under the plea of ill health.

In October of the same year, he is seen fighting bravely in Italy. The next year he was called by Bonaparte to the Council of State, and the year following, (1801,) took the place of Lucien Bonaparte as Ambassador to the Court of Madrid. He was soon after appointed to the command of the Neapolitan army, where he remained inactive till 1805, when he was made Colonel General of the Cuirassiers, and received the Grand Eagle of the Legion of Honour. In the following campaigns of Prussia and Poland, he distinguished himself, and in 1807, was appointed Governor of Warsaw. After the peace of Tilsit, he was sent into Spain, where he won but few laurels and indulging in unjust, unmanly complaints, was finally superseded by Augereau. Two years of disgrace and exile followed. But in 1812, in the Russian campaign, he appears again, and exhibits the same great qualities of a commander, and fighting bravely at Polotsk, receives the long withheld though long deserved Marshal's baton.

The next year, he commanded at Dresden, when it was assailed by the allies; and after their repulse held possession of it till the disasters that overtook the French army, left him once more at the mercy of the allies, and he was compelled to capitulate. He returned to France after the restoration, and was given, by Louis, a seat in the Chamber of Peers.

On the landing of Napoleon from Elba, he retired into the country and remained there inactive, till the second overthrow of the Empire at Waterloo. On the king's return he was honoured with the order of St. Louis and presented with the portfolio of the war ministry. In the autumn of the same year, however, he retired because he could not give his consent to the treaty of Paris. But two years after he was made Minister of the Marine, from whence he passed to the War Office. While in this department he succeeded in getting a law passed by which no man was to receive a commission in the army till he had served two years as a soldier. This thoroughly democratic measure, sprung from his experience of the superior efficiency of those officers who had arisen from the ranks, and also, perhaps, from a desire to pay a compliment to his own career. In 1819, being strongly opposed to the proposed change in the law of elections, he resigned his office, and never after appeared in public life.

The great characteristics of St. Cyr, were clear-sightedness on the field of battle; perfect method in all his plans, and a cold, deep spirit. However, he might fail in a great campaign—on the field where an engagement was to take place, he was regarded one of the ablest tacticians in the army. His eye took in the enemy's position, and his own at a glance, and he saw at once the best course to be taken. In forming his plans he seemed to omit no detail necessary to success, while the moral feeling of the two armies was not forgotten. The latter he calculated with the same nicety he did numbers; and it is interesting to observe what reliance he always placed upon it. He possessed, to a certain extent, that combination which distinguished Napoleon, and belonged more or less to all his great Generals, viz: clearness and rapidity of thought. But this power in him arose from a different cause than with them. Napoleon, and Ney, and Massena, and Kleber, possessed strong minds and strong imaginations also, yet they were so well balanced as only to strengthen each other. The imagination never became so excited as to confuse the operations of reason, while the judgment never acquired such a mastery as in Moreau, that inspiration and impulse could have no control. Cool, clear-headed, and self-collected, they planned with the sobriety of reason, and yet kept it in such abeyance that in moments of excitement they could be carried away by the impulse of genius. Their imaginations acted as a powerful stimulant to the mental powers, giving them greater rapidity, without forcing them into confusion; but St. Cyr possessed none of this impulsiveness. He frequently *acted* as if he did, but his most headlong movements were as much the result of calculation as his soberest plans. Consummate art took the place of a vivid imagination with him. He could *calculate* the inspirations of genius, and knew when he *ought* to be moved by impulse; his mind had great rapidity of movement, but it was the rapidity of mere logic. There was a certainty in his operations on which one could depend, and he himself placed the most implicit confidence in his own judgment. He had all the qualities of a great commander, and but for his unsocial disposition, and cold, repulsive nature, would doubtless, early have attained to the highest honours of the Empire. Napoleon rewarded the brave, but lavished his choicest favour on the brave that *loved him.* Never governed by attachment himself, how could St. Cyr expect others to be swayed by it in their treatment of him. Nevertheless, Napoleon always treated him with justice, and frequently rewarded him with places of trust. The neglect to make him marshal; when, on assuming the imperial crown, he made out that immortal list, was apparently undeserved; and gave rise, perhaps justly, to some charges of favouritism.

St. Cyr was an obstinate man in the prosecution of his own plans, and equally so in his opposition to those which differed from them; and though ready to condemn others, when thwarted or condemned himself, he flew into a passion, and his head became filled with all forms of suspicion. Thus, when he and Moreau could not agree, and he found there was a clique around the commander-in-chief, arrayed against him—instead of performing his duty bravely, and winning back that confidence which others had unjustly deprived him of—he first became remiss and inactive, then fierce and condemnatory, and finally threw up his command. He ought to have known that was no way either to screen himself from unjust charges, or win his way to power. He did not seem to know the meaning of the device, "I bide my time." Thus also in Spain, when placed over the army destined to act in Catalonia, he became peevish, complaining and foolish. It was true, the army was not an effective one; but on the other hand, the enemy he had to contend with was not a dangerous one. Besides, it was the greatest compliment Napoleon could pay him, to appoint him over a poor army from which he expected victory. The Emperor knew it was badly conditioned, but he could not help it, and the only remedy of the evil, in his power, was to place an able and skillful commander over it. A poor general would have insured its ruin. Yet St. Cyr, instead of winning confidence and renown, by executing great things with small means, began to grumble. Ney, when conducting the retreat from Russia, created means where an ordinary man would have declared it impossible; and out of his very defeats and disasters, wove for himself the brightest wreath that hangs on his tomb. But St. Cyr not only complained, though successful in all his engagements—winning every battle—but accused Napoleon of placing him there on purpose to ruin him, because he had belonged to the army of the Rhine, under Moreau; and this splenetic and ridiculous statement of his, has been taken up and incorporated in English histories, as an evidence of the Emperor's meanness.* How such an accusation could have received a sober thought, is passing strange.

Napoleon, at the head of the French empire, nourished such a hostility to Moreau, for winning the battle of Hohenlinden, which he, as First Consul,

---

* This silly accusation has found its way into one of our school books, "Camp and Court of Napoleon," which contains many errors, in fact—as, for instance, it states that Moncey was at the battle of Marengo, when he was on the Tessino, and knew nothing of the engagement till it was over. It says, also, that he was in the Russian expedition, when he was not. Mr. Alison reiterates the same nonsense.

sent him there on purpose to gain, and on whose success depended his own—that years after he transferred it to one of Moreau's Generals, by placing him over a poor army in Spain, at a time he was straining every nerve to subdue the kingdom. The simple statement of the charge, and the circumstances connected with it, shows it to be the absurdest thing that ever entered a diseased brain. Besides, Napoleon did not take this round about way to disgrace those who were displeasing to him. St. Cyr ought to have seen this after he was superseded by Augereau; and not have incorporated such a silly charge into his work.

Offended and proud, he left his command to hurry Augereau to assume his place, thus evincing openly his comtempt for the rebuke the Emperor had given him for his folly. Two years of disgrace and exile, showed that Napoleon knew a shorter way to ruin the Generals that offended him.

The truth is, St. Cyr was placed where he was compelled to put forth great efforts without winning much renown. It was hard work without corresponding reward, but he should have waited patiently for the latter on some more fortunate field; remembering that a good General is known by his sacrifices as much as by his victories. Once resigning his command in anger, and once disgraced for the same reason, argues very poorly for the amiability of the man.

Previous to this, in 1807, he fought bravely in the campaign of Prussia and Poland, and especially at Heilsberg, though there was no opportunity offered for great actions, as he commanded only a division under Soult. But in 1812, as before remarked, in the great Russian expedition, he had an opportunity to distinguish himself, and won that place among the renowned leaders that followed Napoleon, which his services richly merited.

BATTLE OF POLOTSK.

In the first battle of Polotsk, in the advance to Moscow, Oudinot, with his corps, was assaulted by Wittgenstein, and the French Marshal was wounded. St. Cyr immediately succeeded him as commander-in-chief of the army, composed of thirty thousand men. This was what he had long desired. Disliking to serve under any other officer, the moment his actions were unfettered, he exhibited his great qualities as a military leader. He immediately adopted his own plan of operations, and with that clearness of perception and grasp of knowledge which distinguished him, proceeded to put it in execution. For a whole day after the engagement in which Oudinot was wounded, he kept the Russian General quiet, by sending proposals respecting the removal of the wounded, and by making demonstrations of a retreat. But as soon as darkness closed over the armies, he began in silence to rally his men, and arranging them in three columns, by five in the morning was ready for battle. The signal was given—the artillery opened its destructive fire, and rousing up the Russian bear ere the morning broke, his three columns poured in resistless strength on the enemy, carrying every thing before them. But even in the moment of victory, St. Cyr came very near being killed. A French battery, suddenly charged by a company of Russian horse was carried, and the brigade sent to support it being overthrown and borne back over the cannon that dared not open lest they should sweep down their own troops; spread disorder in their flight. The cannoniers were sabred at their pieces, and the French horse, overwhelmed in the general confusion, also fled, overturning the commander-in-chief and his staff, and sending terror and dismay through the ranks. St. Cyr was compelled to flee on foot, and finally threw himself into a ravine to prevent being tramped under the hoofs of the charging horse. The French cuirassiers, however, soon put an end to this sudden irruption, and drove the daring dragoons into the woods. The victory was complete, and a thousand prisoners remained in the hands of St. Cyr, and the Marshal's baton was given him as a reward for his bravery.

Here he remained for two months, while Wittgenstein kept at a respectful distance. In the meantime Moscow had blazed over the army of the Empire, and the disheartened and diminished host was about to turn its back on the smouldering capital and flee from the fury of a northern winter. Wittgenstein, who had not been idle, though he dared not to attack St. Cyr, had, by constant reinforcements, more than doubled his army. The French commander, on the other hand, had carried on a partizan warfare for two months; which, together with sickness and suffering, had reduced his army one half—so that in the middle of October he had but seventeen thousand men, while the Russian army amounted to fifty-two thousand. To add to the peril of his position, another Russian army, under Steingell, was rapidly moving down to hem him in; while Napoleon, three hundred miles in the rear, was sealing his fate by tarrying around Moscow. Macdonald was the only person from whom he could hope for succour, and he sent pressing requests to him for reinforcements. But that brave commander had already discovered signs of defection in his Prussian allies, and dared not weaken his force. St. Cyr, therefore, was left to meet his fate alone. As if on purpose to insure his ruin, he was without intrenchments, not having received orders from the Emperor to erect them. Secure of his prey, the Russian General, on the 18th October, bore down with his overwhelming force on the French lines.

The battle at once became furious. St. Cyr was one of the first struck. Smitten by a musket ball, he could neither ride his horse nor keep his feet—still he would not retire. Every thing depended on his presence and personal supervision; for the struggle against such fearful odds was to be a stern one. Pale and feeble, yet self-collected and clear minded as ever, he was borne about by his officers, amid the storm of battle, cheering on his men, again and again to the desperate charge. Seven times did the Russian thousands sweep like a resistless flood over the partial redoubts, and seven times did St. Cyr, steadily hurl them back, till night closed the scene, and fourteen thousand men slept on the field of victory they had wrung from the grasp of fifty thousand. When the morning dawned, the Russian General seemed in no hurry to renew the attack. St. Cyr arose from his feverish couch, where the pain from his wound, and his intense anxiety had kept him tossing the long night; and was borne again to the field of battle. He perceived at once that the hesitation of the enemy did not arise from fear of a repulse, but from some expected manœuvre, which was to be the signal of assault; and so he stood in suspense, hour after hour, firmly awaiting the approach of the dense masses that darkened the woods before him, till, at ten o'clock, an aid-de-camp was seen spurring at a furious gallop over the bridge, the hoofs of his horse striking fire on the pavements as he dashed through the village towards the commander-in-chief. Steingell, with thirteen thousand Russians had come, and was rapidly marching along the other side of the river to assail him in rear. Hemmed in between these two armies, St. Cyr must inevitably be crushed. Imagine, for a moment, his desperate condition. Polotsk stands on the left side of the Dwina, as you ascend it, with only one bridge crossing the river to the right bank. Behind this wooden town, St. Cyr had drawn up his forces, in order of battle, with the formidable masses of the Russian army in front, threatening every moment to overwhelm him. In the meantime, word was brought that thirteen thousand fresh troops were approaching the bridge on the other side, cutting off all hopes of retreat. Here were two armies, numbering together more than sixty thousand men, drawing every moment nearer together, to crush between them fourteen thousand French soldiers, commanded by a wounded General. But St. Cyr, forgetting his wound, summoned all his energies to meet the crisis that was approaching. He gave his orders in that quiet, determined tone, which indicates the settled purpose of a stern and powerful mind. Unseen by Wittgenstein, he despatched three regiments across the river to check the progress of Steingell, while he, with his weakened forces, should withstand the shock of the

Russian army before him as best he could. Thus the two armies stood watching each other, while the roar of artillery on the farther side, approached nearer and nearer every moment, showing that the enemy was sweeping before him the few regiments that had been sent to retard him. At length the French batteries, which had been planted on the farther bank of the Dwina to protect the camp, were wheeled round, ready to fire on the new enemy, which was expected every moment to emerge into view. At this sight, a loud shout of joy rolled along the Russian lines, for they now deemed their prey secure. But the Russian general still delayed the signal of attack, till he should see the head of Steingell's columns.

In consternation the French generals gathered around St. Cyr, urging him to retreat, but he steadily refused all their counsel and urgent appeals, declaring that with his first retrograde movement, the Russian army would descend upon him, and that his only hope was in delay. If Steingell did not make his appearance before dark, he could retreat under the cover of night; but to fall back now, was to precipitate an attack that was most unaccountably delayed. For three mortal hours he stood and listened to the roar of the enemy's cannon, shaking the banks of the river as it mowed its way towards the bridge—now gazing on the opposite shore, now on the fifty thousand Russians before him in order of battle and now on his own band of heroes, till his agitation became agony. Minutes seemed lengthened into hours, and he kept incessantly pulling out his watch, looking at it, and then at the tardy sun, which his eager gaze seemed almost to push down the sky.

The blazing fire-ball, as it stooped to the western

horizon, sending its flashing beams over the battle array on the shores of the Dwina, never before seemed so slow in its motions. St. Cyr afterwards declared that he never, in his life, was so agitated as in the three hours of suspense he then endured. The shock and the overthrow can be borne by a brave heart, but in a state of utter uncertainty, to stand and watch the dial's face, on whose slow-moving shadow rests everything, is too much for the calmest heart.

At length, when within a half-hour's march of the bridge, Steingell halted. Had he kept on a few minutes longer, the head of his columns would have appeared in sight, which would have been the signal of a general attack. Nothing could be more favourable to St. Cyr than this unexpected halt; and a dense fog soon after spreading over the river, wrapping the three armies in its folds, hastened on the night, and relieved his anxious heart. The artillery was immediately sent over the bridge, and his divisions were pressing noiselessly as possible after it, when Legrand foolishly set fire to his camp, so as not to let it fall into the hands of the enemy. The other divisions followed his example, and in a moment the whole line was in a blaze. This rash act immediately revealed to the enemy the whole movements. Its batteries opened at once—the roused columns came hurrying onward, while blazing bombs, hissing through the fog in every direction, fell on the town which blazed up in the darkness, making a red and lurid light, by which the two armies fought—the one for existence, the other for victory. Amid the burning dwellings the wounded Marshal stood, and contested every inch of ground with the energy of despair; and slowly retiring over the blazing timbers, by the light of the conflagration, brought off his army in perfect order, though bleeding at every step. It was three o'clock in the morning before the Russians got possession of the town. In the meantime, St. Cyr had gained the farther bank, and destroyed the bridge in the face of the enemy, and stood ready for Steingell, who had soundly slept amid all the uproar and strife of that wild night. The latter seemed under the influence of some unaccountable spell, and could not have acted worse, had he been bribed by the French. In the morning, when he aroused himself for battle, St. Cyr was upon him, and after relieving him of one-sixth of his army, drove him into the wood several miles from the place of action. Ten thousand Russians had fallen in these three days of glory to St. Cyr.

This brave marshal, though wounded, was compelled, on account of dissensions among the generals, to keep the command of his troops, and commence his retreat. Reversing Napoleon's mode of retreat from Moscow, he, with ten thousand men, kept nearly fifty thousand at bay; so that they did not make more than three marches in eight days. After eleven days of toil, and combat, and suffering, in which he, though wounded, had exhibited a skill, courage, and tenacity, seldom surpassed, he at length effected a junction with Victor, who had marched from Smolensko to meet him.

After the termination of that disastrous campaign, he is seen next year at Dresden, struggling to uphold the tottering throne of Napoleon. With twenty thousand men he was operating round the city, and fearing that the allies would make a demonstration upon it, wrote to that effect to Napoleon, who was combating Blucher in Silesia. But the latter did not agree with him, and kept pushing his projects in the quarter where he then was, when the astounding intelligence was brought him that the allied forces were marching on Dresden. St. Cyr saw at once his danger; and prepared, as well as his means permitted, to meet it. But after some fierce fighting with Wittgenstein's advanced guard—his old foe of Polotsk, in Russia—he retired within the redoubts of Dresden, and patiently waited the result.

BATTLE OF DRESDEN.

A hundred and twenty thousand soldiers, with more than five hundred pieces of cannon, covered the heights that overlooked his entrenchments. It was the latter part of August, and everything was smiling in summer vegetation, when this mighty host pitched their tents on the green hills that encircled the city.

On the evening of their approach, St. Cyr wrote to Napoleon the following letter: "*Dresden*, 23d. Aug. 1813; *ten at night*. At five this afternoon the enemy approached Dresden, after having driven in our cavalry. We expected an attack this evening; but probably it will take place to-morrow. Your Majesty knows better than I do, what time it requires for heavy artillery to beat down enclosure walls and palisades." The next night at midnight he despatched another letter to him, announcing an immediate attack, and closing up with, "We are determined to do all in our power; but I can answer for nothing more with such young soldiers." Immediately on the reception of the first letter, Napoleon surrendered his command to Macdonald, and turned his face towards Dresden. Murat was despatched in hot haste, to announce his arrival and re-assure the besieged. In the midst of his guards, which had marched nearly thirty miles a day since the commencement of the war, he took the road to the city.

To revive his sinking troops, he ordered twenty thousand bottles of wine to be distributed among them, but not three thousand could be procured. He, however, marched all next day, having dispatched a messenger to the besieged to ascertain the exact amount of danger. Said Napoleon to the messenger Gourgaud, "*Set out immediately for Dresden, ride as hard as you can, and be there this evening—see St. Cyr, the King of Naples, and the King of Saxony—encourage every one. Tell them I can be in Dresden to-morrow with forty thousand men, and the day following with my whole army. At day-break visit the outposts and redoubts—consult the commander of Engineers as to whether they can hold out. Hurry back to me to-morrow at Stolpen, and bring a full report of St. Cyr's and Murat's opinion as to the real state of things.*" Away dashed Gourgaud in hot haste, while the Emperor hurried on his exhausted army. Gourgaud did not wait till day-break before he returned. He found every thing on the verge of ruin—the allied army was slowly enveloping the devoted city, and when, at dark, he issued forth from the gates, the whole summer heavens were glowing with the light of their bivouac fires, while a burning village near by threw a still more baleful light over the scene. Spurring his panting steed through the gloom, he at midnight burst in a fierce gallop into the squares of the Old Guard, and was immediately ushered into the presence of the anxious Emperor The report confirmed his worst fears. At daylight the weary soldiers were aroused from their repose, and

10*

though they had marched a hundred and twenty miles in four days, pressed cheerfully forward; for already the distant sound of heavy cannonading was borne by on the morning breeze. At eight in the morning, Napoleon and the advanced guard, reached an elevation that overlooked the whole plain in which the city lay embosomed; and lo, what a sublime yet terrific sight met their gaze. The whole valley was filled with marching columns, preparing for an assault; while the beams of the morning sun were sent back from countless helmets and bayonets that moved and shook in their light. Here and there columns of smoke told where the batteries were firing, while the heavy cannonading rolled, like thunder over the hills. There, too was the French army, twenty thousand strong, packed behind the redoubts, yet appearing like a single regiment in the midst of the host that enveloped them. Courier after courier, riding as for life, kept dashing into the presence of the Emperor, bidding him make haste if he would save the city. A few hours would settle its fate. Napoleon, leaving his guards to follow on, drove away in a furious gallop, while a cloud of dust along the road, alone told where his carriage was whirled onward. As he approached the gates, the Russian batteries swept the road with such a deadly fire, that he was compelled to leave his carriage and crawl along on his hands and knees over the ground, while the cannon balls whistled in an incessant shower above him.

Suddenly and unannounced, as if he had fallen from the clouds, he appeared at the Royal Palace, where the King of Saxony was deliberating on the terms of capitulation. Waiting for no rest, he took a single page so as not to attract the enemy's fire, and went forth to visit the outer works. So near had the enemy approached, that the youth by his side was struck down by a spent musket ball. Having finished his inspection, and settled his plans, he returned to the Palace, and hurried off couriers, to the different portions of the army, that were advancing by forced marches towards the city. First, the indomitable guards and the brave cuirassiers, eager for the onset, came pouring in furious haste over the bridge. The over-joyed inhabitants stood by the streets, and offered them food and drink; but though weary, hungry and thirsty, the brave fellows refused to take either, and hurried onward towards the storm that was ready to burst on their companions. At ten o'clock, the troops commenced entering the city—infantry, cavalry and artillery pouring forward with impetuous speed—till there appeared to be no end to the rushing thousands. Thus without cessation, did the steady columns arrive all day long, and were still hurrying in, when at four o'clock, the attack commenced. The batteries, that covered the heights around the city, opened their terrible fire, and in a moment Dresden became the target of three hundred cannon, all trained upon her devoted buildings. Then commenced one of war's wildest scenes. St. Cyr replied with his artillery, and thunder answered thunder, as if the hot August afternoon, was ending in a real storm of heaven. Balls fell in an incessant shower in the city, while the blazing bombs traversing the sky, hung for a moment like messengers of death over the streets, and then dropped with an explosion, that shook the ground among the frightened inhabitants. Amid the shrieks of the wounded, and the stern language of command, was heard the heavy rumbling of the artillery and ammunition wagons through the streets,—and in the intervals, the steady tramp, tramp of the marching columns, still hastening in to the work of death—while over all, as if to drown all; like successive thunder claps where the lightning falls nearest, spoke the fierce batteries that were exploding on each other. But the confusion and death, and terror that reigned through the city, as the burning buildings shot their flames heavenward, were not yet complete. The inhabitants had fled to their cellars, to escape the balls and shells that came crashing every moment through their dwellings; and amid the hurry and bustle of the arriving armies, and their hasty tread along the streets, and the roll of drums, and rattling of armour and clangour of trumpets, and thunder of artillery, the signal was given for the assault—*three cannon shots from the heights of Raecknitz.* The next moment, six massive columns with fifty cannon at their head, began to move down the slopes—pressing straight for the city. The muffled sound of their heavy measured tread, was heard within the walls, as in dead silence and awful majesty they moved steadily forward upon the batteries.

It was a sight to strike terror into the heart of the boldest, but St. Cyr marked their advance with the calmness of a fearless soul, and firmly awaited the onset that even Napoleon trembled to behold. No sooner did they come within the range of artillery than the ominous silence was broken by its deafening roar. In a moment, the heights about the city were in a blaze; the fifty cannon at the head of those columns belched forth fire and smoke; and amid the charging infantry, the bursting of shells, the rolling fire of musketry, and the explosion of hundreds of cannon, St Cyr received the shock. For two hours the battle raged with sanguinary ferocity. The plain was covered with dead—the suburbs were overwhelmed with assailants, and ready to yield every moment—the enemy's batteries were playing within fifteen rods of the ramparts—the axes of the pioneers were heard on the gates; and shouts, and yells, and execrations rose over the walls of the city. The last of St. Cyr's reserve were in the battle, and had been for half an hour, and Napoleon began to tremble for his army. But at half past six, in the hottest of the fight, the Young Guard arrived, shouting as they came, and were received in return with shouts by the army, that for a moment drowned the roar of battle. Then Napoleon's brow cleared up, and St. Cyr, for the first time, drew a sigh of relief.

The gates were thrown open, and the impetuous Ney, with the invincible Guard, poured through one like a resistless torrent on the foe, followed soon after by Murat, with his headlong cavalry. Mortier sallied forth from another; and the Young Guard, though weary and travel-worn, burst with loud cheers on the chief redoubt—which, after flowing in blood, had been wrested from the French—and swept it like a tornado.

Those six massive columns, thinned and riddled through, recoiled before this fierce onset, and slowly surged back, like a receding tide; from the walls. In the meantime, dark and heavy clouds began to roll up the scorching heavens, and the distant roll of thunder mingled with the roar of artillery. Men had turned this hot August afternoon into a battle-storm, and now the elements were to end it with a fight of their own. In the midst of the deepening gloom, the allies, now for the first time aware that the Emperor was in the city, drew off their troops for the night. The rain came down as if the clouds were falling, drenching the living and the dead armies; yet Napoleon, heedless of the storm, and knowing what great results rested upon the next day's action, was seen hurrying on foot through the streets to the bridge, over which he expected the corps of Marmont and Victor, to arrive. With anxious heart he stood and listened, till the heavy tread of their advancing columns through the darkness, relieved his suspense; and then, as they began to pour over the bridge, he hastened back, and traversing the city, passed out at the other side, and visited the entire lines that were now formed without the walls. The bivouac fires shed a lurid light over the field, and he came at every step upon heaps of corpses, while groans and lamentations issued from the gloom in every direction; for thousands of wounded, uncovered and unburied, lay exposed to the storm, dragging out the weary night in pain. Early in the morning, Napoleon was on horseback, and rode out to the army. Taking his place beside a huge fire that was blazing and crackling in the centre of the squares of the Old Guard, he issued his orders for the day. Victor was on the right; the resistless Ney on the left, over the Young Guard, while St. Cyr and Marmont were in the centre, which Napoleon commanded in person.

The rain still fell in torrents, and the thick mist shrouded the field as if to shut out the ghastly spectacle its bosom exhibited. The cannonading soon commenced, but with little effect, as the mist concealed the armies from each other. A hundred and sixty thousand of the allies, stretched in a huge semicircle along the heights, while Napoleon, with a hundred and thirty thousand in the plain below, was waiting the favourable moment in which to commence the attack. At length the battle opened on the right, where a fierce firing was heard as Victor pressed firmly against an Austrian battery. Suddenly, Napoleon heard a shock like a falling mountain. While Victor was engaging the enemy in front, Murat, unperceived in the thick mist, had stolen around to the rear, and without a note of warning, burst with twelve thousand cavalry on the enemy. He rode straight through their broken lines, trampling under foot the dead and dying. Ney was equally successful on the left, and as the mist lifted, it showed the allied wings both driven back. The day wore away in blood—carts, loaded with the wounded, moved in a constant stream into the city; but the French were victorious at all points; and when night again closed over the scene, the allied armies had decided to retreat.

It was in this battle Moreau fell. He had just returned from the United States, at the urgent solicitation of the Emperor Alexander, to take up arms against his country.

This was his first battle, and Napoleon killed him. About noon, on the last day of the fight, he noticed a group of persons on an eminence, half a mile distant. Supposing they were watching his manœuvres, he called a Captain of Artillery, who commanded a battery of eighteen or twenty pieces, and pointing to them said; "*Throw a dozen bullets into that group, at one fire, perhaps there are some little Generals in it.*" He obeyed, and it was immediately seen to be agitated. One of the balls had struck Moreau's leg just below the knee, and cutting it off, passed through his horse, carrying away the other leg also. The next day, a peasant picked up one of the boots, with the leg in, which the surgeon had left on the field, and brought it to the King of Saxony, saying it belonged to a superior officer. The boot, on examination, was found to be neither of English or French manufacture, and they were still in doubt. The same day, the advance guards, while in pursuit of the enemy, came upon a little spaniel that was roaming over the field, moaning piteously for its master. Around its neck was a collar, on which was written, "*I belong to General Moreau.*"

Both legs of the unfortunate General had to be amputated, wich he bore with stoical firmness, calmly smoking a cigar during the painful operation. It is a little singular, that by this same battery and same captain, another French traitor who occupied a high rank in the Russian army, General St. Priest, was afterwards killed under similar circumstances. Napoleon gave the order in that case as in this.

The death of Moreau cast a gloom over the kingly group that assembled to hold a council of war, and on the 28th, the morning after the battle, the allied army was in full retreat, and the blood-stained field was left in the hands of the French.

But what a field it was! For two days a thousand cannon had swept it, and three hundred thousand men had struggled upon it in the midst of their fire. The grassy plain was trodden into mire, on which nearly twenty thousand men, mangled, torn, and bleeding, had been strewn. Many had been carried into the city during the night; but some stark an stiff in death—some reclining on their elbows, pale and ghastly, and calling for help; others writhing in mortal agony amid heaps of the slain, still covered the ground. Others which had been hastily buried the day before, lay in their half covered graves—here a leg and there an arm, sticking out of the ground, while to crown the horror of the scene, multitudes of women were seen roaming the field, not to bind up the wounded, but to plunder the dead. They went from heap to heap of the slain, turning over the mangled bodies and stripping them of their clothing; and loaded down with their booty, gathered it in piles beside the corpses. Unmolested in their work, they made the shuddering field still more ghastly by strewing it with half-naked forms. White arms and bodies stretched across each other, or dragged away from the heaps they had helped to swell, made the heart of even Napoleon turn faint as he rode over the scene of slaughter. Oh, what a comment on war, and what a cure for ambition and the love of glory was this field! The terrified and horror-stricken inhabitants came out from the cellars of their burnt dwellings and strove to relieve this woe by burying the dead and succouring the wounded.

After the disasters that soon befell other portions of the French army under Vandamme, Macdonald, and Oudinot; St. Cyr was ordered back to Dresden, with thirty thousand men, under the expectation of soon evacuating it again after he had destroyed the fortifications around it: but Napoleon, changing his plan, sent him word to keep it to the last extremity. The disastrous battle of Leipsic rendered his situation desperate, for it shut him off from all reinforcements. Previously the allies had placed twenty thousand men before the city to observe it. Against these, St. Cyr advanced, and routed them, and thus opened the country about to the foragers. But when Leipsic fell the allies again directed their attention to the place, and St. Cyr saw their victorious armies once more hem him in. Insufficient supplies had already weakened his men, so that he had the mere shadow of an army, while the multitudes of the sick and wounded added to the burdens that oppressed him. The maimed and wounded which he had been ordered to send by boats to Torgau, could not be got off. Only three thousand were sent, though multitudes, hearing they were to leave their fetid hospitals, crawled out to the banks of the river, and when they found all the boats were filled and they were to be left behind, refused to return to the city and lay down in rows along the shore. Wasted with sickness and wounds, these ranks of spectres lay all night in the cold to be ready for the next boat that should appear. In the meantime the famine and suffering increased in the city. St. Cyr could not hear a word from Napoleon, and was left without orders, to save his army as he could. But the soldiers were depressed and spiritless—the German auxiliaries deserted him, and the ammunition becoming exhausted, he was driven to desperation. In this hopeless condition he resolved to sally forth and cut his way through the fifty thousand that environed him, and joining the garrison at Torgau and Wittenberg, fight his way back to the Rhine.

Carrying out this bold determination, he sallied forth with his fifteen thousand men. Vain and last effort! His weary, half-famished soldiers staggered back from the shock, and were compelled to flee into the city All hope was gone. The bread-shops were closed and the mills silent, though the miserable crowds pressed around them, threatening and beseeching by turns. Famine stalked through the streets, followed by pestilence, and woe, and death. The meat was exhausted, and the starving soldiers fell on their horses, and devoured them. Thirty were slain every day; and at length, around the putrid carcasses in the streets, poor wretches were seen quarreling for the loathsome food,—even the tendons were chewed to assuage the pangs of hunger. Two hundred bodies were carried every day from the hospitals to the church-yard, where they accumulated so fast that none were found to bury them; and they were "laid naked in ghastly rows along the place of sepulture." The dead tumbled from the overloaded carts—and over the corpses that thus strewed the streets, the wheels passed, crushing the bones with a sound that made even the drivers shudder. Some were hurried away before they were dead, and shrieked out as they fell on the hard pavement. Multitudes were thrown into the river, some of whom, revived by the cold water, were seen flinging about their arms and legs in a vain struggle for life. Silent terror, and faintness, and despair, filled every heart. Amid this accumulation of woe, St. Cyr moved with his wonted calmness, though the paleness on his cheek told how this suffering around him wrung his heart. He endured and suffered all as became his brave spirit; and then finding there was no hope, (for he no longer had men that could fight,) he consented to capitulate. He offered to surrender the city on condition he should be allowed to return with his soldiers to France, not to fight again till regularly exchanged. The terms were agreed to, and he marched out of the city; but so wan and worn were the soldiers, that he himself said, that probably not more than one-fourth would ever reach the Rhine. He was spared the trial of conducting this ghost of an army back to France. The allies, with the faithlessness of barbarians, had no sooner got him in their power, than they marched him and his army into Bohemia as prisoners of war. Had Napoleon perjured himself in this manner, the world would have rung with the villanous deed. The brave St. Cyr firmly protested against this violation of the laws of civilized nations, and hurled scorn and contempt on the sovereigns who thus stamped themselves with infamy in the sight of the world, threatening them with future vengeance for the deed. It was all in vain, for he had fallen into the hands of victors who were moved neither by sentiments of honour nor sympathy for the brave.

The course of St. Cyr, on the abdication of Napoleon, and his return and final overthrow, has been already spoken of. He died in March, 1830, and sleeps in the cemetery of Père-la-Chaise. A noble monument crowns his grave, and he rests in peace amid the heroes by whose side he fought.

St. Cyr was a humane man, and abstained from those excesses which stained the reputation of so many of the military leaders of his time. He was possessed of great talents, and deserved all the honours he received His "Journal des Opérations de l'Armée de Catalogne en 1808–9, sur le commandment du Général Gouvion St. Cyr," is an able work, though tinged with acrimony against Napoleon which is as unjust as his conduct was foolish.

VI.

MARSHAL LANNES.

Principle on which Napoleon chose his officers—Passage of Lodi—Battle of Montebello—Battle of Marengo—Siege of Saragossa—Battle of Aspern, and Death of Lannes.

BONAPARTE always chose his Marshals on the eclectic principle. Wherever he found *one great* quality, he laid it under contribution. The great error, even with sensible men is, they bring every one to a single standard and judge him by a single rule. Forgetting the variety everywhere visible in nature, and that the beauty and harmony of the whole depend on the difference of each part, they wish to find in every man that proportion and balance of all his qualities which would make him perfect. Disappointed in this, they seek the nearest approximation to it; and hence prefer an ordinary intellect, if well balanced, to a great one, if great only in some particular direction. Forgetting that such a character is unbalanced, only because it has at least *one* striking quality, they reject its aid, or content themselves with more prudent, mediocre minds. This may do for a merchant, but not for a government or military leader. The collection of twenty thousand common minds furnishes no additional strength, while the union of one-twentieth of that number, each of which possesses force in only one direction, gives immense power. It is true, one well balanced intellect is needed to control these conflicting energies, and force them to act in harmony on one great plan, or they will only waste themselves on each other. Bonaparte was such a controlling mind, and he cared not how one-sided the spirits were he gathered about him, if they only had force: he was after *power*, acting in whatever direction. A combination of men, each of whom could do one thing well, must do all things well. Acting on this principle, he never allowed a man of any striking quality to escape him. Whether it was the cool and intrepid Ney, or the chivalric Murat—the rock-fast Macdonald, or the tempestuous Junot—the bold and careful Soult, or the impetuous Lannes, it mattered not. He needed them all, and he thus concentrated around him the greatest elements of strength that man can wield. It is fearful to see the spirits Napoleon moulded into his plans, and the combined energy he let loose on the armies of Europe. Knowing the moral power of great and striking qualities, he would have no leader without them. In this he showed his consummate knowledge of human nature, especially of Frenchmen. Enthusiasm, and the reliance on one they never trusted in vain in battle, will carry an army farther than the severest discipline. A company of conscripts would follow Ney as far as a body of veterans a common leader. So would a column charge with Lannes at their head, when with a less daring and resolute man they would break and fly. Moral power is as great as physical, even where every thing depends upon hard blows. Mind and will give to the body all its force —so do they also to an army. The truth of this was witnessed and proved in our struggle with the parent country.

Jean Lannes was born in Lectoure, a small town in Normandy, in April, 1769. His father was a humble mechanic, and designing his son for a similar occupation, he bound him out, at an early age, as an apprentice. In ordinary times young Lannes would probably have remained in the humble station in which his birth had placed him, and become in time, perhaps, a passable shoemaker or carpenter. But the call which the Revolution sent forth for the military talent of France, could not be resisted, and young Lannes ran away from his master, and enlisted as a common soldier in the army. Soon after, he was sent with the army that operated on the Pyrenean frontier. Here he soon exhibited the two striking traits of his character—traits which eminently fitted him for the scenes in which his life was to pass—viz., reckless daring and unconquerable resolution. These qualities shining out in the heat of battle and in the most desperate straits, soon won for him the regard of his officers, and he was made chief of brigade. In this rank he fought under Lefebvre, but soon after, for some cause known only to the Convention, which yet scarcely knew the cause of anything it did, he was deprived of his commission, and returned to Paris. Amid the conflicting elements that surrounded the young soldier in the French capital, he soon found work to do. An ardent republican, his bold politics and bolder manner could not long escape the notice of government, and he was sent to the army in Italy. As chief of a battalion at Milesimo, he conducted himself so gallantly, and fought with such desperate impetuosity, that he arrested Napoleon's attention in the hottest of the engagement, and he made him Colonel on the spot.

Crossing the Po, soon after, under the enemy's fire, he was the first to reach the opposite bank; and finally crowned his brilliant exploits at Lodi, where he was made general of brigade, and soon after of division.

After the successive victories of Montenotte, Milesimo and Dego, Napoleon resolved to push on to Milan. In his progress he was forced to cross the Adda, at Lodi. Twelve thousand Austrian infantry, and four thousand cavalry, with a battery of thirty cannon, stood at the farther extremity of the bridge he was to cross, to dispute its passage. On the first of May, he arrived at Lodi with his army. The Austrian cannon and musketry began immediately to play on the bridge, so that it seemed impossible to reconnoitre the ground. But Napoleon, sheltering his men behind the houses of the town, sallied out into the midst of the deadly storm, and immediately arranged his plan. Forming a column of seven thousand picked men, he placed himself at their head and rushed on the bridge; but the cannon balls and grape-shot and the bullets of the infantry swept every inch of the narrow defile, and rattled like an incessant shower of hail-stones against its stony sides. So incessant and furious was the discharge, that a cloud of smoke lay like a dense fog round it—yet into its very bosom moved the intrepid column. The sudden volley that smote their breasts made those bold men reel and stagger back. For a moment the column wavered and balanced on the pass—for a thousand had already fallen, and it was marching straight into a volcano of fire; but the next moment, seeing themselves supported by the tirailleurs that were fording the stream beneath the arches, the soldiers shouted, " *Vive la Repub lique!*" and, receiving the storm of cannon-balls and grape-shot on their unshrinking bosoms, rushed forward and bayoneted the artillery-men at their guns. Lannes was the *first man across, and Bonaparte the second.* Spurring his excited steed on the Austrian ranks, he snatched a banner from the enemy, and just as he was about to seize another, his horse sunk under him. In a moment the swords of half a dozen cuirassiers glittered above him, and his destruction seemed inevitable. But extricating himself with incredible exertion from his dying steed, he arose amid the sabre strokes that fell like lightning around him; and leaping on the horse of an Austrian officer behind him, slew him with a single stroke, and hurling him, from his saddle, seated himself in his place, and then, wheeling on the enemy, charged the cuirassiers like a thunderbolt, and fought his way through them single-handed, back to his followers. It is said that Napoleon never forgot the bearing of Lannes on that occasion. The fury of a demon seemed to possess him, and the strength of ten men appeared to be concentrated in his single arm. No wonder Bonaparte promoted him on the spot. His own daring was reckless enough, but Lannes' was still more so, and it seems almost a miracle that he escaped death.

Napoleon, whom his soldiers here, for the first time, gave the title of "the little corporal," in honour of his courage, was, ever after, accustomed to speak of this sanguinary struggle as "the terrible passage of the bridge of Lodi." It was by such acts of heroic valour that Lannes acquired the sobriquet in the army of "Orlando" and "Ajax." A few months after, he exhibited the same fearlessness of character and headlong courage, at the passage of the bridge of Arcola

During all this bloody struggle, Lannes never left Bonaparte; but advancing when he advanced, charging like fire by his side, and covering his person with his own body from the bullets that mowed everything down around them—he received three wounds, which well nigh relieved him of his life. He was suffering from a wound when he entered the battle, but it did not prevent him from doing deeds of incredible daring. Nothing shows the personal exposure and personal daring of the generals, who, one after another, rose to be marshals and dukes, more than the frequency with which they were wounded in their earlier career. Here, after three pitched battles, Murat, Ney, Macdonald, Berthier, and Lannes, were all wounded.

One cannot follow him through all his after career, but must select out those particulars in which he exhibited his most striking qualities. Lannes was frank, even to bluntness, and so impatient of restraint that he sometimes became insubordinate, but was always brave, and firm as a rock in the hour of battle. Indeed, his very impatience of control, and frequent outbursts of passion, when crossed in his purpose, made him rise in excitement and increase in daring, the greater the obstacles that opposed him. Always heading his columns in the desperate onset, and exposing his person where death reaped down the brave fastest, he so fastened himself in the affections of his soldiers, that they would follow him into any extremity. By the openness of his character and brilliancy of his exploits, he fixed himself deeply also in the heart of Napoleon, who always wished him by his side, and leaned on him in battle as he did on Ney. But the impetuosity of his character demanded constant action, and he grew irritable and unmanly when compelled to suffer without resistance. He could encounter any obstacle against which he was allowed to dash, and would enter any danger where he could swing the arm of defiance; but he had none of the martyr-spirit in him. Pinion him, and he would become frantic under suffering. He needed self-control and the discipline of calm and collected thought. Trained in the camp, and educated in the roar of battle, he was all action and excitement. Yet his excitement made him steady. In the midst of falling thousands and the shock of armies, his mind worked with singular clearness and power. It needed the roar of cannon and the tumult of a battle-field, to balance the inward excitement which drove him on. Hence, in his earlier career, he could not be trusted alone with an army, and Bonaparte knew it. But he learned the duties of a great leader fast, and Napoleon says himself of him, "I found him a dwarf, I lost him a giant."

In the campaign of Egypt, he appears the same great General, and fought at Aboukir and Acre as he had done before at Lodi and Arcola. At Acre, he nearly lost his life, and was carried from the field of battle severely wounded. But in the march from Alexandria to Cairo, across the desert, he exhibited that impatience and irritability before mentioned. In the midst of a boundless plain of sand, without water, parched by the sun, and surrounded by troops of Bedouins; the army gave way to despair, and Murat and Lannes among the rest. Wherever there was a battery to be stormed, or an army of eighty thousand men to be annihilated, none spurred more joyously into the battle than they. But to bear up against the solitude and silence of the desert—against hunger and thirst, and a burning sun—foes that could not be routed or even assailed, required more self-control than either possessed. They became dispirited and desperate, and dashed their plumed hats to the ground and trampled them in the sand; and it is said, even conspired to return to Alexandria with the army. Ney and Macdonald never would have acted thus.

Selected by Bonaparte, as one of the eight officers to return with him to France, he played an important part in that conspiracy by which the government of France was overthrown, and the commander-in-chief of the army became the First Consul of the Empire.

Bonaparte, having resolved to overthrow the imbecile Directory, and take the power into his own hands, assembled around him the most determined spirits the army could furnish. On the morning that he mounted his steed and rode towards the Tuileries—resolved to stake everything on one bold move, and pass the power of France into his own hands—seven men, as yet only partially known to fame, were assembled in the palace, sworn to his interests, and bound to his destiny. Those seven names afterward made Europe tremble. They were Moreau, Murat, Marmont, Macdonald, Berthier, Lefebvre, and Lannes. Only one was wanting—the intrepid Ney. Napoleon felt the loss of him, and when about to present himself before the bar of the Ancients, said, "*I would give, at this moment, two hundred millions to have Ney by my side.*"

Being employed a while in France, Lannes afterwards joined the army destined to Italy, and shared largely in the glory of that brilliant campaign. He accompanied Napoleon over the St. Bernard; or rather, he went over five days before him. The van guard, composed of six regiments, was placed under his command, and he set out at midnight for the top of the pass. While Bonaparte was still at Martigny, Lannes was rushing down into Italy, and had already opened his musketry on the Austrians. When the whole army was stopped by the fort of Bard, he was still sent on with the advance guard by another path to take possession of the valley of Ivrea.

BATTLE OF MONTEBELLO.

But one of the most remarkable actions of his life illustrating best the iron will and unsurpassed bravery of the man, was his battle with the Austrians at Montebello, which gave him the title of Duke. Still leading the vanguard he had carried over the St. Bernard, he came upon the Po, and upon nearly eighteen thousand Austrians, admirably posted, with their right wing resting on the Apennines, and their left reaching off into the plain; while the whole field was swept by batteries that lined the hill-sides. When he beheld this strong array, and discovered their position, he saw at once that he must retreat, or fight with no hope, except to maintain his ground till Victor, five or six miles in the rear, could come up. Independent of the superior position of the Austrians, they had between seventeen and eighteen thousand, while Lannes could muster only about eight thousand men, or less than half the number of his enemy. But his rear rested on the Po, and fearing the effect of a retreat in such a disastrous position, he immediately resolved to hazard an attack. The cheerfulness with which his soldiers advanced to this unequal combat shows the wonderful power he wielded over them. They were not only ready to march on the enemy, but advanced to the charge with shouts of enthusiasm. There can scarcely be a more striking instance of valour than the behaviour of Lannes on this occasion. There was no concealment of the danger—no chance of sudden surprise—and no waiting the effect of some other movement on which his own would depend. It was to be downright hard fighting, and he knew it; fighting, too, against hopeless odds for the first few hours. But all the heroic in him was aroused, and his chivalric bearing before his army inspired them with the highest ardour. Especially after the battle was fairly set, and it was necessary to make one man equal to three, he seemed endowed with the spirit of ten men. He was everywhere present, now heading a column in a charge—now rallying a shattered division—and now fighting desperately, hand to hand, with the enemy. Without waiting the attack of the Austrians, he formed his troops *en echelon*, and advanced to the charge. Two battalions marched straight on the murderous artillery, which, stationed in the road, swept it as the cannon did the bridge of Lodi. The third battalion endeavored to carry the heights, while Watrin, with the remainder, marched full on the centre. The battle at once became terrific. Before the furious onset of the French, the Austrians were driven back, and seemed about to break and fly, when a reserve of the Imperialists came up, and six fresh regiments were hurled on their exhausted ranks. The heights of Rovetta had been carried, but the fresh onset was too heavy for the victorious troops, and they were driven in confusion down the hill. The centre staggered back before the superior numbers and the heavy fire of the artillery; but still Lannes rallied them to another and another effort. Under one of the most destructive fires to which a division was perhaps ever exposed, he supported his men by almost superhuman efforts. Standing himself where the shot ploughed up the ground in furrows about him, he not only coolly surveyed the danger, but by his commands and presence held his men for a long time in the very face of death. But it was impossible for any column, unless all composed of such men as Lannes, long to withstand such a fire; and they were on the point of turning and fleeing, when one of the divisions of Victor's corps arrived on the field and rushed with a shout into the combat. This restored for a time the fight. The Austrians were again repulsed, when, bringing up a fresh reserve, they forced the French a second time to retire. Now advancing and now retreating, the two armies wavered to and fro, like mist when it first meets the rising blast. As division after division of Victor's corps came up, the French rallied; till at length, when they had all arrived, and the two armies stood twelve to eithteen thousand—the whole French force and the whole Austrian reserve in the field—the combat became dreadful. Though pressed by such superior numbers, and wasted by such commanding and hotly-worked batteries, Lannes refused to yield one inch of the sanguinary field. It is said that his appearance in this battle was absolutely terrific. Besmeared with powder and blood and smoke, he rode from division to division, inspiring courage and daring in the exhausted ranks—rallying again and again the wasted columns to the charge, and holding them by his personal heroism and reckless exposure of his life, hour after hour, to the murderous fire. General Rivaud, battling for the heights, and the brave Watrin, charging like fire on the centre—cheered at every repulse by the calm, stern voice of Lannes—fought as Frenchmen had not fought before during the war. The moral power which one man may wield, was never more visible than on this occasion. Lannes stood the rock of that battle-field, around which his men clung with a tenacity that nothing could shake. Had he fallen, in five minutes that battle would have been a rout. On his life hung victory, and yet it seemed not worth a hope, in the steady fire through which he constantly galloped. From eleven in the mornng till eight at night, for nine long hours, did he press with an army first of six, then of twelve thousand, on one of eighteen thousand, without intermission or relief. It was one succession of onsets and repulses, till darkness began to gather over the scene. One fourth of his army had sunk on the field where they fought. At length Rivaud, having carried the heights, came down like an avalanche on the centre, while Watrin led his intrepid column for the last time on the artillery. Both were carried, and the Austrians were compelled to retreat. Bonaparte arrived just in time to see the battle won.* He rode up to Lannes, surrounded by the remnants of his guard, and found him soiled with blood—his sword dripping in his exhausted hand—his face blackened with powder and smoke—and his uniform looking more as if it had been dragged under the wheels of the artillery during the day, than worn by a living man. But a smile of exultation passed over his features, as he saw his commander gazing with pride and affection upon him; while the soldiers, weary and exhausted as they were, could not restrain their joy at the victory they had won.

* Allison, with his accustomed correctness, says, "At length the arrival of Napoleon with the division of Gardanne, decided the victory.' This reminds us of h'z Account of the taking of the President by the Endymion.

Such was the terrible battle of Montebello; and Lannes, in speaking of it afterwards, said in referring to the deadly fire of the artillery, before which he held his men with such unflinching firmness, "*I could hear the bones crash in my division, like hail-stones against the windows.*"* A more terrific description of the effect of cannon-shot on a close column of men, could not be given. I have known of single-handed sea-fights of frigate with frigate, where the firing was so close and hot that the combatants could hear the splitting of the timbers in the enemy's ship at every broadside, but never before heard of a battle where the bones could be heard breaking in the human body, as cannon balls smote through them. Yet no one would ever have thought of that expression, had it not been suggested to him by what he actually heard. At all events, Lannes never fought a more desperate battle than this, and as evidence that Napoleon took the same view of it, he gave him the title of Duke of Montebello, which his family bear with just pride to this day.

BATTLE OF MARENGO.

Bonaparte did not forget the great qualities of a commander he exhibited on this occasion, and ever afterwards placed him in the post of danger. In the battle of Marengo, which took place a few days after, he performed prodigies of valour. Wandering over this renowned battle-field, Lannes was recalled to my mind at almost every step. The river Bormida crosses the plain between the little hamlet of Marengo,

---

* As Bonaparte was riding over the field of battle afterwards, with Lannes, and saw the heaps of the dead on every side, he shrugged his shoulders, saying, "Au diable, this has been rather a serious affair." "Yes," replied Lannes, "I could hear the bones crash in my division, like hail-stones against windows."

of some half a dozen houses, and Alessandria, where crosses the plain between the little hamlet of Marengo, the Austrians lay encamped. Coming out from the city in the morning, and crossing the Bormida under a severe fire of the French, they deployed into the open field, and marched straight on Victor, posted just before Marengo. He had stationed himself behind a deep and muddy stream—resembling, indeed, in its banks and channel, a narrow canal rather than a rivulet—and sustained the shock of the enemy with veteran firmness, for two hours; but overpowered by superior numbers he was fast losing his strength, when Lannes came up and restored the combat. There, divided only by this narrow ditch—across which the front ranks could almost touch bayonets—did the tirailleurs stand for two hours, and fire into each other's bosoms, while the cannon, brought to within pistol shot, opened horrible gaps in the dense ranks at every discharge, which were immediately filled with fresh victims. It did not seem possible, as I stood beside this narrow stream, over which I could almost leap, that two armies had stood and fired into each other's faces, hour after hour, across it.

But I do not design to go into the particulars of this battle. Austrian numbers, and the two hundred Austrian cannon, were too much for Victor and Lannes both together. The little stream of Fontanone was carried, and these two heroes were compelled to fall back on the second line. This, after a desperate resistance, was also forced back. Victor's corps, exhausted by four hours' fighting, finally gave way, and broke and fled towards Lannes' division, which alone was left to stay the reversed tide of battle. Seeing that all now rested on him, he put forth one of those prodigious efforts, for which he was remark able in the hour of extreme danger. Forming his men into squares, he began slowly to retreat. The Austrian army moved *en masse* upon him, while eighty pieces of cannon sent an incessant shower of round and grape shot through his dense ranks, mowing them down at every discharge like grass. Still he held the brave squares firm. Against the charge of cavalry, the onset of infantry, and the thunder of eighty cannon, he opposed the same adamantine front. When pressed too hard by the infantry, he would stop and charge bayonet—then commence again his slow and heroic retreat. Thus he fought for two hours—retreating only two miles in the whole time—leaving entire ranks of men on almost every foot of ground he traversed. But between the steady onset of the Hungarian infantry, which halted every ten rods and poured a deadly volley on his steady squares, and the headlong charge of the Imperial cavalry, sweeping in a fierce gallop around them, and the awful havoc of those eighty cannon, incessantly playing on the retreating masses—the trial became too great for human endurance. Square after square broke and fled, and the field was covered with fugitives crying, "*Tout est perdu, sauve qui peut.*" Still Lannes, unconquered to the last, kept those immediately about him unshaken amid the storm and devastation. Scorning to fly, unable to stand, he allowed his men to melt away before the destructive fire of the enemy; while the blowing up of his own caissons, which he could not bring away, added tenfold terror to the thunder of cannon that shook the field. He, and the Consular Guard also in square, moved like "living citadels" over the plain, and furnished a wall of iron, behind which Bonaparte was yet to rally his scattered army, and turn a defeat into a victory.

From early in the morning till three o'clock in the afternoon, the battle had raged with ceaseless fury, when the head of Desaix's column, with banners flying and trumpets sounding, was seen advancing with rapid step over the plain. Immediately at the commencement of the battle, Bonaparte despatched his aids-de-camp with urgent haste for Desaix. But as the report of the first cannon fired on Marengo, rose dull and heavy on the morning air, the hero of Egypt stood and listened; and as he heard the distant and heavy cannonading, like the roll of far-off thunder, come booming over the plain, he suspected the enemy he was after at Novi, was on the plains of Marengo, and despatched Savary in haste to the former place to see. Finding his suspicions true, he immediately put his army in motion, and was miles on his way, when the dust of fierce riders in the distance told him he was wanted. Sending forward his aids-de-camp on the fleetest horses to announce his approach, he urged his excited army to the top of its speed. At length, as he approached the field, and saw the French army in a broken mass, rolling back, he could restrain his impatience no longer, and dashing away from the head of his column, spurred his steed over the plain, and burst in a fierce gallop into the presence of Napoleon. A short council of the generals was immediately held, when most advised a retreat. "What think you of it?" said Napoleon to Desaix Pulling out his watch, he replied, "The battle is lost, but it is only three o'clock; there is time to gain another." Delighted with an answer corresponding so well with his own feelings, he ordered him to advance, and with his 6,000 men hold the whole Austrian force in check, while he rallied the scattered army behind him. Riding among them, he exclaimed, "Soldiers, you have retreated far enough; you know it is always my custom to sleep on the field of battle." The charge was immediately beat, and the trumpets sounded along the lines. A masked battery of twelve cannon opened on the advancing column of the Austrians, and before they could recover their surprise, Desaix was upon them in a desperate charge. "Go," said he to his aid-de-camp, "tell the First Consul I am charging, and must be supported by the cavalry," A volley of musketry was poured in his advancing column, and Desaix fell pierced through the heart by a bullet. His fall, instead of disheartening his men, inspired them with redoubled fury, and they rushed on to avenge his death. Napoleon, spurring by where the hero lay in death, exclaimed, "It is not permitted me to weep now." No, every thought and feeling was needed to wring victory from that defeat. The battle again raged with its wonted fury. But the tide was turned by a sudden charge of Kellerman at the head of his cavalry, which cutting a column of two thousand men in two, made fearful havoc on the right and left. Soon the whole Austrian army were in full retreat, and being without a commanding officer, broke and fled in wild confusion over the plain. "To the bridge! to the bridge!" rose in terrified shouts, as the turbulent mass rolled back towards the Bormida. Their own cavalry, also in full retreat, came thundering through the broken ranks; and trampling down the fugitives, added to the destruction that already desolated the field. All were hurrying to the bridge, which was soon choked by the crowds that sought a passage; and horses, and riders, and artillery, and infantry, were rolled together into the Bormida, that grew purple with the slain. Melias, the Austrian general, who at three o'clock, supposing the battle won, had retired to his tent, now rallied the remnants of his few hours before victorious, but now overthrown army, on the further shores of the river. Twelve thousand had disappeared from his ranks since the morning sun shone upon them, flushed with hope and confidant of victory. The combat had lasted for twelve hours, and now the sun went down on the field of blood. Over the heaps of the slain, and across the trampled field, Savary, the aid-de-camp and friend of Desaix, was seen wandering in search of the fallen chief. He soon discovered him by his long and flowing hair, (he had already been stripped naked by those after the spoils,) and carefully covering his body with the mantle of a hussar, had him brought to the head-quarters of the army. Desaix saved Bonaparte from a ruinous defeat at Marengo, and saved him, too, by not waiting for orders, but moving immediately towards where the cannonading told him the fate of the army and Italy was sealing. Had Grouchy acted thus, or had Desaix been in his place at Waterloo, the fate of that battle and the world would have been different.

Lannes wrought wonders on this day, and was selected by Napoleon, in consideration of his service, to present to government the colours taken from the enemy. This calls to mind a scene which took place in Paris just before Bonaparte set out on this expedition. The news of Washington's death had just been received, and Bonaparte thus announced it to his army; "Washington is dead! That great man fought against tyranny; he consummated the independence of his country. His memory will be ever dear to the French people, as to all freemen of both worlds, and most of all to French soldiers, who, like him and the soldiers of America, are fighting for equality and freedom." Ten days' mourning were appointed, and a solemn ceremony performed in the Church of the Invalides. Under the solemn dome Bonaparte assembled all the authorities of France, and the officers of the army, and there, in their presence, Lannes presented to the Government ninety-six colours, taken in Egypt. Berthier, then Minister of War, sitting between two soldiers, both a hundred years old, shaded by a thousand standards, the fruits of Bonaparte's victories; received them from the hand of Lannes, who pronounced a warlike speech, as he presented them. The young Republic of France went into mourning for the Father of the American Republic, and this was the funeral ceremony.

Soon after this, Lannes was sent as an ambassador to Portugal, and feeling too much the power Bonaparte and France wielded, treated with that independent nation, as if its king and ministers had been subordinates in the army. He was better at the head of a column than in the cabinet, and got no honour to himself from his office as ambassador. This very bluntness and coarseness, which rendered him fit only for the camp and the battle-field, and which indeed was the cause of his receiving this appointment, were sufficient reasons for his not having it. Being commander of the Consular Guard, he administered its chest and disbursed the money intrusted to him with such prodigality and recklessness, that there was a general complaint. It was done with the full knows ledge and authority of Napoleon, yet he reproved him for it when the excitement became too great to be any longer disregarded. This exasperated Lannes so much that he indulged in the most abrupt language towards the First Consul, and resolved to replace the money that had been expended. But from all his victories, he had little left, and Augereau was compelled to loan him the sum he needed, saying: "There, take this money; go to that ungrateful fellow for whom we have spilt our blood; give him back what is due to the chest, and let neither of us be any longer under obligations to him." But Napoleon could not afford to lose two of his best generals, and thinking it was better to keep such turbulent spirits apart, sent Augereau to the army and Lannes as ambassador to Portugal.

Recalled to the army, he fought at Austerlitz, Jena, Eylau, and Friedland with his accustomed valour. In the campaign of Eylau, at the battle of Pultusk, he advanced with his corps of 35,000 men in the midst of driving snow-squalls, and knee-deep in mud, up to the very muzzles of a hundred and twenty cannon.

In 1808, he was sent to join the army in Spain. In crossing the mountains near Mondragon he came very near losing his life. His horse stumbled and in the effort to rally fell back on him, crushing his body dreadfully by his weight. He who had stormed over so many battle-fields, and been hurled again and again from his seat amid trampling squadrons as his horse sunk under him, and yet escaped death, was here, on a quiet march, well nigh deprived of his life.

The surgeon,—who had seen a similar operation performed by the Indians in Newfoundland,—ordered a sheep to be skinned immediately, and the warm pelt sewed around the wounded Marshal's body. His cry

tremities in the meantime were wrapped in hot flannels, and warm drinks were given him. In ten minutes he was asleep, and shortly after broke into a profuse perspiration, when the dangerous symptoms passed away. Five days after he led his columns into battle at Tuedla, and completely routed an army of forty thousand men.

SIEGE OF SARAGOSSA.

The next year he was appointed to take charge of the siege at Saragossa, which had been successively under the command of Moncey and Junot. The camp was filled with murmurs and complaints. For nearly a month they had environed the town in vain. Assault after assault had been made; and from the 2d of January, when Junot took the command, till the arrival of Lannes in the latter part of the month, every night had been distinguished by some bloody fights, and yet the city remained unconquered. Lannes paid no heed to the complaints and murmurs around him, but immediately, by the promptitude and energy of his actions, infused courage into the hearts of the desponding soldiery. The decision he was always wont to carry into battle was soon visible in the siege. The soldiers poured to the assault with firmer purpose, and fought with more resolute courage. The apathy which had settled down on the army was dispelled. New life was given to every movement; and on the 27th, amid the tolling of the tower bell, warning the people to the defence, a grand assault was made, and after a most sanguinary conflict the walls of the town were carried; and the French soldiers fortified themselves in the convent of St. Joseph.

12

Unyielding to the last, the brave Saragossans fought on; and, amid the pealing of the tocsin, rushed up to the very mouths of the cannon, and perished by hundreds and thousands in the streets of the city. Every house was a fortress, and around its walls were separate battle-fields, where deeds of frantic valour were done. Day after day did these single-handed fights continue, while famine and pestilence walked the city at noon-day, and slew faster than the swords of the enemy. The dead lay piled up in every street, and on the thick heaps of the slain the living mounted and fought with the energy of despair for their homes and their liberty. In the midst of this incessant firing by night and by day, and hand-to-hand fights on the bodies of the slain, ever and anon a mine would explode, blowing the living and dead, friend and foe, together in the air. An awful silence would succeed for a moment, and then over the groans of the dying would ring again the rallying cry of the brave inhabitants. The streets ran torrents of blood, and the stench of putrified bodies loaded the air. Thus for three weeks did the fight and butchery go on within the city walls, till the soldiers grew dispirited, and ready to give up the hope of spoils if they could escape the ruin that encompassed them. Yet theirs was a comfortable lot to that of the besieged. Shut up in the cellars with the dead—pinched with famine, while the pestilence rioted without mercy and without resistance—they heard around them the incessant bursting of bombs, and thunder of artillery, and explosions of mines, and crash of falling houses, till the city shook, night and day, as if within the grasp of an earthquake. Thousands fell daily, and the town was a mass of ruins. Yet unconquered, and apparently unconquerable, the inhabitants struggled on. Cut of the dens they had made for themselves amid the ruins, and from the cellars where there were more dead than living, men would crawl to fight, who looked more like spectres than warriors. Women would man the guns, and, musket in hand, advance fearlessly to the charge; and hundreds thus fell, fighting for their homes and their firesides. Amid this scene of devastation—against this prolonged and almost hopeless struggle of weeks—against the pestilence that had appeared in his own army, and was mowing down his own troops—and above all, against the increased murmurs and now open clamors of the soldiers, declaring that the seige must be abandoned till reinforcements could come up—Lannes remained unshaken and untiring. The incessant roar and crash around him—the fetid air—the exhausting toil, the carnage and the pestilence, could not change his iron will. He had decreed that Saragossa, which had heretofore baffled every attempt to take it, should fall. At length, by a vigorous effort, he took the convent of St. Lazan, in the suburbs of the town, and planted his artillery there, which soon levelled the city around it with the ground. To finish this work of destruction by one grand blow, he caused six mines to be run under the main street of the city, each of which was charged with three thousand pounds of powder. But before the time appointed for their explosion arrived, the town capitulated. The historians of this seige describe the appearance of the city and its inhabitants after the surrender as inconceivably horrible. With only a single wall between them and the enemy's trenches, they had endured a siege of nearly two months by 40,000 men, and continued to resist after famine and pestilence began to slay faster than the enemy. Thirty thousand cannon balls and sixty thousand bombs had fallen in the city, and fifty-four thousand of the inhabitants had perished. Six thousand only had fallen in combat, while forty-eight thousand had been the prey of the pestilence. After the town had capitulated, but twelve thousand were found able to bear arms, and they looked more like spectres issuing from the tombs than living warriors.

Saragossa was taken; but what a capture! As Lannes rode through the streets at the head of his victorious army, he looked only on a heap of ruins, while six thousand bodies still lay unburied in his path. Sixteen thousand lay sick, while on the living, famine had written more dreadful characters than death had traced on the fallen. Infants lay on the breasts of their dead mothers, striving in vain to draw life from the bosoms that never would throb again. Attenuated forms, with haggard faces and sunken eyes and cheeks, wandered around among the dead to search for their friends—corpses bloated with famine lay stretched across the threshold of their dwellings, and strong-limbed men went staggering over the pavements, weak from want of food, or struck with the pestilence. Woe was in every street, and the silence in the dwellings was more eloquent than the loudest cries and groans. Death and famine, and the pestilence, had been there in every variety of form and suffering. But the divine form of Liberty had been there too, walking amid those heaps of corpses and ruins of homes, shedding her light through the subterranean apartments of the wretched, and with her cheering voice animating the thrice-conquered, yet still unconquered, to another effort, and blessing the dying, as they prayed for their beloved city.

But she was at last compelled to take her departure, and the bravest city of modern Europe sunk in bondage. Still her example lives, and shall live to the ond of time, nerving the patriot to strike and suffer for his home and freedom, and teaching man everywhere how to die in defending the right. A wreath of glory surrounds the brow of Saragossa, fadeless as the memory of her brave defenders. Before their achievements—the moral grandeur of their firm struggle, and the depth and intensity of their sufferings—the bravery and perseverance of the French and Lannes sink into forgetfulness. Yet, it was no ordinary task, the latter had given him, and it was by no ordinary means that he executed it. It required all the iron in his nature to overcome the obstacles that encompassed him on every side.

The renown which belongs to him from the manner in which he conducted this siege to its issue, has been somewhat dimmed by the accusations English historians have brought against him. He is charged with having, three days after the siege, dragged the tutor and friend of Palafox from his bedside, where he was relieving his wants and administering to him the consolations of religion, and bayoneting him and another innocent chaplain on the banks of the Ebro. He is charged, also, with levying a contribution of 50,000 pairs of shoes and 8,000 pairs of boots, and medicines, &c., necessary for a hospital, on the beggared population. He is accused of rifling a church of jewels to the amount of 4,687,000 francs, and appropriating them all to himself; and worst of all, of having ordered monks to be enveloped in sacks and thrown into the river, so that when their bodies were thrown ashore in the morning, they would strike terror into others. He is also accused of violating the terms of capitulation, by sending the sick Palafox the commander-in-chief, a close prisoner to France, when he had promised to let him retire wherever he chose. These are Mr. Alison's allegations; but as Madame d'Abrantes is the only authority he gives, they are all to be doubted, at least in the *way* they are stated, while some of them carry their falsehood in their very inconsistency; and one hardly knows which to wonder at most, the short-sighted pique of Madame Junot, (alias d'Abrantes,) which could originate them, or the credulity or national prejudice of Mr. Alison, which could endorse them.

Junot had been unsuccessful in conducting the siege, and had been superseded in the command by Lannes, who had won the admiration of Europe by his success. That Junot's wife should feel this, was natural; and that her envy should cause her to believe any story that might meet her ear, tending to disparage her husband's rival, was woman-like. Besides, Junot received less of the spoils than he would have done, had he been commander-in-chief. This also warped the fair historian's judgment—especially the loss of the jewels of our Lady of the Pillar, which she declares Lannes appropriated to himself. All this was natural in *her*, but how Mr. Alison could suppose any one would believe that Lannes wreaked his entire vengeance against the city of Saragossa and its brave inhabitants, by spearing two harmless priests on the banks of the Ebro, is passing strange. He must find some other reason for the act before any one will believe it. But the accusation that he drowned a few monks to frighten the rest, is still more laughable. One would think that Lannes considered himself in danger from monkish conspiracies, to resort to this desperate method of inspiring terror. If this story was to be believed at all, one would incline to think that he did it for mere amusement, to while away the tedious hours, in a deserted, ruined, famine-struck, and pestilence-struck city. To inspire a sepulchre and hospital with terror, by drowning a few monks, was certainly a very original idea of his.

In the storming of Ratisbon, Lannes exhibited one of those impulsive deeds which characterized him. Seeing a house leaning against the ramparts, he immediately ordered the artillery against it, which soon broke down the walls, and left them a sort of stepping-stones to the tops of the walls of the city. But such a destructive fire was kept up by the Austrians on the space between the French and it, that they could not be induced to cross it. At length Lannes seized a scaling-ladder, and rushing into and through the tempest of balls that swept every foot of the ground, planted it firmly against the ruined house, and summoned his men to follow. Rushing through the fire, they rallied around him, scaled the walls, and poured into the city, and opened the gates to the army.

But now we come to the close of Lannes' career. He had passed through three hundred combats, and proved himself a hero in fifty-three pitched battles. Sometimes the storm swept over him, leaving him unscathed; sometimes, desperately wounded, he was borne from the field of his fame, but always rallied again to lead his host to victory. But his last battle-field was at hand, and one of the strongest pillars of Napoleon's throne was to fall amid clouds and darkness.

BATTLE OF ASPERN.

In the summer of 1809, after Vienna had fallen into his hands, Napoleon determined to pass the Danube and give the Archduke Charles battle, on the farther shore. The Danube, near Vienna, flows in a wide stream, embracing many islands in its slow and majestic movement over the plain. Bonaparte resolved to pass it at two points at the same time, at Nussdorf, about a mile above Vienna; and against the island of Lobau, farther down the river. Lannes took charge of the upper pass, and Massena of the lower—the two heroes of the coming battle of Aspern. Lannes, failing in his attempt, the whole army was concentrated at Lobau. On the evening of the 19th of May, Bonaparte surprised the Austrians on the island, and taking possession of it and the other islands around it, had nothing to do but throw bridges from Lobau to the northern bank of the Danube, in order to march his army over to the extended plains of Marchfield, that stretched away from the bank to the heights of Bisomberg, where lay the Archduke with a hundred thousand men. Through unwearied efforts, Bonaparte was able to assemble on the farther shore, on the morning of the 21st, forty thousand soldiers. The Archduke saw, from the height he occupied, every movement of the French army; which seemed by its rashness and folly, to be rushing into the very jaws of destruction.

It was a cloudless summer morning, and as the glorious sun came flashing over the hill tops, a forest of glittering bayonets sent back its beams. The grass and the flowers looked up smilingly to the blue heavens, unconscious of the carnage that was to end the day.

Just as the sun had reached its meridian, the command to advance was heard along the heights, answered by shouts that shook the earth, and the roll of drums and thousands of trumpets, and wild choruses of the soldiers. While Bonaparte was still struggling to get his army over the bridge, and Lannes' corps was on the farther side, and Davoust in Vienna; the Austrian army of eighty thousand men came rolling down the mountain-side and over the plain, like a resistless flood. Fourteen thousand cavalry accompanied this magnificent host, while nearly three hundred cannon came trundling, with the sound of thunder over the ground. The army advanced in five massive columns, with a curtain of cavalry in front to conceal their movements and direction. Bonaparte looked with an unquiet eye on this advancing host, while his own army was still separated by the Danube. In a moment the field was in an uproar. Lannes, having at length crossed, took possession of Essling, a little village that stood half a mile from the Danube; and Massena of Aspern, another village, standing at the same distance from the river, and a mile and a half from Essling. These two villages were the chief points of defence between which the French army was drawn up in line. Around these two villages, in which were entrenched these two renowned leaders, were to be the heat and strength of the battle. Three mighty columns were seen marching with firm and rapid steps on Aspern, while towards Essling, where the brave Lannes lay, there seemed a countless host moving. Between, thundered the two hundred and ninety pieces of cannon, as they slowly advanced, enveloping the field in a cloud of smoke, blotting out the noon-day sun, and sending death and havoc amid the French ranks. As night drew on, the conflict became indescribably awful. Bursting shells, explosions of artillery, and volleys of musketry, were mingled with shouts of victory and cries of terror; while over all, as if to drown all, was heard at intervals the braying of trumpets and strains of martial music. The villages in which Massena and Lannes maintained their ground with such unconquerable firmness, took fire, and burned with a red flame over the nightly battle-field, adding ten-fold horror to the work of death. But I do not intend to describe the first day's battle, as I shall refer to it again when speaking of Massena and Bessieres, who fought with a desperation and unconquerable firmness that astonished even Napoleon.

At eleven o'clock at night the uproar of battle ceased, and through the slowly retiring cloud of war that rolled away towards the Danube, the stars came out one by one, to look on the dead and the dying. Groans and cries loaded the midnight blast, while the sleeping host lay almost in each other's embrace. Bonaparte, wrapped in his military cloak, lay stretched beside the Danube, not half a mile from the enemy's cannon. The sentinels could almost shake hands across the narrow space that separated them; and thus the living and the dead slept together on the hard-fought field, while the silent cannon, loaded with death, were pointing over the slumbering hosts. Lulled by the Danube, that rolled its turbulent flood by his side, and canopied by the stars, Napoleon rested his exhausted frame while he revolved the disastrous events of the day, and pondered how he might redeem his error. Massena had lost most of Aspern; but Lannes still held Essling, and had held it during one of the most sanguinary struggles of that fiercely fought battle.

Early in the morning, as soon as the light broke over the eastern hills, the two armies were again on their feet, and the cannon opened anew on the walls of living men. The French troops were dispirited, for the previous day had been one of defeat; while the Austrians were full of hope. But the rest of Lannes' corps had crossed the Danube during the night; while Davoust, with nearly thirty thousand more, was marching with flying colours over the bridge. The Archduke had also received reinforcements, so that two armies of about a hundred thousand each, stood ready to contest the field on the second day. At the commencement of the onset, Lannes was driven for the first time from Essling; but St. Hiliare coming up to his aid, he rallied his defeated troops and led them back to the charge, re-took the place, and held it, though artillery, infantry and cavalry thundered upon it with shocks that threatened to sweep the village itself from the plain.

At length, Bonaparte, tired of acting on the defensive, began to prepare for his great and decisive movement on the centre. Massena was to hold Aspern, Davoust to march on Essling, while Lannes—the brave Lannes, who had fought with such courage, and almost superhuman energy, for two days—was ordered, with Oudinot, to force the centre and cut the Austrian army in two. Bonaparte called him to his side, and from his station behind the lines which overlooked the field, pointed out to him the course he wished him to take. Lannes spurred to his post, and when all was ready, Napoleon came riding along the lines to animate the soldiers in the decisive onset that was about to be made. The shouts of "*Vive l'Em-*

pereur!" with which they received him, were heard above the roar of battle, and fell with an ominous sound upon the Austrian lines. Apprised by the shouts where the Emperor was passing, they immediately turned their cannon in that direction, hoping by a chance shot to strike him down. General Monthier was killed by his side, but he himself passed unhurt through the fire. In a few minutes, Lannes' terrible columns were on the march, and moved with rapid step over the field. Two hundred cannon were placed in front, and advanced like a rapidly moving wall of fire over the cumbered ground. Behind was the cavalry—the irresistible horsemen that had swept so many battle-fields for Napoleon, and before the onset of which the best infantry of Europe had gone down.

The Imperial Guard formed the reserve. Thus arrayed and sustained, those steady columns entered the close fire of the Austrian batteries and the deadly volleys of the infantry. Lannes knew that the fate of the battle was placed in his hands, and that the eye of Napoleon was fixed with the deepest anxiety upon him. He felt the weight of Europe on his shoulders, and determined to sustain it. In front, clearing a path for his strong legions, went the artillery, rending the serried lines as though they had been threads of gossamer. Around the threatened point the whole interest of the battle gathered, and the most wasting and destructive fire opened on Lannes' steady ranks. But nothing could resist the weight and terror of their shock. Through and through the Austrian lines they went, with the strength of the inrolling tide of the sea. Into the wild battle-gorge thus made by their advance the cavalry plunged at headlong gallop, shaking their sabres above their heads, and sending their victorious shouts over the roar of the artillery. They dashed on the ranks with such fury, that whole battalions broke and fled, crying, "All is lost." Amid this confusion and dismay still advanced the firm column of Lannes. On, on it moved with the strength of fate itself, and Bonaparte saw with delight his favourite Marshal wringing the crown from Germany, and placing it on his head. At length the enveloped host pierced to the reserve grenadiers of the Austrian army, and the last fatal blow seemed about to be given. In this dreadful crisis the Archduke showed the power and heroism of Napoleon himself. Seeing that all was lost without a desperate effort, and apparently not caring for his life if defeat must be endured, he spurred his steed among the shaking ranks, rallying them by his voice and bearing, and seizing the standard of Zach's corps, which was already yielding to the onset, charged at their head like a thunder-bolt. His generals, roused by his example, dashed into the thickest of the fight, and at the head of their respective divisions fell like successive waves upon the head of Lannes' column. Those brave officers, almost to a man, sunk before the fire that received them; but that dreadful column was checked for the first time in its advance, and stood like a rock amid its foes. The Austrians were thrown into squares, and stood in checkers on the field. Into the very heart of these, Lannes had penetrated and stopped. The empire stopped with him, and Napoleon saw at once the peril of his chief. The brave cuirassiers, that had broken the best infantry of the world, were immediately ordered to the rescue. Shaking the ground over which they galloped—their glittering armour rattling as they came—they burst into the midst of the enemy and charged the now steady battalions with appaling fury. Round and round the firm squares they rode, spurring their steeds against the very points of the bayonets, but in vain. Not a square broke, not a battalion fled; and, charged in turn by the Austrian cavalry, they were compelled to fall back on their own infantry. Still Lannes stood amid the wreck and carnage of the battle-field around him. Unable to deploy so as to return the terrific fire that wasted him, and disdaining to fly, he let his ranks melt away beside him. Being in squares, the Austrians could fire to advantage, while Lannes could only return it from the edges of his column. Seeing that he dare not deploy his men, the Archduke advanced the cannon to within five rods of them, and there played on the dense masses. Every discharge opened huge gaps, and men seemed like mist, before the destructive storm. Still that shivering column stood as if rooted to the ground, while Lannes surveyed with a flashing eye the disastrous field from which he saw there was no relief. Amid this destruction, and in this crisis, the ammunition began to fail, and his own cannon were less hotly worked. Just then, too, the news began to fly over the field, that the bridges across the Danube had been carried away by the heavy boats that had been floated down against them. Still Lannes disdained to fly, and seemed to resolve to perish in his footsteps. The brave Marshal knew he could not win the battle; but he knew also, he could die on the spot where he struggled for an Empire. Bonaparte, as he looked over the disordered field from his position, saw at once that the battle was lost. Still, in this dreadful crisis he showed no agitation or excitement. Calm and collected, as if on a mere review, he surveyed the ruin about him, and, by his firm bearing, steadied the soldiers and officers amid whom he moved. Seeing that no time was to be lost if he would save the remnant of his army—for the bridges were fast yielding to the swollen stream—he ordered a general retreat. Lannes and his army then began to retire over the field. In a moment the retreat became general, and the whole army rolled heavily towards the bridge that crossed to the island of Lobau. As they concentrated on the shore, it became one mighty mass, where not a shot could fall amiss.

The Archduke, wishing to turn this retreat into a total route, immediately advanced with his whole army upon them. His entire artillery was brought up and arranged in a semi-circle around this dense mass, crowding on to the bridges, and poured its concentrated storm into their midst with horrible effect. It seemed as if nothing could prevent an utter overthrow; but Lannes, cool and resolute as his Emperor, rallied his best men in the rear, and covered the retreating and bleeding army. With Massena by his side, now steadying his troops by his words and actions, now charging like fire on the advancing lines, these two heroes saved the army from burial in the Danube.

Lannes never appeared to better advantage than on this occasion. His impetuosity was tempered by the most serious and thoughtful actions, and he seemed to feel the importance of the great mission with which he had been entrusted. At length, dismounting from his horse to escape the tempest of cannon balls which swept down every thing over the soldiers' heads, he was struck by a shot as he touched the ground, which carried away the whole of the right leg, and the foot and ankle of the left. Placed on a litter, he was immediately carried over the bridge into the island, where Bonaparte was superintending some batteries with which to protect the passage. Seeing a litter approach him, Napoleon turned, and, lo, there lay the bleeding and dying Lannes. The fainting Marshal seized him by the hand, and in a tremulous voice exclaimed, "Farewell, sire. Live for the world, but bestow a passing thought on one of your best friends, who in two hours will be no more."

The roar of battle was forgotten, and reckless alike of his defeat and the peril of his army, of all, save the dying friend by his side, Napoleon knelt over the rude couch and wept like a child. The lip that had seemed made of iron during the day, now quivered with emotion, and the eye that had never blenched in the wildest of the battle, now flowed with tears. The voice of affection spoke louder than the thunder of artillery, and the marble-hearted monarch wept. And well he might. For there before him, mangled and torn, lay the friend of his youth, and the companion of his early career—he who charged by his side at Lodi and Arcola—saved his army at Montebello, and Italy at Marengo—who opened Ratisbon to his victorious army—nay, the right hand of his power—broken and fallen forever. "Lannes," said he, in his overpowering emotion, "do you not know me? it is the Emperor, it is Bonaparte, your friend; you will yet live." "I would that I might," replied the dying hero, "for you and my country, but in an hour I shall be no more." Soon after he fainted away, and then became delirious. He lingered thus for nine days, now charging in his frantic dreams at the head of his column, now calling wildly on the Emperor to come to him, and now raving about his cruel fate. He would not hear of death, and when told that he must die, that nothing could save him— "Not save a Marshal of France!" he exclaimed, " and a Duke of Montebello! Then the Emperor shall hang you." No, death spares neither Marshals nor Dukes, and the hero of so many combats had fought his last battle.

Lannes was prodigal of money, notwithstanding the attempt of Mr. Alison to make him covetous; frank even to bluntness, and unconscious of fear. In the midst of battle, his penetrating eye detected every movement with precision. Napoleon himself says of him: "Lannes was wise, prudent, and withal bold; gifted with imperturbable *sang froid* in presence of the enemy." There was not a General in the French army that could manœuvre thirty thousand infantry on the field of battle so well as he, and had he lived, would have become as distinguished for his military skill as he was for his bravery. His intellect was developing rapidly, and Napoleon was astonished at the growth of his understanding. In a few years more, he would have been one of the ablest Generals of his time. The rashness of youth was rapidly giving way to the reflection of the man, and his character was forming on a solid and permanent basis. He was but forty years of age when he died. His soldiers loved him like children, and a poor officer never was forgotten by him. His wife, whom he married in poverty, and from the lower ranks of life, partook of his generosity and kindness.

The eldest son of Lannes, the present Duke of Montebello, married, not many years ago, in Paris, a daughter of Charles Jenkinson, an English gentleman.

VII.

MARSHAL MONCEY.

His Early Life.—Operations in Spain—The Presentation by Napoleon of his Son to him and the National Guard—His noble efforts in behalf of Ney—Reception of Napoleon's body when brought from St. Helena.

THERE can be no greater contrast than that between Moncey and most of Napoleon's other Marshals. The moral qualities in him predominated over the mental, and while he did every thing right, he did nothing brilliant. Notwithstanding the injustice of it, the world will insist on judging every man by the same standard, without regard to the natural temperament or mental constitution. For the quiet, upright and charitable life a man naturally of a mild spirit and equable feelings leads, he receives all the praise of one who has combatted his fierce propensities, and by a long process of self-discipline, chastened his spirit and corrected his actions. The world seems to forget he is acting out his natural tendencies, and to be rash, positive, an encroaching, would require a painful effort. Being without force of will and the concentration of purpose which loves action, and seeks great accomplishments, he is not at home in the violence of political revolutions or the fierce tumult of battle. In following the peaceful and even path he treads, he is consulting his own tastes and inclinations, yet men point to him as a model. He may be a good man, and worthy of all admiration; yet were the world filled with such, it would stagnate. Such men never make reformers—conceive and execute vast plans, or push the race onward towards its final goal.

Neither will men average character. They will not allow for the peculiar nature with which one is endowed, nor let his good and bad qualities balance each other. A man of strong and vivid imagination, and impetuous spirit, may not only exhibit more principle, show more self-control, and acquire greater virtue in disciplining himself to the point from which errors are still committed, than he who is without spot or blame,—but his actions if mingled up would take a higher level. One error "covers a multitude" of virtues in this world.

Moncey and Murat were as different as light and darkness—neither one could have been the other by any possible training. The career of the former was like a stream flowing through valleys—steady and equable—that of the latter like a rushing wave—now breaking in grandeur on the shore, and now retiring out of sight into the deep. The former cultivates our sentiments, the latter kindles our imagination and awakens our emotions. Murat was a chivalric knight—Moncey an honest man. One went down like a gallant ship at sea—the other slowly wasted away in the peaceful port where he sought shelter and repose. But, if Moncey was not a brilliant man, he exhibited in the early part of his career the qualities of a good general, and received the reward of his bravery and success in being made Duke of Cornegliano and Marshal of the Empire.

Rose-Adrien de Moncey was born at Bezançon, in July, 1754. His father was lawyer of the town parliament, and designed to fit his son for his own peaceful pursuits. But, young Adrien, seized with a love for military life so common to youth, enlisted when but fifteen years old, in the infantry. His father thinking that the rigours of a camp-life would soon disgust him, let him remain six months and then procured his discharge. He, however, soon ran away and enlisted in another regiment of infantry. His father seeing the force of his inclinations, left him to pursue his own course, and he served as grenadier for three years. Having been engaged in no battle in that time, and receiving no promotion, he concluded to abandon his musket and return home, where he commenced the study of law. But a garrison being in the town, it awakened all his old habits and tastes and drew him away from his studies. As a natural result, he again became a soldier, and in about four years reached the rank of sub-lieutenant of dragoons. The Revolution breaking out, a new life opened to him, and he entered at once on his successful career. Draughted into a battalion of light-infantry, he went up rapidly to captain, chief of battalion, and general of division. During the first campaigns of the Republic he distinguished himself as a brave and upright officer.

In 1794, he was sent to the Western Pyrennees, to defend the frontiers of France against the invasions of Spain. After the success of Dugomier in the East, it was resolved to invade Spain in turn by Catalonia and Navarre. The army advanced in three columns through three different passes—Moncey commanded the third. He forced the passage appointed to him, took St. Sebastian, and on the next day fired the gates of Tolosa. Constant successes followed the army, which filled the Convention with joy. The representative Garrau, after enumerating the extraordinary victories that had been gained, closed with saying, "The soldiers of this army are not men—they are either demons or gods." The whole state of French affairs was changed in that quarter, and as it was attributed chiefly to the energy and skill of Moncey, he was nominated commander-in-chief. Hearing of his nomination, he wrote to the Convention not to ratify it, as he did not deem himself qualified for the station. But the Convention paid no heed to his remonstrance, and he was proclaimed "Commander-in-chief of the army in Spain." He soon showed that the government had not misplaced its confidence; for pursuing his success, he beat the Spaniards at Lecumberry and Villa Nova,—passed the Deva, overcame the enemy at Villa Real and Mont Dragon,—took Bilboa,—routed the enemy at Vittoria, and overrun all Biscay. The court at Madrid, alarmed at the rapid advance of the republican general, offered terms of peace, which were accepted, and the victorious Moncey left the field of his fame, and returned to France. In 1796, he was sent to command the army on the side of Brest. Having used all his endeavour to heal the divisions in Vendée, he was appointed at the end of the year to command the first military division at Bayonne. Here he remained idle, while the French army was filling the world with its deeds, along the Nile and around the Pyramids; and winning laurels in the Alps and by the Rhine.

When Bonaparte was appointed First Consul, Moncey, then at Paris, received the command of the fifteenth military division at Lyons. Soon after, when the former commenced operations in Italy, the latter was despatched thither with fifteen thousand men

While the former was descending from the heights of St. Bernard, the latter was leading his army of fifteen thousand men over the pass of St. Gothard. His historians have made him present at the battle of Marengo, but on the day of that great victory to the French, he was guarding the Tessino, awaiting orders from Bonaparte.

In 1801, he was made chief inspector of the *gens d'armerie*, and three years after received his Marshal's baton. Grand officer of the Legion of Honour, President of the Electoral College of his own department, and Duke of Cornegliano, followed in rapid succession.

In 1808, when Napoleon invaded Spain, Moncey was sent into Valencia at the head of ten thousand men, to watch the country between the Lower Ebro and Carthagena, and if he thought it advisable, to attack Valencia itself. Hearing at Cuenca that an army of thirty thousand men was gathered to attack him, and that the insurrection in the province was rapidly increasing, he resolved to march on the city of Valencia. He immediately, according to his instructions, sent a despatch to General Chabran, whom he supposed to be at Tortosa, to march also towards the city, and effect a junction with his army there on the 27th or 28th of the month. In the mean time, he moved forward with his small army towards the place.

Forcing the river Cabriel, he continued his march without serious interruption, and took up his position at Otriel. But hearing that the patriots to the number of twelve thousand were intrenching themselves at Cabrillas on his left, he turned aside to attack them. As he came up to them, his experienced eye saw immediately the advantageous position they had taken. Their centre was behind a deep, narrow defile, lined with precipitous rocks, on which were gathered multitudes of armed peasantry, while the two wings stretched along the side of a steep and rocky mountain. Opening his artillery on the centre, and keeping his cavalry hovering about the defile, in order to draw off the attention of the enemy, he despatched General Harispe to turn their flank. The plan was successful, and the enemy was routed at all points. Continuing his march he arrived before Valencia on the 27th, but General Chabran was not there, nor could he get any tidings of him. He, however, disposed his forces to the best advantage, opened his artillery, and summoned the city to surrender. But a walled town, filled with eighty thousand inhabitants, and surrounded by trenches flooded with water, so that no approach could be made except through the gates, was not likely to yield to an army of ten thousand men without a struggle. Moncey then undertook to carry it by assault—a foolish attempt, unless, as is reported, a smuggler had promised to betray the place.

The assault was unsuccessful—the people were in arms; and a friar traversing the streets, with a cross in one hand and a sword in the other, roused them by his fiery words to the highest pitch of enthusiasm. In the meantime, no intelligence having been received of Chabran, and the ammunition being nearly expended, and a thousand wounded men encumbering his troops; he concluded to raise the siege, and fell back to Quarte. Hearing at this place that the Spanish General was on the march for Almanza to intercept the communication of the French army, he resolved to advance and attack him before he could leave the kingdom of Murcia, from which he was hastening. In carrying out this plan, Moncey, though now fifty four years of age, exhibited a vigour of resolution and rapidity of movement that would have honoured the youngest General in the army.

Serbelloni was impeded in his march by the sudden appearance of the French Marshal before him, and hastily took position behind the river Xucar.

Moncey, however, forced the passage, and Serbelloni retired to some heights that commanded the high road to Almanza, designing to take possession of the defiles before the town, and there dispute the entrance with the enemy. But Moncey's rapidity of movement again defeated him; for marching all night, he drew up his army in the principal gorge and saluted the Spaniards as they approached in the morning with a discharge of artillery. Having dispersed them, he entered the town in triumph.

The whole province soon after arising in arms, his position became perilous, and Caulincourt was sent to reinforce him. Thus strengthened, he began to march back on Valencia. But Savary entrusted with the chief command for a short time in this department, arrested his movements with so little ceremony, that he was offended, and returned to Madrid. Soon after, he was ordered to besiege Saragossa. Arriving before the city, he summoned the inhabitants to surrender and prevent the slaughter that must ensue if the siege was carried on. In a few days, however, he was susperseded by Junot.

Moncey's operations were not very brilliant, and could nct well be with so small a force, still he killed and wounded, in the several battles he fought, a number equal to his entire army, showing that he was anything but an inactive and inefficient leader. Napier, in speaking of his operations in Valencia, gives him great credit, and says, 'Marshal Moncey, whose whole force was at first only eight thousand French, and never exceeded ten thousand men, continued marching and fighting, without cessation, for a month, during which period he forced two of the strongest mountain passes in the world—crossed several large and difficult rivers—carried the war into the very streets of Valencia, and being disappointed of assistance from Catalonia, extricated his division from a difficult situation, after having defeated his opponents in five actions, killed and wounded a number of them, equal in amount to the whole of his own force, and made a circuit of three hundred miles, through a hostile and populous country, without having sustained any serious loss; without any desertion from the Spanish battalions incorporated with his own, and what was of more importance, having those battalions much increased by desertions from the enemy." In another place he says, "Moncey, though an old man, was vigorous, active, and decided."

Recalled to Paris by Napoleon, he was sent into Flanders to repel the English, who were threatening a descent upon Antwerp. The failure of that expedition leaving him without active employment, he was appointed to the command of the army of reserve in the North. When Napoleon projected his fatal Russian campaign, Moncey, then an old man, threw in his strenuous remonstrance against it. After its disastrous termination, he did but little till the allies invaded France. When Napoleon, in that crisis of his life, roused himself to meet the storm that was darkening over his throne, he saw, with his far-reaching glance, that the enemy might approach to Paris; and among his last dispositions was the reorganiza-

the National Guard, over which he placed the veteran Moncey.

On the Monday previous to his setting out for the army, to make his last stand for his Empire; he assembled the officers of the National Guard in the Palace of the Tuilleries, and there, in solemn pomp, committed his son to their charge. The Empress advanced first into the apartment, followed by Madame Montesquieu carrying the infant king—already proclaimed King of Rome. The innocent child, but three years old, was dressed in the uniform of the National Guard, and his blue eyes sparkled with delight at the gay ornaments that now, for the first time adorned his vestments, while his golden locks clustered in ringlets about his neck. Taking him by the hand, Napoleon stepped into the midst of the circle of officers, and thus addressed them: "Gentlemen, I am now to set out for the army, and I entrust to you that which I hold dearest in the world—my wife and son. Let there be no political dissensions; let the respect for property, regard for order, and above all, the love of France, fill every bosom. I do not conceal from you that in the struggle that is to come, the enemy may approach on Paris, but a few days will end the affair. Before they arrive I will be on their flanks and rear, and annihilate those who dare violate our country." After he had closed his address, a silence like that of the grave succeeded, and he took the child in his arms and presented him to the aged Moncey. The old man, who had stood so many battle shocks unmoved, was now unnerved: and the quivering lip and swimming eye told of the deep emotions that mastered him, as he received the sacred trust. "This," said Napoleon, "is your future sovereign." He then presented the child to the other officers, and, as with sad and serious countenance he walked uncovered through their ranks, sudden shouts of enthusiasm filled the apartment; and amid the cries of "*Vive l'Empereur*," and "*Vive le roi de Rome*," tears burst from eyes unaccustomed to weep.

On Tuesday morning, at three o'clock, Napoleon left his palace for the army, never to see his wife and son again.

At length the allied armies approached Paris; and soon the heights around the city were covered with their victorious legions. But previous to this the Empress and her son, by order of Napoleon, had left Paris. Still the National Guard combated bravely, and Marshal Moncey, firm and steadfast to the end, struggled on after all hope was gone, and remonstrated against submission until Marmont's defection ruined every thing. He then resigned his command to the Duke of Montmorency, and, faithful to the last, retired with a few troops to Fontainebleau, to Napoleon. After the abdication of the Emperor, he gave in his adhesion to the new government, and was confirmed in his office of Inspector General of the Horse of the King's household, and in the June following, made Chevalier of Saint Louis, and two days after, Peer of France.

When the news of Napoleon's landing reached Paris, he addressed the Gens d'Armes, reminding them of the oath they had taken, to be faithful to the King. He himself never swerved from his new allegiance; and after the second overthrow of Napoleon at Waterloo, was appointed, as the oldest of the Marshals, to preside at the trial of Ney. But the firm and upright old soldier not only refused to sit in the Council of War, but drew up an able and bold remonstrance to the King, against the act. The letter came to light a few years after, and was first published in this country, and though Moncey, then in favour, saw fit to deny its authenticity, it was in terms that rather confirmed than weakened the common belief of its authorship. The published letter, not corresponding in every particular with the written one, allowed him to disavow it, for the sake of the King, who did not wish to take the obloquy of having treated so noble an appeal with disregard. He says: "Placed in the cruel alternative to disobey your Majesty, or violate my conscience, I am forced to explain myself to your Majesty. I do not enter into the question of the guilt or innocence of Marshal Ney: your justice, and the equity of his judges, must answer for that to posterity, which weighs in the same balance, kings and their subjects." After speaking of the general peace and security which were established, and that there was no cause for this high-handed act of cruelty, except that the allies wished to take vengeance on one whose very name reminded them of their humiliation, he begs the King to refuse his sanction to it. "As for myself," he says, in true nobility of spirit, "My life, my fortune, all that I hold most dear, belongs to my King and my country; *but my honour is my own;* and no power can rob me of it. What, shall I pronounce upon the fate of Marshal Ney! Permit me, Sire, to ask your Majesty, where were these accusers when Ney was marching over the field of battle? Ah! if Russia and the allies are not able to pardon the victor of Borodino, can France forget the hero of Beresina? Shall I send to death one to whom France owes her life—her families, their children, their husbands, and parents? Reflect, Sire; it is, perhaps, the last time that truth shall come near your throne.

"It is very dangerous, very impolitic to push the brave to despair. Ah, if the unhappy Ney had accomplished at Waterloo what he had so often done before, perhaps he would not have been drawn before a military commission. Perhaps those who to-day demand his death would have implored his protection. * * * * *" Nobly said, brave Moncey, in this trying hour of France, when each was seeking to preserve his own head or fortune. This single act should make him immortal. Braving the hatred of the king and the vengeance of the allies, he on whose life was no stain, here interposed himself between an old companion in arms and death. His place, his fortune, and his liberty he regarded light as air when put in the balance with his honour and with justice. To any but a Bourbon's heart, this appeal would not have been in vain, and that unhappy race would have been saved another stain on its character, and England a dishonour which she never can wipe from her history.

This bold refusal of the oldest Marshal to be president of the council of war to try Ney, accompanied with such a noble appeal to the king, and deep condemnation of the allies, awakened, as was to be expected, the deepest indignation. The only reply to it, was a royal order, depriving him of his rank as Marshal, and condemning him, without trial, to three months' imprisonment. This order was countersigned by Marshal St. Cyr, to his everlasting disgrace. He had better died on the field of his fame, or been shot like Ney, by kingly murderers, than put his signature to such a paper. If all the Marshals had en tered their solemn protest against the act, as Moncey did, it is doubtful whether Ney would have been slain.

The disgrace and imprisonment of the old Marshal, without even the farce of a trial, was in perfect keeping with the despotic injustice that had beforehand resolved on Ney's death. But what a pitiful exhibition of kingly violence was this shutting up an old man over sixty years of age, whose head had whitened in the storm of battle, and on whose name was no stain or even reproach, for daring in the nobleness of his nature, to refuse to condemn an old companion in arms, by whose side he had fought so long and bravely for France and for freedom.

When power departed from Napoleon, most of his Marshals, in their eagerness to save their hard-earned honours, and rank, and fortune, showed themselves wanting in some of the noblest qualities of man. But Moncey, unmoved by all his reverses, still kept his honour bright and his integrity unshaken; and the night that he laid his grey hairs on his prisoner's pillow, witnessed a nobler deed than the day that looked on his most victorious battle-field.

Louis XVIII. was not long in perceiving the bad policy of this petty tyranny; and when the three months' imprisonment was ended, he reinstated him in his rank, and in 1820 named him commandant of the 9th military division, and soon after chevalier of the order of Saint Esprit.

In the inglorious Spanish war of 1823, Moncey, then nearly seventy years of age, was appointed over the fourth corps. He marched into Spain, fought several battles, and finally sat down in regular siege before Barcelona. The capitulation of this city, after some severe fighting, ended the war; and Moncey returned to France, and received the grand cross of Saint Louis, and a seat in the Chamber of Peers.

In the late Revolution of 1830, Moncey took no part. He had long foreseen the storm which Charles X. by determining to keep up the Bourbon reputation for folly, was gathering over his head, and saw without regret the overthrow of his throne. His age and sorrow for the death of his only son, who in leaping a ditch in a hunting excursion, accidently discharged his gun and killed himself, had driven him from public life. But when the Bourbon throne went down again, he replaced with joy his old cockade of 1792.

After the death of Marshal Jourdan, in 1834, he was appointed Governor of the Invalides. Nothing could be more touching than the sight of this old veteran, now eighty years of age, among the mutilated and decrepid soldiers of Napoleon. Sustained by two servants, he would drag himself from hall to hall amid the blessings of those old warriors, many of whom had seen him in the pride of manly strength and courage, lead his columns into battle. Nearly two hundred officers and more than three thousand men, the wreck of the grand army, were assembled here, and the oldest Marshal of the Empire placed at their head. How striking the contrast which Moncey and those few thousand men in their faded regimentals, presented to the magnificent army which Napoleon led so often to victory From the Pyramids, from Lodi, Arcola, Marengo, Austerlitz, Jena, Wagram, and Borodino, where the eye rests on mighty armies, moving to battle and to victory amid the unrolling of standards and pealing of trumpets; the glance returns to the bowed form and grey hairs, and trembling voice of Moncey, as he moves on the shoulders of his attendants, through the ranks of these few aged soldiers, who have come maimed from almost every battle-field of Europe, to die in the bosom of France.

Time had taken what the sword left. Napoleon, the spell-word which had startled Europe, was now spoken in mournful accents, and the fields in which they had seen him triumph, were but as dim remembrances. On a far distant isle that mighty spirit had sunk to rest, and the star that had illumined a hemisphere, had left the heavens forever. What ravages time makes! Who would have thought, as he gazed on the aged Moncey borne carefully along, his feeble voice saluting his old companions in arms, that fire had ever flashed from that eye, and amid the uproar of cannon and shock of cavalry he had carried death through the ranks of the enemy; and that those bowed and limping soldiers had shouted on the fierce-fought fields of Austerlitz, Borodino and Wagram, or sent up their war-cry from the foot of the Pyramids?

The old soldiers loved to see the form of Moncey in their midst, and greeted him wherever he went with words of affection and respect. Indeed, all who knew him loved him, for his private life was as spotless as his military career. He was the friend of humanity, the patron of education, and the firm supporter of every benevolent scheme. Upright and kind, he was ever true to himself and merciful to his enemies. No acts of cruelty marred his conquests, and even his captives learned to love him. His face indicated the humane and generous character he exhibited. He was not a brilliant man, but, as Napoleon once said, "*he was an honest man.*" He was not wanting in intellectual qualities, but they predominated too much over his impulsive ones, to render him capable of those great and chivalrous actions which characterized so many of Napoleon's generals. Those sudden inspirations which so often visit genius in the hour of danger or excitement, he was an utter stranger to. He did all things well, and preserved through a long career the respect and confidence of the Emperor; for though he never flattered him in power, he never betrayed him in misfortune. His natural character was better suited to the military tactics of Wellington than Napoleon; who—decided, impetuous, and rapid himself—wished to have around him men of similar character and temperament.

The closing up of Moncey's life presents, perhaps, the most affecting scene in it. When the remains of Napoleon, a few years ago, were brought from St. Helena, Moncey, though nearly ninety years of age, was still governor of the Hotel des Invalides, and hence was appointed to receive them in the name of those disabled veterans. All France was agitated as the time drew near when the vessel was expected that bore back the dead Emperor to her shores. The insulted hero had already slept too long amid his foes, and when the vessel that was wafting him home swept down on the coast of France, the excitement could scarcely have been greater, had he been landing with sword in hand.

On the day of solemn procession in Paris, the whole city was abroad, and Napoleon in the height of his power never received more distinguished honour, than when dead he was borne through the capital of his former empire. As the procession passed through the streets, the beat of the muffled drum, and the prolonged and mournful blast of the trumpet as it rose and fell through the solemn requiem, and all the signs of a nation's woe, filled every heart with the profoundest grief.

There, beside the coffin, marched the remnants of the Old Guard, once the pride and strength of the Emperor, and the terror of Europe; and there, too, walked Napoleon's old war-horse, covered with the drapery of mourning, on whose back he had galloped through the battle; and over all drooped the banner of France, heavy with crape—all—all mourning in silence for the mighty dead.

The church that was to receive the body was crowded in every part of it, waiting its arrival, when the multitude was seen to part in front, and an old man bowed with years, his white locks falling over a whiter visage, and seemingly ready himself to be laid in the tomb, was borne through the throng in a large arm-chair, and placed at the left of the main altar, beside the throne. Covered with decorations and honours, that contrasted strangely with his withered form, and almost lifeless features, he sat and listened to the heavy dirge that came sweeping through the church, as if memory was trying in vain to recall the past. *That was Marshal Moncey*, now nearly ninety years of age, brought hither to welcome his old commander back to his few remaining soldiers. As the funeral train slowly entered the court, the thunder of cannon shook the solid edifice, blending in their roar with the strains of martial music. They, too, seemed conscious beings, and striving with their olden voices to awaken the chieftain for whom they had swept so many battle-fields. But drum and trumpet tone, and the sound of cannon, fell alike on the dull ear of the mighty sleeper. His battles were all over, and his fierce spirit gone to a land where the loud trumpet of war is never heard.

As the coffin approached, the old invalid soldiers drew up on each side of the way, in their old uniform, to receive it. The spectacle moved the stoutest heart.

The last time these brave men had seen their emperor was on the field of battle, and now, after long years, his coffin approached their midst. The roar of cannon, and the strains of martial music brought back the days of glory, and as their eyes met the pall that covered the form of their beloved chief, they fell on their knees in tears and sobs, and reached forth their hands in passionate sorrow. Overwhelmed with grief, and with the emotions that memory had so suddenly wakened, this was the only welcome they could give him. On swept the train till it entered the church; and as the coffin passed through the door, heralded by the Prince de Joinville with his drawn sword in his hand, the immense throng involuntarily rose, and a murmur more expressive than words, filled the house. The king descended from his throne to meet it, and the aged Moncey, who had hitherto sat immovable and dumb, the mere "phantom of a soldier," suddenly struggled to rise. The soul awakened from its torpor, and the dying veteran knew that Napoleon was before him. But his strength failed him—with a feeble effort he sunk back in his chair, while a flash of emotion shot over his wan and wasted visage like a sunbeam, and his eye kindled a moment in recollection. It was a striking spectacle—that silent coffin and that old Marshal together. Nothing could be more appropriate either, than this reception of Napoleon's body. The old soldiers, and the oldest Marshal of the Empire welcoming him back to a resting place in their midst—to sleep where they could keep guard, and visit his tomb.

Soon after this event Moncey died, and his only son being dead, his title of Duke of Cornegliano was conferred on M. Duchene, who married his only surviving daughter.

VIII.

MARSHAL MACDONALD.

His Early Life—Battle of Trebbia—Quarrel with Napoleon—His Passage of the Splugen—Charge at Wagram—Defence at Leipsic—His Character

It is astonishing to see what resolute and iron men Bonaparte gathered around him. Everything that came near him seemed to run in his mould, or rather, perhaps, he would confide in no one who did not partake more or less of his character. Some as much unlike him as men could well be, and worthy of no regard, he had around him, because he could use them, but to none such did he trust his armies or commit the fate of a battle. Those whom he trusted with his fate and fortunes, he knew by stern experience to be men that never flinched in the hour of peril, and were earth-fast rocks amid the tumult of a battle-field. He *tried* every man before he committed the success of his great plans to him. Rank and fortune bought no places of trust from him. He promoted his officers on the field of the slain, and gave them titles amid the dead that cumbered the ground on which they had proved themselves heroes by great deeds. When Bonaparte rode over one of his bloody, yet victorious battle-fields, as was ever his custom after the conflict, he saw from the spots on which the dead lay piled in largest heaps, where the heat and crisis of the battle had been. From his observatory

he had watched the whole progress of the strife and when he rode over the plain it was not difficult to tell what column had fought bravest, or what leader had proved himself worthiest of confidence; and on the spot where they *earned* their reward he *gave* it, and made the place where they struggled bravest and suffered most, the birth-place of their renown. This custom of his furnished the greatest of all incitements to desperate valour in battle. Every officer knew that the glass of his emperor swept the field where he fought, and the quick eye that glanced like lightning over every object was constantly on him, and as his deeds were, so would his honours be. This strung the energies of every ambitious man—and Bonaparte would have none others to lead his battalions—to their utmost tension. What wonder is it, then, that great deeds were wrought, and Europe stood awestruck before enemies that seemed never to dream of defeat?

Macdonald was one of those stern men Bonaparte loved to have in his army. He knew what Macdonald attempted to do he would never relinquish till he himself fell, or his men fled. There was as much iron and steel in this bold Scotchman, as in Bonaparte himself. He had all his tenacity and invincibility without his genius.

Macdonald was the son of a Scotchman, of the family of Clanronald, who fought under the standard of Prince Charles Edward, on the fatal field of Culloden; and after its disastrous issue, fled to France, and settled in Sancerre. There the subject of this sketch was born, in November, 1765, and received the name of Etienne Jaques Joseph Alexandre Macdonald. He belonged to the army before the revolution, and during its progress took the republican side. He was an aid-de-camp in the first Republican army that advanced on the Rhine at the declaration of war, and distinguished himself throughout that miserably conducted campaign. At the battle of Jemappe, he fought with such bravery that he was promoted to the rank of Colonel. Engaged in almost every battle in the Low Countries, he was appointed to lead the van of the army at the North; and in the winter campaign of 1794, performed one of those deeds of daring for which he was afterwards so distinguished. The batteries of Nimeguen swept the river Waal, so that it was deemed impossible to cross it with any considerable force, yet Macdonald led his column over the smooth ice and through the deadly fire that devoured his ranks, and routed the enemy. For this gallant deed he was made general of brigade. In 1796, at Cologne and Dusseldorf, he commanded the army, and soon after was sent by the Convention into Italy.

After the conquest of the Papal states, in 1798, he was made governor of Rome. In his new capacity, he exhibited other talents than those of a military leader. He could scarcely have been placed in a more trying position than the one he occupied as governor of the Eternal City. The two factions—one of which acted with the revolution, and the other against it—kept the population in a perpetual ferment. Insurrections and popular outbreaks occurred almost every day, while the indignity that had been offered the Pope, and the indiscriminate pillage of the Vatican, palaces, and churches, exasperated the upper classes beyond control, and it required a strong arm to maintain French authority in the city. Macdonald did as well, perhaps, as any one could have done in his circumstances.

An insurrection soon after having broken out at Frosinone, which he found himself unable to quell, except with the destruction of a large number of his own men; he ordered the houses to be fired and the insurgents massacred. Mack at length drove him from Rome, but being in turn compelled to evacuate it, Macdonald re-entered, and finally left it to conquer Naples.

The entrance of the French into the latter city was over heaps of corpses, for the inhabitants of every class down to the miserable lazzaroni fought with the desperation of madmen for their homes. And even after the army had entered within the walls, it could advance only by blowing up the houses; and finally conquered by obtaining, through the treachery of a Neapolitan, the castle of St. Elmo, from whence the artillery could be brought to bear on the town below. The famous Parthenopeian Republic was immediately established, and Macdonald entrusted with the supreme command. Mack, who had charge of the army opposed to the French, was an inefficient man. His forces outnumbered those of the French three to one, but he lacked the nerve to contend with Bonaparte's generals. When Nelson heard of his appointment as commander-in-chief of the forces in the south of Italy, he remarked, "Mack cannot travel without five carriages. I have formed my opinion of him."

That was the great difficulty with many of the continental generals—they could not submit to the hardships and exposures and constant toil that such men as Ney and Macdonald and Napoleon cheerfully encountered. But another man soon led his armies into southern Italy. The invincible Suwarrow who had never yet turned his back on a human foe, began to sweep down through the peninsula. Macdonald could not contend with the superior force now brought against him, and commenced a masterly retreat toward Tuscany, which tested his skill as a general more than any other act of his life.

Still advancing north, he came upon Suwarrow at the river Trebbia, and there for three days endured the shock of the entire Russian army. After the first day's battle, the two armies bivouacked on opposite sides of the river, to wait for the morning light to renew the combat.

At 6 o'clock the Russians advanced to the attack. Macdonald, finding that he must fight, though anxious to delay till Moreau could come up, poured his battalions across the river, but after a most desperate struggle, was compelled to retire again over the Trebbia. The quiet stream swept with a gentle murmur between the foemen, while the watch-fires of both camps were reflected from its placid bosom. All was still as the moonlight sleeping there, when three French battalions, mistaking their orders, advanced into the river, and began to fire on the Russian outposts. Both armies taken by surprise, supposing a grand attack was to be made, rushed to arms. In a moment all was hurry and confusion. The artillery on either bank opened their fire—the cavalry plunged headlong into the water—the infantry followed after—and there, in inextricable confusion, the two armies, up to their middle in water, fought by moonlight, while the closely advanced cannon played on the dark masses of friend and foe with dreadful effect.

This useless slaughter at length being stopped, the

two weary hosts again lay down to rest on the shore, so near, that each could almost hear the breathing of the other. Early in the morning they prepared for the third and last day's battle, and at ten o'clock Macdonald advanced to the attack. His men, up to their arm.-pits in water, moved steadily across the river in the face of a murderous fire. The battle was fiercely contested, but the French were finally driven again over the Trebbia with great loss, and next day were compelled to retreat.

The battle of Trebbia was one of the severest that had yet been fought, and though Macdonald was blamed for his tactics, he there evinced that indomitable courage and tenacity which afterwards so distinguished him. As it was, had Suwarrow received no reinforcements, or had Macdonald been aided to the same extent, the issue of it would doubtless have been different. Nearly thirty thousand men had fallen during these three terrible days. The courage, the tenacity and firmness of the troops on both sides, were worthy of that field on which nineteen hundred years before, the Romans and Carthagenians had battled for Italy.

In the revolution of the 18th Brumaire, which overthrew the Directory and made Bonaparte First Consul, Macdonald was by his side, and with Murat, Lefebre, Marmont, Lannes and others, passed the power of France over into his hands.

For the service he rendered on this occasion, Napoleon appointed him to the command of the army in the Grisons. A letter from him to General Regnier, then with the army in Egypt, shews his exalted views of Napoleon. In an extract, he says: "Since you left, we have been compelled to lament over the capriciousness of fortune, and have been defeated everywhere, owing to the impotence of the old tyrannical Directory. At last Bonaparte appeared—upset the audacious government, and seizing the reins, now directs with a steady hand the car of the revolution to that goal all good men have long waited to see it reach. Undismayed by the burden laid upon him, this wonderful man reforms the armies—calls back the proscribed citizens—flings open the prison in which innocence has pined—abolishes the old revolutionary laws—restores public confidence—protects industry—revives commerce, and making the republic triumphant by his arms, places it in that high rank assigned it by Heaven."

In 1802 he was sent as ambassador to Copenhagen, where he remained a year. On his return he was appointed grand officer of the Legion of Honour. But soon after he incurred the displeasure of Bonaparte by his severe condemnation of the trial and sentence of Moreau. Macdonald had fought beside the hero of Hohenlinden—they had planned and counselled together, and he felt keenly the disgrace inflicted on his old companion in arms. Fearless in court as he was in battle, he never condescended to flatter, nor refrained from expressing his indignation against meanness and injustice. His words, which were uttered without disguise, and couched in the plain, blunt terms of a soldier, were repeated to Napoleon, who afterwards treated him with marked coolness. Too proud to go where he was not received as became his rank, and equally disdaining to make any efforts to produce a reconciliation when he had told what he considered the simple truth, he kept away from court altogether.

Bonaparte seemed to have forgotten him, and let him remain inactive, while Europe was resounding with the great deeds of the Generals that were leading his victorious armies over the Continent. Macdonald felt this keenly. He who had fought so manfully the bloody battle of the Trebbia, performed such prodigies of valour in Italy, and finally, to the astonishment of the world, led his army in mid-winter over the Splugen amid hurricanes of snow and falling avalanches; did not deserve this neglect from one whom he had served so faithfully, and in whose hands he had helped to place the supreme power of France. Bonaparte, in his towering and unjust pride, allowed a few expressions—unjust, it is true—but springing from the very excellences of that character which made him the prop of his throne, to outweigh the *years* of service he had rendered, and the glorious victories he had brought to his standard.

The campaign of Austerlitz with its "Sun" of glory—Jena and its victories—Eylau and its carnage and doubtful issue—Friedland with its deeds of renown and richly bestowed honours, passed by and left Macdonald unnoticed and uncalled for. Thus years of glory rolled away. But in 1807, Bonaparte, who either thought that he had sufficiently punished him, or felt that he could dispense no longer with his powerful aid, gave him command of a corps under Eugene Beauharnois. He advacced into Styria, fought and captured the Austrian General, Meerfeldt— helped to gain the victory of Raab, and soon afterwards saved Napoleon and the Empire at Wagram, by one of the most desperate charges recorded in the annals of war. Created Marshal on the field of battle, he was next appointed to the government of

Gratz, where he exhibited the nobler qualities of justice and mercy. The bold denouncer of what he deemed injustice in his Emperor was not likely to commit it himself. By the severe discipline he maintained among the troops—preventing them from violating the homes and property of the inhabitants—and by the equity and moderation with which he administered the government entrusted to him, he so gained the love and respect of the people, that on his departure they made him a present of 100,000 francs, or nearly $20,000, and a costly box of jewels, as a wedding gift for one of his daughters. But he nobly refused them both, replying, "Gentlemen, if you consider yourselves under any obligation to me, repay it by taking care of the three hundred sick soldiers I am compelled to leave with you."

Not long after he was made Duke of Tarentum, and in 1810 was appointed to command the army of Augereau in Catalonia, who had been recalled. Acting in conjunction with Suchet he carried on for a while a species of guerilla warfare for which he was by nature little fitted. In 1812, he commanded the tenth corps of the Grand Army in its victorious march into Russia, and was one of the surviving few, who, after performing prodigies of valour, and patiently enduring unheard of sufferings in that calamitous retreat; struggled so nobly at Bautzen, and Lutzen, and Leipsic, to sustain the tottering throne of Napoleon. He never faltered in his attachment; nor refused his aid till Bonaparte's abdication and exile to Elba. He was strongly opposed to his mad attempts to relieve Paris, which ended in his immediate overthrow. He declared to Berthier that the Emperor should retire to Lens and there fall back on Augereau, and choosing out a field where he could make the best stand, give the enemy battle. "Then," he said, "if Providence has decreed our final hour, we shall at least die with honour." Unwavering in his attachment to the last, when the allies had determined on the Emperor's abdication, he used every effort to obtain the most favourable terms for him and his family. This generous conduct, so unlike what Bonaparte might have expected from one whom he had treated so unjustly, affected him deeply. He saw him alone at Fontainbleau, and in their private interview previous to his departure for Elba, acknowledged his indebtedness to him, expressed his high regard for his character, and regretted that he had not appreciated his great worth sooner. At parting he wished to give him some memorial of his esteem, and handing him a beautiful Turkish sabre, presented by Ibrahim Bey when in Egypt, said, "It is only the present of a soldier to his comrade."

When the Bourbons re-ascended the throne, Macdonald was made a Peer of France, and never after broke his oath of allegiance. Unlike Murat, and Ney, and Soult, and other of Napoleon's generals, he considered his solemn oath sacred, and though when sent to repel the invader, his soldiers deserted him at the first cry of "Vive l'Empereur," he did not follow their example, but making his escape hastened to Paris to defend Louis. After the final overthrow of Napoleon at Waterloo, he was promoted from one post of honour to another, till he was made Governor of the 21st Military Division, and Major General of the Royal Guard. He visited soon after Scotland, and hunting up his poor relatives, bestowed presents upon them, and finally, on the overthrow and abdication of Charles X., gave his allegiance to Louis Philippe.

This brief outline of his history gives us space to speak more fully of the three great acts of his life. When commanding the army in the Grisons, Macdonald was ordered by Napoleon to pass the Spluger with his forces, in order to form the left wing of his army in Italy.. This was in the Campaign of Italy, after Bonaparte's return from Egypt. Though no braver or bolder man than Macdonald ever lived, he felt that the execution of the First Consul's commands was well nigh impossible, and sent General Dumas to represent to him the hopelessness of such an undertaking. Bonaparte heard him through, and then with his usual recklessness of difficulties replied, "I will make no change in my dispositions. Return quickly and tell Macdonald that an army can always pass in every season where two men can place their feet." Like an obedient officer he immediately set about preparations for the herculean task before him.

PASSAGE OF THE SPLUGEN.

THE present pass over this mountain is a very different thing from the one which Macdonald and his fifteen thousand men traversed. There is now a carriage way across, cut in sixteen zig-zags along the breast of the mountain. But the road he was compelled to take was a mere bridle path, going through the gorge of the *Cardinel*. To understand some of the difficulties that beset him and his army, imagine a gloomy defile leading up to the height of *six thousand five hundred feet* above the level of the sea, while the raging of an Alpine storm and the rapid sweep of avalanches across it, add tenfold horror to the wintry scene. First comes the deep, dark defile called the Via Mala, made by the Rhine, here a mere rivulet, and overhung by mountains often three thousand feet high. Along the precipices that stoop over this mad torrent the path is cut in the solid rock— now hugging the mountain wall like a mere thread, and now shooting in a single arch over the gorge that sinks three hundred feet below. Strangely silent snow peaks pierce the heavens in every direction, while from the slender bridges that spring from precipice to precipice over the turbulent stream, the roar of the vexed waters can scarcely be heard. After leaving this defile the road passes through the valley of Schams, then winding up the pine-covered cliffs of La Rafla, strikes on to the bare face of the mountain— going sometimes at an angle of forty-five degrees—and finally reaches the naked summit, standing bleak and cold in the wintry heavens. This was the Splugen-pass over which Macdonald was commanded to lead his army of 15,000 men in mid-winter.

It was on the 20th of November he commenced his preparations. A constant succession of snow-storms had filled up the entire path, so that a single man on foot would not have thought of making the attempt. But when Macdonald had made up his mind to do a thing, that was the end of all impossibilities. The cannon were dismounted and placed on sleds, to which oxen were attached—the ammunition divided about on the backs of mules, while every soldier had to carry, besides his usual arms, five packets of cartridges and five days' provisions. The guides went in advance, and stuck down long black poles to indicate the course of the path beneath, while be hind them came the workmen clearing away the snow, and behind them still, the mounted dragoons, with the most powerful horses of the army, to beat down the track. The first company had advanced, in this manner, nearly half way to the summit, and were approaching the hospice, when a low moaning was heard among the hills, like the voice of the sea before a storm. The guides understood too well its meaning, and gazed on each other in alarm. The ominous sound grew louder every moment, till suddenly the fierce Alpine blast swept in a cloud of snow over the breast of the mountain, and howled like an unchained demon through the gorge below. In an instant all was confusion, and blindness, and uncertainty. The very heavens were blotted out, and the frightened column stood and listened to the raving tempest, that threatened to lift the rock-rooted pines that shrieked above them from their places, and bring down the very Alps themselves. But suddenly another still more alarming sound was heard amid the storm—"an avalanche! an avalanche!" shrieked the guides, and the next moment an awful white form came leaping down the mountain, and striking the column that was struggling along the path, passed straight through it into the gulf below, carrying thirty dragoons and their horses along with it in its wild plunge. The black forms of steeds, and their riders, were seen, for one moment, suspended in mid-heavens, and in the next, disappeared among the ice and crags below. The head of the column immediately pushed on and reached the hospice in safety, while the rear, separated from it by the avalanche, and struck dumb by this sudden apparition crossing their path with such lightning-like velocity, and bearing to such fearful death their brave comrades, refused to proceed, and turned back to the village of Splugen.

For three days the storm raged amid the mountains, filling the heavens with snow, and hurling avalanches into the path, till it became so choked up that the guides declared it would take fifteen days to open it again. But fifteen days Macdonald could not spare. Independent of the urgency of his commands, there was no way to provision his army in these savage solitudes, and he *must* proceed. He therefore ordered four of the strongest oxen that could be found to be led in advance by the best guides. Forty peasants followed behind, clearing away and beating down the snow. Two companies of sappers came after to give still greater consistency to the track, while on their heels marched the remnant of the company of the dragoons, part of which had been borne away by the avalanche, three days before. The post of danger was given them at their own request. They presented a strange sight amid those Alpine solitudes. Those oxen with their horns just peering above the snow, toiled slowly on, pushing their unwieldly bodies through the drifts, while the soldiers up to their arm-pits struggled behind. Not a drum or bugle note cheered the solitude, or awoke the echoes of those silent peaks. The footfall gave back no sound in the soft snow, and the words of command seemed smothered in the very atmosphere. Silently, noiselessly the vast but disordered line stretched itself upward, with naught to break the deep stillness of the wintry noon, save the fierce pantings of the horses and animals, as with reeking sides they strained up the ascent.

This day and the next being clear and frosty, the

separate columns passed in safety, with the exception
of those who sunk in their footsteps overcome by the
cold. The successful efforts of the columns, these
two days, induced Macdonald to march all of the
remaining troops over the next day; and so ordering the whole army to advance, he commenced, on the
5th of December, the passage. But fresh snow had
fallen the night previous, filling up the entire track,
so that it had all to be made over again. The guides,
expecting a wind and avalanches after this fresh fall
of snow, refused to go, till they were compelled to by
Macdonald. Breast deep the army waded up the
difficult and desolate path, making in six hours but six
miles, or *one mile an hour*. They had not advanced
far, however, when they came upon a huge block of
ice, and a newly fallen avalanche, that entirely filled
up the way. The guides halted before these new
obstacles and refused to proceed, and the head of the
column wheeled about and began its march down the
mountain. Macdonald immediately hastened forward; and placing himself at the head of his men,
walked on foot, with a long pole in his hand to sound
the treacherous mass he was treading upon, and
revived the drooping spirits of the soldiers with words
of encouragement. "Soldiers," said he, "your destinies call you into Italy; advance and conquer first
the mountain and the snow—then the plains and the
armies." Ashamed to see their General hazarding his
life at every step where they had refused to go, they
returned cheerfully to their toil. But before they
could effect the passage the voice of the hurricane was
again heard on its march, and the next moment a
cloud of driving snow obliterated every thing from
view. The path was filled up, and all traces of it

swept utterly away. Amid the screams of the guides, the confused commands of the officers, and the howling of the storm, there came at intervals the rapid thunder-crash of avalanches.

Then commenced again the stern struggle of the army for life. The foe they had to contend with was not one of flesh and blood. To sword-cut, bayonet-thrust, and the blaze of artillery, the strong Alpine storm was alike invulnerable. On the serried column and straggling line, it thundered with the same reckless power, while over all, the drifted snow lay like one vast winding-sheet. No one who has not seen an Alpine storm, can imagine the fearful energy with which it rages through the mountains. The light snow, borne aloft on its bosom, is whirled and scattered like an ocean of mist over all things. Such a storm now piled around them the drifts which seemed to form instantaneously, as by the touch of a magician's wand. All was mystery and darkness, gloom and affright. The storm had sounded its trumpet for the charge, but no note of defiance replied. The heroes of so many battle-fields stood in still terror before this new and mightier foe. Crowding together, as though proximity added to their safety, the frightened soldiers crouched and shivered to the blast that seemed to pierce their very bones with its chilling cold. But the piercing cold, and drifting snow, and raging storm, and concealed pitfalls, were not enough to complete this scene of terror. Avalanches fell in rapid succession from the top of the Splugen. Scaling the breast of the mountain with a single leap, they came with a crash on the shivering column, bearing it away to the destruction that waited beneath. The extreme density of the atmosphere, filled as it was with snow, imparted infinite terror to these mysterious messengers of death, as they came down the mountain declivity. A low, rumbling sound would be heard amid the pauses of the storm; and as the next shriek of the blast swept by, a rushing as of a counterblast smote the ear; and before the thought had time to change, a rolling, leaping, broken mass of snow burst through the thick atmosphere, and the next moment plunged with the sound of thunder, far, far below, bearing away a whole company of soldiers to its deep, dark resting place. One drummer carried over the precipice, fell unhurt to the bottom of the gulf, and crawling out from the mass of the snow which had broken his fall, began to beat his drum for relief. Deep down, amid the crushed forms of avalanches, the poor fellow stood, and for a whole hour beat the rapid strains which had so often summoned his companions to arms. The muffled sound came ringing up the face of the precipice, the most touching appeal that could be made to a soldier's heart. But no hand could reach him there, and the blows grew fainter and fainter, till they ceased altogether, and the poor drummer lay down to die. He had beaten his last reveillè, and his companions passed mournfully on, leaving the Alpine storm to sing his dirge.

On the evening of the 6th of December, the greater part of the army had passed the mountains, and the van had pushed on as far as Lake Como. From the 26th of November to the 6th of December, or nearly two weeks, had Macdonald been engaged in this perilous pass. Nearly two hundred men had perished in the undertaking, and as many more mules and horses.

One can never in imagination see that long strag

gbng line, winding itself like a huge anaconda over the lofty snow-peak of the Splugen, with the indomitable Macdonald feeling his way in front, covered with snow, while ever and anon huge avalanches sweep by him, and the blinding storm covers his men and the path from his sight, and hear his stern, calm, clear voice, directing the way;—without feelings of supreme wonder. There is nothing like it in modern history, unless it be Suwarrow's passage of the Glarus while pressed by a superior enemy. Bonaparte's passage over the St. Bernard—so world-renowned—was mere child's play compared to it. That pass was made in pleasant weather, with nothing but the ruggedness of the ascent to obstruct his progress. Suwarrow, on the contrary, led his mighty army over the Pragel, breast-deep in snow, with the enemy on every side of him, mowing down his ranks without resistance. Macdonald had no enemy to contend with but nature—but it was nature alive and wild. The path by which he conducted his army over the Splugen was nearly as bad in summer, as the St. Bernard the time Napoleon crossed it. But in midwinter to *make* a path, and lead an army of fifteen thousand men through hurricanes and avalanches, where the foot of the chamois scarce dared to tread, was an undertaking from which even Bonaparte himself might have shrunk. And Napoleon never uttered a greater untruth, than when he said, " The passage of the Splugen presented, without doubt, some difficulties, but winter is by no means the season of the year in which such operations are conducted with the most difficulty; the snow is then firm, the weather settled, and there is nothing to fear from the avalanches, which constitute the true and only danger to be apprehended in the Alps.'

Bonaparte would have us suppose that no avalanches fall in December, and that the passage of the Splugen in the midst of hurricanes of snow, was executed in "settled weather." What then must we think of *his* passage of the St. Bernard, in summer time, without a foe to molest him, or an avalanche to frighten him.

But Macdonald's difficulties did not end with the passage of the Splugen. To fulfil the orders of Napoleon, to penetrate into the valley of the Adige, he, after arriving at Lake Como, began the ascent of the Col Apriga, which also was no sooner achieved, than the bleak peak of Mount Tonal arose before him. A mere sheep-path led over this steep mountain, and the army was compelled to toil up it in single file through the deep snow. When he arrived at the summit, which was a small flat, about fifty rods across, he found the Austrians there, prepared to dispute the passage with him. This narrow flat lay between two enormous glaciers, that no human foot could scale, and across it the enemy had built three entrenchments, forming a triple line, and composed chiefly of huge blocks of ice, cut into regular shapes, and fitted to each other. Behind these walls of ice, the Austrians lay waiting the approach of the exhausted French. The grenadiers clambering up the slippery path, formed in column and advanced with firm step on the strong entrenchments. A sheet of fire ran along their sides, strewing the rocks with the dead. Pressing on, however, they carried the external palisades, but the fire here becoming so destructive they were compelled to retreat, and brought word to Macdonald that the entrenchments could not be forced Eight days after, however, he ordered a fresh column under Vandamme, to attempt to carry them by assault

Under a terrible discharge the intrepid column moved up to the icy wall, and though a devouring fire mowed down the men, so fierce was the onset, that the two external forts were carried. But the fire from the inner intrenchment, and from a blockhouse that commanded the position of the French, was too terrific to withstand; and after bravely struggling against such desperate odds they were compelled to retreat. On the snowy summit of the Tonal—among the glaciers, and scattered around on the huge blocks of ice, lay the brave dead, while the wintry sun flashed mournfully down on the bayonets of the retreating and wounded column. Nothing daunted,—Macdonald by a circuitous route over two other mountain ridges, at length reached the Adige, and fulfilled the extraordinary commands of Napoleon.

The passage of Napoleon over the St. Bernard was a magnificent feat, but the passage of the Splugen, by Macdonald, was a *desperate* one. One was attended with *difficulties* alone, the other with danger—one was executed in safety, the other with the loss of whole companies. This latter fact alone, is sufficient to prove which was the most difficult and dangerous. Suwarrow was driven up his pass by the cannon of the French, and led his bleeding thousands over the snow, while the enemy's muskets were continually thinning his defenceless ranks. Macdonald led *his* column through an awful gorge, and up a naked Alpine peak, when the tempest was raging, and the snow flying, and the avalanches falling in all the terror of a wintry hurricane. Bonaparte led *his* army over the San Bernard, in the delightful month of summer, when the genial sun subdues the asperity of the Alps; and without an enemy to molest him. Which achievement of these three stands lowest in the scale, it is not difficult to determine.

BATTLE OF WAGRAM.

But it is at Wagram that we are to look for Macdonald's greatest deed. One never thinks of that terrific battle, without feelings of the profoundest wonder at his desperate charge, that then and there saved Napoleon and the Empire. The battle of Aspern had proved disastrous to the French. The utmost efforts of Napoleon could not wring victory from the hands of the Austrians. Massena had stood under a tree while the boughs were crashing with cannon balls over head, and fought as never even *he* fought before. The brave Lannes had been mangled by a cannon shot, and borne away while the victorious guns of the enemy were still playing on his heroic, but flying column; and the fragments of the magnificent army, that had in the morning moved from the banks of the Danube in all the confidence of victory, at nightfall were crowded and packed in the little island of Lobau. Rejecting the counsel of his officers, Bonaparte resolved to make a stand here, and wait for reinforcements to come up. No where does his exhaustless genius show itself more than in this critical period of his life. He revived the drooping spirits of his soldiers by presents from his own hands, and visited in person the sick in the hospitals; while the most gigantic plans at the same time, strung his vast energies to their utmost tension.

From the latter part of May to the first of July, he remained cooped up in this little island, but not inactive. He had done every thing that could be done on the *spot*, while orders had been sent to the different armies to hasten to his relief; and never was there such an exhibition of the skill and promptitude with which orders had been issued and carried out. At two o'clock in the afternoon, the different armies from all quarters first began to come in, and before the next night they had all arrived. First with music and streaming banners appeared the columns of Bernadotte, hastening from the banks of the Elbe, carrying joy to the desponding hearts of Napoleon's army. They had hardly reached the field before the stirring notes of the bugle, and the roll of drums in another quarter, announced the approach of Vandamme from the provinces on the Rhine. Wrede came next from the banks of the Lech, with his strong Bavarians, while the morning sun shone on Macdonald's victorious troops, rushing down from Illyria and the Alpine summits, to save Bonaparte and the Empire. As the bold Scotchman reined his steed up beside Napoleon, and pointed back to his advancing columns, he little thought that two days after the fate of Europe was to turn on his single will. Scarcely were his troops arranged in their appointed place, before the brave Marmont appeared with glittering bayonets and waving plumes, from the borders of Dalmatia. Like an exhaustless stream, the magnificent armies kept pouring into that little isle; while, to crown the whole, Eugene came up with his veterans from the plains of Hungary. In two days they had all assembled, and on the evening of the 4th of July, Napoleon glanced with exultant eye over a hundred and eighty thousand warriors, crowded and packed into the small space of two miles and a half in breadth, and a mile and a half in length. Congratulations were exchanged by soldiers who last saw each other on some glorious battle-field, and universal joy and hope spread through the dense ranks that almost touched each other.

Bridges had been constructed to fling across the channel; and, during that evening, were brought out from their places of concealment, and dragged to the bank. In *ten minutes* one was across, and fastened at both ends. In a little longer time two others were thrown over, and made firm to the opposite shore. Bonaparte was there, walking backwards and forwards in the mud, cheering on the men, and accelerating the work, which was driven with such wonderful rapidity, that by three o'clock in the morning, six bridges were finished and filled with the marching columns. He had constructed two bridges lower down the river, as if he intended to cross there in order to distract the enemy from the *real* point of danger. On these the Austrians kept up an incessant fire of artillery, which was answered by the French from the island with a hundred cannon, lighting up the darkness of the night with their incessant blaze. The village of Erzerdorf was set on fire, and burned with terrific fierceness—for a tempest arose as if in harmony with the scene, and blew the flames into ten-fold fury. Dark clouds swept the midnight heavens, as if gathering for a contest among themselves —the artillery of the skies was heard above the roar of cannon, and the bright lightning that ever and anon rent the gloom, blent in with the incessant flashes below—while blazing bombs, traversing the air in every direction, wove their fiery net-work over the heavens, making the night wild and awful as the last day of time. In the midst of this scene of terror, Napoleon remained unmoved, heedless alike of the storm of the elements and the storm of the artillery; and though the wind shrieked around him, and the dark Danube rolled its turbulent flood at his feet, his eye watched only the movements of his rapid columns over the bridges, while his sharp quick voice gave redoubled energy to every effort. The time—the scene—the immense results at stake—all harmonized with his stern and tempestuous nature. His perceptions became quicker—his will firmer, and his confidence of success stronger. By six o'clock in the morning, a hundred and fifty thousand infantry and thirty thousand cavalry stood in battle array on the shores of the Danube, from whence a month before the Austrians had driven the army in affright. The clouds had vanished with the night, and when the glorious sun arose over the hill-tops, his beams glanced along a countless array of helmets—and nearly three hundred thousand bayonets glittered in his light. It was a glorious spectacle: those two mighty armies standing in the early sunlight amid the green fields, while the air sparkled with the flashing steel that rose like a forest over their heads. Nothing could exceed the surprise of the Austrians, when they saw the French legions across the river, and ready for battle.

The battle, the first day, was fierce and sanguinary, and clearly indicated the sternness with which the field would be contested. Bonaparte, at the outset, had his columns—converged to a point—resting at one end on the Danube, and radiating off into the field, like the spokes of a wheel. The Austrians, on the contrary, stood in a vast semi-circle, as if about to enclose and swallow up their enemy. Macdonald's division was among the first brought into the engage

ment, and bravely held its ground during the day
When night closed the scene of strife, the Austrians
had gained on the French. They nevertheless sounded
a retreat, while the exhausted army of Napoleon lay
down on the field of blood, to sleep.

Early in the morning, the Austrians taking advan
tage of their success the day before, commenced the
attack, and the thunder of their guns at day-light
brought Napoleon into his saddle. The field was
again alive with charging squadrons, and covered
with the smoke of battle. From day-light till nearly
noon the conflict raged without a moment's cessation.
Every where, except against the Austrians' left,
the French were defeated. From the steeples of
Vienna, the multitude gazed on the progress of the
doubtful fight, till they heard the cheers of their countrymen above the roar of cannon, driving the flying
enemy before them, when they shouted in joy, and
believed the victory gained. But Napoleon galloped
up, and restoring order in the disordered lines, ordered
Davoust to make a circuit, and ascending the plateau
of Wagram, carry Neusiedel. While waiting the result of this movement, on the success of which depended all his future operations, the French lines
under Napoleon's immediate charge were exposed to
a most scourging fire from the enemy's artillery, which
tore them into fragments. Unable to advance, and
too distant to return the fire, they were compelled to
stand, as idle spectators, and see the cannon-shot
plough through them. Whole battalions, driven
frantic by this inaction in the midst of such fearful
carnage, broke and fled. But every thing depended on
the infantry holding firmly their position till the effect

of Davoust's assault was seen. Yet, nothing but Napoleon's heroic example kept them steady. Mounted on his milk-white charger, Euphrates, given him by the king of Persia, he slowly rode backward and forward before the lines, while the cannon balls whistled and rattled about him — casting ever and anon an anxious look towards the spot where Davoust was expected to appear with his fifty thousand brave followers. For a *whole hour* he thus rode in front of his men, and though they expected every moment to see him shattered by a cannon ball, he moved unscathed amid the storm. At length Davoust was seen sweeping over the plateau of Wagram, and finally appeared with his cannon on the farther side of Neusiedel. In a moment the plateau was covered with smoke as he opened his artillery on the exposed ranks of the enemy. A smile lighted up Napoleon's countenance, and the brow that had been knit like iron during the deadly strife of the two hours before, as word was constantly brought him of his successive losses, and the steady progress of the Austrians— cleared up, and he ordered Macdonald, with eight battalions, to march straight on the enemy's centre, and pierce it.

CHARGE OF MACDONALD.

This formed the crisis of the battle, and no sooner did the Archduke see the movement of this terrible column of eight battalions, composed of sixteen thousand men, upon his centre; than he knew that the hour of Europe's destiny and of his own army had arrived. He immediately doubled the lines at the threatened point, and brought up the reserve cavalry, while two hundred cannon were wheeled around the spot on which such destinies hung, and opened a steady fire on the approaching column. Macdonald ordered a hundred cannon to precede him, and answer the Austrian batteries, that swept every inch of ground like a storm of sleet. The cannoniers mounted their horses, and started on a rapid trot with their hundred pieces, approached to within half a cannon shot, and then opened on the enemy's ranks. The column marched up to this battery, and with it, at its head, belching forth fire like some huge monster, steadily advanced. The Austrians fell back, and closed in on each other, knowing that the final struggle had come. At this crisis of the battle, nothing could exceed the sublimity and terror of the scene. The whole interest of the armies was concentrated here, where the incessant and rapid roll of cannon told how desperate was the conflict. Still Macdonald slowly advanced, though his numbers were diminishing, and the fierce battery at his head was gradually becoming silent. Enveloped in the fire of its antagonist, the guns had one by one been dismounted, and at the distance of a mile and a half from the spot where he started on his awful mission, Macdonald found himself without a protecting battery, and the centre still unbroken. Marching over the wreck of his guns, and pushing the naked head of his column into the open field, and into the devouring cross fire of the Austrian artillery, he continued to advance. The carnage then became terrible. At every discharge, the head of that column disappeared, as if suddenly engulphed, while the outer ranks, on either side, melted away like snow wreaths on the river's brink. No pen can describe the intense anxiety with which Napoleon watched its progress. On just such a charge rested his empire at Waterloo, and in its failure his doom was sealed. But all the lion in Macdonald's nature was roused, and he had fully resolved to execute the dread task given him or fall on the field. Still he towered unhurt amid his falling guard, and with his eye fixed steadily on the enemy's centre, moved sternly on. At the close and fierce discharges of these cross batteries on its mangled head, that column would sometimes stop and stagger back, like a strong ship when smitten by a wave. The next moment the drums would beat their hurried charge, and the calm, steady voice of Macdonald ring back through his exhausted ranks, nerving them to the desperate valour that filled his own spirit. Never before was such a charge made, and it seemed at every moment that the torn and mangled mass must break and fly.

The Austrian cannon are gradually wheeled around till they stretch away in parallel lines like two walls of fire on each side of this band of heroes, and hurl an incessant tempest of iron against their bosoms. But the stern warriors close in and fill up the frightful gaps made at every discharge, and still press forward. Macdonald has communicated his own settled purpose to conquer or die, to his devoted followers. There is no excitement—no enthusiasm such as Murat was wont to infuse into his men when pouring on the foe his terrible cavalry. No cries of "*Vive l'Empereur*," are heard along the lines; but in their place is an unalterable resolution that nothing but annihilation can shake. The eyes of the army and the world are on them, and they carry Napoleon's fate as they go. But human strength has its limits, and human effort the spot where it ceases forever. No living man could have carried that column to where it stands but the indomitable leader at its head. But now he halts and casts his eye over his little surviving band that stands all alone in the midst of the enemy. He looks back on his path, and as far as the eye can reach, he sees the course of his heroes by the black swath of dead men that stretches like a huge serpent over the plain. Out of the *sixteen thousand men with which he started but fifteen hundred are left beside him. Ten out of every eleven have fallen*, and here at length the tired hero pauses, and surveys with a stern and anxious eye his few remaining followers. The heart of Napoleon stops beating at the sight, and well it may, for his throne is where Macdonald stands. He bears the Empire on his single brave heart—*he is the* EMPIRE. Shall he turn at last, and sound the retreat? The fate of nations wavers to and fro, for, like a speck in the distance, Macdonald is seen still to pause, while the cannon are piling the dead in heaps around him. "*Will he turn and fly?*" is the secret and agonizing question Napoleon puts to himself. No! he is worthy of the mighty trust committed to him. The Empire stands or falls with him, but shall stand while *he* stands. Looking away to where his Emperor sits, he sees the dark masses of the Old Guard in motion, and the shining helmets of the brave cuirassiers sweeping to his relief. "Forward," breaks from his iron lips. The roll of drums and the pealing of trumpets answer the volley that smites that exhausted column, and the next moment it is seen piercing the Austrian centre. The day is won—the Empire saved—and the whole Austrian army is in full retreat.

Such was the battle of Wagram, and such the charge of Macdonald. I know of nothing equal to it, except Ney's charge at Waterloo, and that was not equal, because it failed.

On riding over the victorious field, Bonaparte came where Macdonald stood amid his troops. As his eye fell on the calm and collected hero, he stopped and holding out his hand said, "*Shake hands, Macdonald—no more hatred between us—we must henceforth be friends, and as a pledge of my sincerity, I will send your marshal's staff, which you have so gloriously earned.*" The frankness and kindness of Napoleon effected what all his neglect and coldness had failed to do—*subdued him.* Grasping his hand, and with a voice choked with emotion, which the wildest uproar of battle could never agitate, he replied, "*Ah! sire, with us it is henceforth for life and death.*" Noble man! kindness could overcome him in a moment. It is no wonder that Bonaparte felt at last that he had not known Macdonald's true worth.

The last great conflict in which he was engaged was the disastrous battle of Leipsic. For two days he fought like a lion; and when all hope was abandoned, he was appointed by Napoleon to form, with Lannistau and Poniatowski, the rear guard of the retreating army while it passed over the only remaining bridge of Lindenau across the Elster. Here he stood and kept the allies at bay, though they swarmed in countless multitudes into the city, making it reel under their wild hurrahs, as they drove before them the scattered remnants of the rear of the French army. Carriages, and baggage-waggons, and char iots, and artillery came thundering by, and Macdonald hurried them over the bridge, still maintaining his post against the headlong attacks of the victorious enemy. Slowly the confused and bleeding mass streamed over the crowded bridge, protected from the pursuing enemy by the steady resistance of Macdonald. The allies were struck with astonishment at this firm opposition in the midst of defeat. Half the disasters of that battle, so fatal to Napoleon, would have been saved but for the rashness of a single corporal. Bonaparte had ordered a mine to be constructed under this bridge, which was to be fired the moment the French army had passed. The corporal to whom this duty had been entrusted, hearing the shouts of the allies as they rolled like the sea into Leipsic, and seeing the tirailleurs amid the gardens on the side near the river, thought the army had all passed, and fired the train. The bridge was lifted into the air with a sound of thunder, and fell in fragments into the river. It is said, the shriek of the French soldiers forming the rear guard, when they saw their only communication with the army cut off, was most appalling. They broke their ranks and rushed to the bank of the river, stretching out their arms towards the opposite shore, where were the retreating columns of their comrades. Thousands, in desperation, plunged into the stream, most of whom perished, while the whole remaining fifteen thousand were made prisoners. But amid the melée that succeeded the blowing up of the bridge, two officers were seen spurring their horses through the dense multitude that obstructed their way. At length, after most desperate efforts, they reached the banks. As they galloped up to the shore on their panting steeds one was seen to be Macdonald, and the other the brave Poniatowski. Casting one look on the chaos of an army that struggled towards the chasm, they plunged in. Their strong chargers stemmed the torrent manfully, and struck the opposite shore. With one bold spring, Macdonald cleared the bank, and galloped away. But the brave and noble Pole reached it only to die. His exhausted steed struggled nobly to ascend the bank, but failing, fell back on his wounded rider, and both perished together in the flood.

Of Macdonald's after-career I have already spoken. He remained firm to Napoleon till his abdication, and then, like all his Generals and Marshals, gave in his allegiance to the Bourbon throne. His firmness of character, which rendered him in all emergencies so decided and invincible, prevented him also from indulging in those excesses and adopting those ultra principles which marred the character of some of the other Marshals. His Scotch education may also have had some influence over him. He gave his adhesion to the Bourbons because it was in the compact with Napoleon, and because under the circumstances he considered it his duty to do so, and no after excitement could shake his fidelity. He was a thorough Scotchman in his fixedness of will. He possessed none of the flexibility of the French character, and but little of its enthusiasm. Bold, unwavering, and determined, he naturally held great sway over the French soldiers Versatile themselves, they have greater confidence in a character the reverse of their own, and will follow farther an iron-willed commander than one possessing nothing but enthusiasm. In a sudden charge you want the headlong excitement, but in the steady march into the very face of destruction, and the firm resistance in the midst of carnage, you need the cool, resolute man.

This trait in Macdonald's character was evinced in his conduct when sent to repel the invasion of Napoleon who was drawing all hearts after him in his return from exile. He repaired to Lyons with his army, but finding that his troops had caught the wild-fire enthusiasm that was carrying everything before it, he addressed them on their duty. It was to no purpose, however, for no sooner did they see the advanced guard of Napoleon's small company, and hear the shout of "*Vive l'Empereur*," with which they rent the air, than they rushed forward, shouting "Vive l'Empereur" in return, and clasped their old comrades to their bosoms. Ney, under similar circumstances, was also borne away by the enthusiasm of the moment, and flinging his hat into the air, joined in the wild cry that shook Europe like an earthquake, and summoned a continent to arms again, and made kings tremble for their thrones. But Macdonald was not a being of such rapid impulses. His actions were the result of reflection rather than of feeling. True to his recent oath, he turned from his treacherous troops and fled, and narrowly escaped being taken prisoner by them.

He was a conscientious soldier—kind in peace—sparing of his men in battle, unless sacrifice was imperiously demanded, and then spilling blood like water. Generous and open-hearted, he spoke his sentiments freely, and abhorred injustice and meanness. Dazzled, as all the world was by the splendid talents and brilliant achievements of Bonaparte, he followed him with a constancy and devotion that evince a generous and noble heart.

To a watchfulness that never slept, and a spirit that never tired, he added exertion that overcame the most insurmountable difficulties, and baffled the plans of all his enemies. He seemed to be unconscious of fatigue, and never for a moment indulged in that lassitude which is so epidemic in an army, and so often ensures its destruction. One cannot put his finger on the spot in the man's life where he acted as if he felt discouraged or ready to abandon everything in despair. He seemed to lack enthusiasm, but had in its place a dogged resolution that was still more resistless. He quietly saw what was to be done, and then commenced doing it in the best possible manner, without the thought of failing in his designs. He was conscious of the mighty force of will, and knew by experience how difficulties vanish by pushing against them.

The Duke of Tarentum, as Macdonald was called in France, had no sons. He had three daughters, two of whom married nobles, and the third a rich banker.

IX.

MARSHAL MORTIER.

His Early Life—Character—Battle of Dirnstein—Burning of Moscow—Blowing up of the Kremlin—His Bravery at Krasnoi.

EDWARD-ADOLPHE-CASIMER-JOSEPH-MORTIER was born for a soldier; and though inferior as a commander to Soult, Ney, Massena, St. Cyr, and Suchet, he nevertheless, played an important part in the great Napoleonic drama, and always exhibited the qualities of a good general.

He was born in Cambray, in 1768, and his father being a rich farmer, was able to give him a good education. Having adopted the republican side in the Revolution, he obtained for his son, when twenty-three years of age, a commission in a regiment of cavalry. Here, by his knowledge and good behaviour, the latter was soon promoted to the rank of adjutant general. On the Rhine, under Pichegru and Moreau, and in Switzerland under Massena, he fought bravely in his place, and was finally promoted to general of a division.

At the rupture of the peace of Amiens, he was ordered to march into Hanover with 25,000 men. With scarcely any opposition, he occupied the country and acted as humanely and uprightly as his orders allowed him; and on the assumption of the imperial crown by Napoleon, was made Marshal of the Em pire. He was in the campaigns of Austerlitz, Jena, Eylau and Friedland—now operating with the main army, and now left by himself to act against detached portions of the enemy; and yet in all circumstances, whether victorious or defeated, exhibiting the same heroism and loftiness of character.

In 1808 he was placed over a part of the army in Spain, and reduced Badajos, after a siege of fifty-five days; but his career in the Peninsula was marked by no brilliant actions. He was ever found humane, generous, and upright, while he bore a part in that unhappy war. In the expedition to Russia, he commanded the Young Guard; but was not called to fight in any great battle till the retreat commenced. At Dresden, Lutzen, and around Paris in that last death-struggle of Napoleon, he bore himself worthy of his renown and won laurels even in defeat.

After the Abdication of Napoleon, Louis made him Peer of France and Knight of St. Louis, and bestowed on him the command of the sixteenth military division. On the return of the Emperor from Elba, Mortier was appointed by Louis, over the army of the north with the Duke of Orleans. But the Prince, finding he could not secure the fidelity of the troops, which the mere mention of Napoleon's name was enough to shake; fled, leaving the command to Mortier, bidding him do what in his "excellent judgment and patriotism," he might think best. Mortier thought it best to join his former Emperor at Paris. He was immediately made Peer, and appointed inspector of the frontiers on the East and North. Napoleon designed to have had him command the Young Guard at Waterloo; but he was taken sick and compelled to remain inactive till the second over throw. Louis XVIII., on his restoration, denied him a seat in the Chamber of Peers; but in 1816 he was elected member of the Chamber of Deputies, made governor of the fifteenth military division, and three years after restored to the Peerage.

After the Revolution of 1830, he gave in his adhesion to Louis Philippe, and retained his rank.

Mortier was a noble-hearted man, of great valour, tempered with prudence, and of incorruptible integrity. Napoleon loved some of his generals for their chivalric devotion to him, while he had no great admiration for their characters—others he tolerated because they were useful; while some few received both his respect and affection. Mortier belonged to the latter class. Napoleon loved the frank, unostentatious and heroic chieftain, whom he had proved in so many trying circumstances.

Mortier was not an impulsive man, though capable of being strongly aroused. His excitement steadied him, and in the moment of extreme peril he was as calm as if in perfect safety. He would manœuvre his men under the murderous fire of a hundred cannon as composedly as in a peaceful review. Having determined what he ought to do, he seemed to give himself no concern about the results to himself.

Tall and well formed, his splendid and commanding figure moved amid the chaos of a battle-field like some ancient hero, while his calm and powerful voice would restore confidence in the very moment of despair. He never murmured like Bernadotte and St. Cyr, as the trying circumstances in which the Emperor placed him. If a sacrifice was to be made, and he was selected as the victim he made no complaint;

and where his duty as a commander placed him, there he stood and fought—apparently caring little whether he fell or was saved in the struggle.

He was less ambitious and vain than many of the other marshals, and was governed by higher principles of action. His selfishness was not constantly interfering with his duty, and he always appears calm and self-sustained amid the tumultuous events in which his life was passed. Better educated than many of the other generals, his mind and feelings were better disciplined, so that the warrior never triumphed over the man. His very chivalry, sprung not so much from the excitement of the moment as from his high sense of honour, which was a part of his nature.

BATTLE OF DIRNSTEIN.

But in the campaign of Austerlitz, at the battle of Dirnstein, he appears in his most chivalric and determined character.

After the capitulation of Ulm, Napoleon continued his progress along the Danube, waiting the moment to strike a mortal blow at the enemy. The Austrians, hearing of the surrender of Mack, began to retreat towards Vienna, pressed by the victorious French. Napoleon moved down the right bank of the Danube, while Mortier, at the head of twenty thousand men, was ordered to keep nearly parallel on the left shore. Murat, with the advanced guard, pressed with his accustomed audacity, towards Vienna. In the mean time, the Russian allies, finding they could not save the capital, crossed over the Danube to the left shore, to escape the pursuit of Napoleon, and effect a junction with reinforcements that were coming up. Mortier was aware of this, and pressed eagerly forward to intercept their march towards Moravia.

As you pass from Dirnstein to Stein, the only road winds along the Danube, and between it and a range of rocky hills, forming a deep and narrow defile. Mortier was at the former place, hastening the march of his columns; and eager to advance, pushed forward with only the single division of Gazan, leaving orders for the army to follow close in the rear. Passing through this defile, he approached Stein at daybreak, and found the rear guard of the Russian army posted on heights in front of the town, sustained by powerful batteries, which swept the road along which he was marching. Notwithstanding his inferiority of numbers and the murderous fire he should be forced to encounter, he resolved immediately to attack the enemy's position.

As the broad daylight of a November morning spread over the Danube, he opened his fire on them, and rushed to the assault. In a short time, the action became desperate, and the grenadiers on both sides could almost touch each other in the close encounter. The Russian troops came pouring back to sustain the rear-guard, while the French advanced with rapid step along the road to aid their companions. With headlong courage on the one side, and steady firmness on the other, the struggle grew hotter every moment. Neither would yield, and Mortier stood hour after hour, amid the wasting storm; till at length he began to grow anxious for the issue, and at eleven o'clock, to hurry up his troops, galloped back to Dirnstein. Spurring furiously along the defile, he came up to Dupont's division—a little beyond the farther entrance—and urged him to redouble his speed. Then, putting spurs to his horse, he again hastened back to the scene of strife. But what was his astonishment, on emerging from the road, to behold a Russian army issuing from the hills, and marching straight for its entrance. Doctoroff, with his whole division, had made a circuitous march during the combat; and, cutting off Mortier's retreat, was about to take possession of the defile. As the Marshal left the main road to escape being taken prisoner himself, and wound along the hill-sides, and saw the dense masses pouring silently into that narrow pass, his heart for a moment stopped beating; for his own doom and that of his brave troops, seemed to be sealed. Crushed between the two armies, there was no hope for him, unless Dupont came to his relief. The morning that had dawned so brightly upon him, had suddenly become black as midnight. But his resolution was immediately taken. There was but one course left for him, unless he intended to surrender; and that was, to march back, and endeavour to cut his way through to his army.

Behold that single division pressed in front by the whole Russian army, and cut off in the rear, slowly retiring towards that silent gorge. Battling back the host that pressed after him, and sent their vollies of grape-shot through his torn ranks; Mortier formed his men into a solid column, and without a drum or trumpet note to cheer them on, moved with a firm step into the dark entrance, resolved to cut his way through, or die in the effort. But a sight, dread enough to appal the stoutest heart, met his gaze as he looked along the narrow strip of road between the rocks and the Danube. As far as the eye could see, there wat nothing but dense battalions of the enemy in order of battle. Without shrinking, however, the steady column moved with fixed bayonets into the living mass. A deadly fire received them, and the carnage at once became dreadful. With the cannon thundering on their rear, and burying their fiery loads in their ranks—swept in front by incessant discharges of musketry—trampled under foot by the cavalry, and crushed between two armies, the escape of that brave division seemed utterly hopeless. Indeed, the work of annihilation had begun with frightful rapidity. Mortier, after the most desperate fighting, had pierced but a little way into the pass, and hope grew fainter every moment, as he surveyed his thinned and wasting ranks, when the thunder of cannon at the farther extremity sent a thrill of joy through his heart. No cannon shot before ever carried such hope to his bosom, for he knew that Dupont was charging along that defile to his rescue. The Russians immediately faced this new foe also, and then commenced the complicated strife of four armies fighting in the form of one long protracted column—Mortier hemmed in between two Russian armies, and Doctoroff between two French ones. But Mortier was naturally the first to go down in this unequal strife. Combating all the morning against overwhelming numbers, and struggling all the afternoon in a deep ravine, crushed between two armies, his noble division had sunk away till nothing but the mutilated fragments remained; and now, as twilight deepened over the Danube, its last hour seemed striking. But perceiving that the fire of Dupont approached steadily nearer, he cheered on his men to another, and still another effort. Under the light of the stars, that now and then twinkled through the volumes of smoke that curtained in the armies, and by the blaze of the artillery, the work of death went on—while an old castle, in which Richard Cœur de Lion once lay imprisoned, stood on the hills above, and looked sternly down on the strife. All along that gorge was one incessant thunder-peal of artillery, to which the blaze of musketry was as the lightning's flash. Amid the carnage that wasted around him, Mortier towered like a pillar of fire before his men, as they closed sternly behind him. Nearly three-fourths of his whole division had fallen in this Thermopylæ, and nothing but its skeleton was left standing. Still he would not yield, but rousing his men by his words and example, cleared a terrible path through the enemy with his sword. With his majestic form rising above the throng that tossed like a wreck on a strong current about him, he was visible to all his men. Sometimes he would be seen completely enveloped by the Russian grenadiers, while his dripping sabre swept in rapid circles round his head, drinking the life of some poor wretch with every blow, as he moved steadily on in the lane he made for himself. Parrying sword cut and bayonet thrust, he trod amid this chaos and death as if above the power of fate. With friends and foes falling like autumn leaves around him, he still remained untouched; and it was owing to his amazing strength alone, and the skill and power with which he wielded his sabre, that he escaped death. His strokes fell like lightning on every side, and under them the strongest grenadier bent like a smitten reed. Struck with admiration at his gallantry, and thinking all was lost, his officers besought him to step into a bark they saw moored to the shore and escape. "No," said he, in the spirit of true heroism, "keep that for the wounded. He who has the honour to command such brave soldiers, should think himself happy to die with them. We have still two guns left, and a few boxes of grape-shot—we are almost through. *Close up the ranks for a last effort.*" And they did close up, and move intrepidly into the fire. But the last of the ammunition was soon gone, and then nothing was left but the bayonet. But just then a cheer burst on their ears over the roar of battle—the cheer of approaching deliverance, and they answered it. That shout was like life to the dead, and that torn and mangled remnant of a column closed up for a final charge. The Russians flew up a side valley before the onset; and with the shout, "France, France, you have saved us!" that weary but heroic band rushed into the arms of their deliverers. A loud hurrah rent the air, and the bloody conflict was done. Nearly six thousand men lay piled in ghastly heaps along the road, while broken muskets and twisted bayonets, scattered here and there, showed how close and fierce the struggle had been.

The deep and solemn silence that succeeded this uproar, was broken only by the groans of the wounded, or the sullen murmur of the Danube, that rolled its bright waters along as calmly as if no deadly strife had stained its banks with blood. The smoke of battle, which had rolled so fiercely over the scene, now hung above the river, or lay along the hill-sides like thin vapour, calm and tranquil; while nature breathed long and peacefully.

Mortier had been out-generalled, but not conquered; and his bearing on this occasion stamped him as a true hero. The decision to cut his way through the enemy or perish—the personal courage he exhibited, and the noble resolution to fall amid his brave followers, when all hope seemed lost, exhibit not only the greatness of the warrior, but the nobleness of the man.

His career, as has been remarked, in Spain, was not a brilliant one; but he appears before us again in his true character in the expedition to Russia. The honourable post of commander of the Young Guard was given to him, and his place was near the Emperor's person. He took no active parts in the great combats through which the Grand Army passed to Moscow, for Napoleon was sparing both of the Young and Old Guard, and would not allow them to be engaged. At Borodino, Ney and Murat, in the midst of the conflict, sent frequently to Napoleon for its aid, and though it marched to the margin of the battle, ready to pour its massive columns on the enemy the moment the French should yield, it remained merely a spectator of the fight.

As the army approached Moscow, Murat and Mortier were ordered to advance on the city. They marched for two days with nothing to eat but bruised wheat and horse-flesh, and at length they came in sight of the enemy drawn up for battle in a strong position. Mortier remonstrated against an attack as hopeless and useless; but Murat, with his accustomed impetuosity, ordered a charge, and two thousand of that reserve of which Napoleon had been so sparing, was left on the field. Mortier immediately wrote to the Emperor, denouncing Murat, and declaring he would not serve under him.

At length Moscow, with its domes, and towers, and palaces, appeared in sight; and Napoleon, who had joined the advanced guard, gazed long and thoughtfully on that goal of his wishes. Murat went forward and entered the gates with his splendid cavalry; but as he passed through the streets, he was struck by the solitude that surrounded him. Nothing was heard but the heavy tramp of his squadrons as he passed along, for a deserted and abandoned city was the meagre prize for which such unparalleled efforts had been made. As night drew its curtain over the splendid capital, Napoleon entered the gates and immediately appointed Mortier governor. In his directions he commanded him to abstain from all pillage. "For this," said he, "you shall be answerable with your life. Defend Moscow against all, whether friend or foe."

The bright moon rose over the mighty city, tipping with silver the domes of more than two hundred churches, and pouring a flood of light over a thousand palaces, and the dwellings of three hundred thousand inhabitants. The weary army sunk to rest; but there was no sleep for Mortier's eyes. Not the gorgeous and variegated palaces and their rich ornaments—nor the parks and gardens, and Oriental magnificence that every where surrounded him, kept him wakeful, but the ominous foreboding that some dire calamity was hanging over the silent capital. When he entered it, scarcely a living soul met his gaze as he looked down the long streets; and when he broke open the buildings he found parlours and bed-rooms and chambers all furnished and in order, but no occupants. This sudden abandonment of their homes betokened some secret purpose yet to be fulfilled. The midnight moon was sailing over the city, when the cry of "fire!" reached the ears of Mortier; and the first light over Napoleon's falling em pire was kindled, and that most wondrous scene of modern time, commenced,

THE BURNING OF MOSCOW.

Mortier, as governor of the city, immediately issued his orders, and was putting forth every exertion, when at daylight Napoleon hastened to him. Affecting to disbelieve the reports that the inhabitants were firing their own city, he put more rigid commands on Mortier, to keep the soldiers from the work of destruction. The Marshal simply pointed to some iron covered houses that had not yet been opened, from every crevice of which smoke was issuing like steam from the sides of a pent-up volcano. Sad and thoughtful, Napoleon turned towards the Kremlin, the ancient palace of the Czars, whose huge structure rose high above the surrounding edifices.

In the morning, Mortier, by great exertions, was enabled to subdue the fire. But the next night, Sept. 15th, at midnight, the sentinels on watch upon the lofty Kremlin saw below them the flames bursting through the houses and palaces, and the cry of "fire! fire!" passed through the city. The dread scene had now fairly opened. Fiery balloons were seen dropping from the air and lighting upon the houses—dull explosions were heard on every side from the shut up dwellings, and the next moment a bright light burst forth, and the flames were raging through the apartments. All was uproar and confusion. The serene air and moonlight of the night before had given way to driving clouds, and a wild tempest that swept with the roar of the sea over the city. Flames arose on every side, blazing and crackling in the storm, while clouds of smoke and sparks in an incessant shower went driving towards the Kremlin. The clouds themselves seemed turned into fire, rolling in wrath over devoted Moscow. Mortier, crushed with the responsibility thus thrown upon his shoulders, moved with his Young Guard amid this desolation, blowing up the houses and facing the tempest and the flames—struggling nobly to arrest the conflagration.

He hastened from place to place amid the blazing ruins, his face blackened with the smoke and his hair and eye-brows singed with the fierce heat. At length the day dawned, a day of tempest and of flame; and Mortier, who had strained every nerve for thirty-six hours, entered a palace and dropped down from fatigue. The manly form and stalwarth arm that had so often carried death into the ranks of the enemy, at length gave way, and the gloomy Marshal lay and panted in utter exhaustion. The day passed away in storm and conflagration; and when night again enveloped the city, it was one broad flame, wavering to and fro in the blast. The wind had increased to a perfect hurricane, and shifted from quarter to quarter as if on purpose to swell the sea of fire and extinguish the last hope. The fire rapidly approached the Kremlin, and soon the roar of the flames and the crash of falling houses, and the crackling of burning timbers were borne to the ears of the startled Emperor. He arose and walked to and fro, stopping convulsively and gazing on the terrific scene. Murat, Eugene, and Berthier rushed into his presence, and on their knees besought him to flee: but he still clung to that haughty palace, as if it were his Empire.

But at length the shout, "The Kremlin is on fire!" was heard above the roar of the conflagration, and Napoleon reluctantly consented to leave. He descended into the streets with his staff, and looked about for a way of egress, but the flames blocked every passage. At length they discovered a postern gate, leading to the Moskwa, and entered it, but they had only entered still farther into the danger. As Napoleon cast his eye around the open space, girdled and arched with fire, smoke and cinders, he saw one single street yet open, but all on fire. Into this he rushed, and amid the crash of falling houses, and raging of the flames— over burning ruins, through clouds of rolling smoke, and between walls of fire he pressed on; and at length, half suffocated, emerged in safety from the heated city, and took up his quarters in the imperial palace of Petrowsky, nearly three miles distant. Mortier, relieved from his anxiety for the Emperor, redoubled his efforts to arrest the conflagration. His men cheerfully rushed into every danger. Breathing nothing but smoke and ashes—canopied by flame, and sparks and cinders—surrounded by walls of fire that rocked to and fro and fell with a crash amid the blazing ruins, carrying down with them red-hot roofs of iron; he struggled against an enemy that no boldness could awe, or courage overcome. Those brave troops had heard the tramp of thousands of cavalry sweeping to battle without fear; but now they stood in still terror before the march of the conflagration, under whose burning footsteps was heard the incessant crash of falling houses, and palaces and churches. The continuous roar of the raging hurricane, mingled with that of the flames, was more terrible than the thunder of artillery; and before this new foe, in the midst of this battle of the elements, the awe-struck army stood powerless and affrighted.

When night again descended on the city, it presented

a spectacle the like of which was never seen before, and which baffles all description. The streets were streets of fire—the heavens a canopy of fire, and the entire body of the city a mass of fire, fed by a hurricane that whirled the blazing fragments in a constant stream through the air. Incessant explosions from the blowing up of stores of oil, and tar, and spirits, shook the very foundations of the city, and sent vast volumes of black smoke rolling furiously towards the sky. Huge sheets of canvass on fire came floating like messengers of death through the flames—the towers and domes of the churches and palaces, glowed with a red heat over the wild sea below, then tottering a moment on their bases were hurled by the tempest into the common ruin. Thousands of wretches, before unseen, were driven by the heat from the cellars and hovels, and streamed in an incessant throng through the streets. Children were seen carrying their parents—the strong, the weak; while thousands more were staggering under the loads of plunder they had snatched from the flames. This, too, would frequently take fire in the falling shower, and the miserable creatures would be compelled to drop it and flee for their lives. Oh, it was a scene of woe and fear inconceivable, and indescribable. A mighty and close packed city of houses, and churches and palaces, wrapped from limit to limit in flames which are fed by a fierce hurricane, is a sight this world will seldom see.

But this was all within the city. To Napoleon without, the spectacle was still more sublime and terrific. When the flames had overcome all obstacles, and had wrapped everything in their red mantle, that great city looked like a sea of rolling fire, swept by a tempest that drove it into vast billows. Huge domes and towers, throwing off sparks like blazing fire-brands, now towered above these waves and now disappeared in their maddening flow, as they rushed and broke high over their tops, scattering their spray of fire against the clouds. The heavens themselves, seemed to have caught the conflagration, and the angry masses that swept them, rolled over a bosom of fire Columns of flame would rise and sink along the surface of this sea, and huge volumes of black smoke suddenly shoot into the air as if volcanoes were working below. The black form of the Kremlin alone, towered above the chaos, now wrapped in flame and smoke, and again emerging into view—standing amid this scene of desolation and terror, like virtue in the midst of a burning world, enveloped but unscathed by the devouring elements. Napoleon stood and gazed on this scene in silent awe. Though nearly three miles distant, the windows and walls of his apartment were so hot that he could scarcely bear his hand against them. Said he, years afterward: "*It was the spectacle of a sea and billows of fire, a sky and clouds of flame, mountains of red rolling flame, like immense waves of the sea, alternately bursting forth and elevating themselves to skies of fire, and then sinking into the ocean of flame below. Oh! it was the most grand, the most sublime, and the most terrific sight the world ever beheld.*"

When the conflagration subsided, Mortier found himself governor of a city of ashes. Nine-tenths of Moscow had sunk in the flames, and the gorgeous capital, with its oriental magnificence—its palaces, and towers, and gardens, was a heap of smoking ruins, amid which wandered half-naked, starving wretches, like spectres around the place of the dead

Napoleon returned to the Kremlin, but the spectacle which the camps of the soldiers presented as he passed through them, was one his eye had never rested on before.* The soldiers had here and there thrown together a few boards to shelter them from the weather, and sprinkled over the soft, wet ground with straw to keep off the dampness, and "there, reclining under silken canopies, or sitting in elegant chairs, with Cashmere shawls and the costliest furs, and all the apparel of the noble and wealthy strewed around them, they fed their camp-fires with mahogany furniture and ornamental work, which had a few days before decorated the palaces of the noble." The half-starved wretches were eating from silver plates, though their only food was a miserable black cake and half-boiled horse-flesh. In the interval between them and the city, were crowds of disbanded soldiers, staggering under the weight of plunder, and among them many Russians, men and women, seeking the camp-fires of their enemies. In the city it was still worse, and an insufferable stench arose from the smoking mass. All discipline was lost, and the disbanded army swarmed through the streets for plunder. This they gathered into the open places, and bartered away with their friends. Thus the poor creatures loaded themselves with gold and silver, and costly apparel, little thinking how valueless the snow-drifts of Russia would soon make them. When Napoleon was again established in the Kremlin, he put a stop to this disorder, and ordered the pillaging to be carried on according to rule.

At length, the reluctant Napoleon turned his back on the towers of Moscow, confessing to the world, that

* *Vide Segur.*

after the loss of a hundred thousand men and incredible toil, he had grasped only a phantom. It was necessary that some one should cover his retreat by remaining in the city, and Mortier was appointed to this unwelcome task. Had the Young Guard been left with him, it would not have been so hopeless an undertaking; but only eight thousand were put under his command, of which not more than a quarter could be relied upon. With this handful of men he was to cover Napoleon's retreat, and when he could hold out no longer, to blow up the Kremlin and join the rear guard of the army. It was necessary for some one to do this for the safety of the army, and the lot fell more naturally on Mortier as governor of the city. That is—a sacrifice was demanded, and it seemed proper that Mortier should be the victim. That he should escape the whole Russian army was not to be expected, and when his friends took their farewell, it was as with one they should never see again. Mortier himself looked on his career as ended, but made no complaint. Without a murmur he set about fulfilling the task allotted him.

As the army withdrew from the city the Cossacks began to swarm around it, and finally drove Mortier and his feeble band into the Kremlin. These were followed by ten thousand Russians, who pressed around the French Marshal. To perform the double task assigned him of defending the city and blowing up the Kremlin, he was compelled, even while he occupied it, to gather immense quantities of powder within it, a single touch of which would send that massive structure broken and shattered towards the heavens. He placed a *hundred and eighty-three thousand pounds* in the vaults below, while he scattered barrels of it through the different apartments above. Over this volcano of his own creation he stood and fought for four days, when the slightest ignition from one of the enemy's guns would have buried him and his soldiers in one wild grave together.

At length, after he had kindled a slow fire-work, whose combustion could be nicely calculated, he led his weary troops out of that ancient structure. But while he marched with rapid steps from the scene of danger, several Cossacks and Russians, finding the imperial palace deserted, rushed into it after plunder. The next moment, the massive pile wavered to and fro like a column of sand, and seeming to rise from the earth, fell with a crash that was heard thirty miles distant. The earth shook under Mortier as if an earthquake was on the march. Huge stones—fragments of wall—thirty thousand stand of arms, and mangled bodies and limbs were hurled in one fierce shower heavenward together, and then sunk over the ruined city. The second act in the great tragedy was now ended, and the last was about to commence.

On his arrival at the army he was again placed over the Young Guard. At the battle of Krasnoi, which Napoleon fought to save Davoust, and which was described in the chapter on that Marshal, Mortier was the principal actor. When Bonaparte with his six thousand Imperial Guard marched into the centre of fifty thousand Russians, protected by powerful batteries, Mortier, with five thousand of the Young Guard—all that was left of that splendid body —was just in advance of him. He and General Roguet commenced the attack. The Russians, able by their overwhelming numbers to crush that handful of French at once, hesitated to advance, and began to cannonade them. Mortier stood with his noble Guard in the midst of this iron storm, willing victims to save Davoust. Having no artillery of his own to answer the murderous batteries of the Russians, and they being beyond the reach of musketry, he had nothing to do but to remain inactive, and let the cannon plough through his ranks. For three mortal hours he stood and saw the horrible gaps which every discharge made. Yet not a battalion broke; and that Young Guard there proved themselves worthy to fight beside the Old Guard of the Empire. In those three hours two thousand of his little band had fallen, and then he was directed to retreat. Steadily and in perfect order, though the enemy were rapidly hemming them in, did that heroic Guard retire before those fifty thousand Russians. Mortier gave orders for them to retreat slowly, and General Laborde, repeating his orders, exclaimed, *"Do you hear, soldiers? the Marshal orders ordinary time. Ordinary time, soldiers!"* and amid that incessant tempest of grapeshot and balls, it *was "ordinary time"* with them. The brave fellows never hastened their steps by a single movement, but marched as calmly out of that storm as if going to their bivouacks.

At Lutzen and Dresden he fought worthy of his former glory, and at the disastrous battle of Leipsic, commanded the Old Guard. He battled for France till the last moment, and when the allied forces invaded his country, and were marching towards Paris, he and Marmont alone were left to arrest them. Napoleon, thinking to draw the enemy after him, had hung on their rear till they were out of his reach, and on the march for the French capital.

But previous to his separation from Napoleon, Mortier combated bravely by his side in those stupendous efforts he put forth to save his Empire. At the battle of Montmirail he fought beside Ney with the greatest heroism. At the commencement of the action he was not on the field, but amid the roar of artillery and the shocks of the bayonet he came up, bringing with him the Old Guard, the cuirassiers, and the Guards of Honour. Napoleon immediately ordered a grand attack on the centre, and while victory stood balancing in the conflict, he brought up the cuirassiers and Guards of Honour. As they rode in their splendid array past him, he said, "Brave young men! there is the enemy! will you let them march on Paris?" "We will not," was the ready response, and shaking their glittering sabres over their heads, they burst with a loud hurrah on the enemy, scattering them like a whirlwind from their path.

At the bloody battle of Craon, he fought on foot at the head of his columns; and amid one of the most wasting fires of artillery, troops were perhaps ever exposed to, steadied his men by his example, and was seen, again and again, with his tall, commanding form rising above his soldiers, to move straight in to the blaze of the enemy's batteries. When the smoke cleared away, there he still stood amid his rent and shattered ranks, sending his calm voice over the tumult, and animating, for the third time, his troops by his courageous words and still more courageous actions.

But when Marmont and Mortier, who had held the positions at Rheims and Soissons, as Napoleon had directed, found themselves cut off from all communication with the Emperor by the interposition of the Russian army, their case became desperate

With only twenty thousand men in all, they slowly retired towards Paris before the formidable masses of the allied forces. The weary army was toiling on, striving to gain the village of Fere-Champanoise, fighting as it went, when twenty thousand horse came thundering upon it and a hundred and thirty guns opened their fire on its shaking squares. Bravely combating, Mortier struggled with his wonted firmness to steady his troops. His five thousand cavalry met the shock of these twenty thousand bravely, but in vain; the hundred and eighty guns sent havoc amid the squares, making huge rents into which the Russian cuirassiers galloped with fierce valour, treading down every thing in their passage. A heavy rolling fire of musketry met each charge, but at length order was lost, and the army, which had patiently dragged its bleeding form over the plain rushed in one confused mass into Fere-Champanoise. A gallant charge of horse from the village, right through the broken ranks, arrested the pursuit til. Mortier and Marmont could rally their troops behind the houses.

The next day a division, under General Pacthod, coming up to join the French army, was surrounded by the Imperial Guards of Alexander, commanded by the Emperor in person, and refusing to surrender, was utterly annihilated. It could not be helped, though the valour the soldiers exhibited, deserved a better reward. Completely surrounded, they formed themselves into squares, and kept up a rolling fire as they retreated towards Fere-Champanoise. Thirteen thousand cavalry galloped around this worn band of six thousand, filling the air with dust, and fell in successive shocks on them in vain, till a battery brought to bear with fatal effect, made a lane through one square, into which they dashed, and sabred it to pieces. The Emperor Alexander, admiring their valour, wished to save them, and ordered them to surrender. General Pacthod refused, and, cheering his men by his actions and words, roused them to the highest pitch of enthusiasm; and though the cannon balls crushed through them with frightful havoc, they moved on unshaken—till their ammunition was exhausted—then weeping in indignation that they had fired their last cartridge, charged bayonet. At length, when half of the whole division had fallen, and the enemy's cavalry was riding through their broken ranks with irresistible fury, General Pacthod delivered up his sword.

A most touching incident occurred during this engagement. In the midst of the fight Lord Londonderry saw a young and beautiful lady, the wife of a French officer, dragged from a calèche by three wretches who were making off with their prey. Galloping up to her rescue, he snatched her from their hands and delivered her to his orderly, to be taken to his own quarters, who, lifting her to the horse behind him, started off, but was scarcely out of sight when a band of Cossacks rushed upon him and piercing him through with a lance, bore off the lady. She was never heard of more. Every exertion was made to discover her fate, but it was never known. Whether a prey to lawless violence, she was released from her sufferings by death, or whether she dragged out her existence a helpless captive, no one can tell.

After this defeat, Mortier and Marmont could no longer keep the field, and fell back on Paris. There they made the last stand for their country, and fought till valour and resistance were no longer of avail, and then delivered up their swords to the enemy. But though together in their retreat, and equally brave in their last defence, they were not alike in their surrender of the city. Mortier's honour is free from the stain that dims the lustre of Marmont's fame.

Sickness, as before stated, prevented Mortier from striking a last blow for Napoleon at Waterloo. If he had commanded the Young Guard on that day, and Murat the cavalry, the fate of the battle and the world might have been changed.

He was retained in the confidence of Louis Philippe; until at length he who had passed through so many battles unscathed, fell a victim to an assassin. On the 28th of July, 1835, as Louis Philippe was going to a review of the National guard, Mortier on horseback close behind, was killed by the explosion of Fieschi's infernal machine. A little delay had allowed the king to pass the spot of danger, but when the smoke lifted, Mortier was seen falling from his horse, dead. He was the most distinguished victim in that attempt to assassinate the King.

X.

MARSHAL SOULT.

His early career—Campaigns with Massena—His Character—Battle of Austerlitz—His first campaign in Spain—Death of Sir John Moore—Storming of Oporto—Retreat from Portugal—Battle of Albuera—Second campaign in Spain—Siege of St. Sebastiani—Soult's last struggle for the Empire.

No American has visited the Chamber of Peers, within the last few years, without being struck with the appearance of Marshal Soult. The old warrior, with his grave and severe look, comes limping into the hall, almost the sole representative of that band of heroes to whom Napoleon committed his Empire, and whose names are indissolubly linked with his through all coming time. He is now about seventy-seven years of age, though erect as a soldier. His head is bald on the top, and the thin hair that remains is whitened by the frosts of age. He is, perhaps, a little over the middle height, rather square built, and evidently once possessed great muscular power. His eye is dark, and now and then exhibits something of its ancient fire, while his brown visage looks as if he had just returned from a long campaign, rather than lived at his ease in Paris. He is extremely bow-legged, which is evidently increased by the wound that makes him limp, and though he wears ample pantaloons to conceal the defect, nothing but petti

coats can ever prevent the lower extremities of the Marshal from presenting the appearance of a parenthesis. He received his wound in storming Monte Creto, at the time when Massena was besieged in Genoa. His voice is rather guttural, and its tone severe, as if belonging to a man who had passed his life in the camp.

No one acquainted with his history, can behold the old veteran limping to his seat, without emotion. One of the chief props and pillars of Napoleon's throne, and one of the principal actors in that great drama which he enacted on the plains of Europe, his presence calls to mind many a fierce fought battle, and many a victory too. During some of those frequently stupid *seances* of the Chamber, I have often wondered, as I looked down on Soult in his seat, whether he, too, was not thinking of his struggles along the Rhine, or his bivouacs in the Alps, or of some of those fearful scenes he witnessed in Spain.

Nicholas-Jean-de-Dieu Soult was born in the small town of Amans, Department of Tarn, the 29th of March, 1769, or about four months after Bonaparte. His father was a country Notary, of no distinction, and apparently unable to control the restless spirit of his boy, let him choose his own course of life. Young Soult could not brook the confinement of study, and read little, and that not of the most instructive kind, and becoming perfectly disgusted with the old parchments of his father, at the age of sixteen entered, as a volunteer, in a regiment of the Royal Infantry. The revolution opened an ample field for his genius, and during the first struggles of the Republic he distinguished himself by his skill and bravery, and rapidly went up from Sergeant to Under-Lieutenant, Adjutant,

Major, Captain, Chief of Battalion, and Colonel—learning the art of war under Luckner, Hoche, Lefebvre, and Jourdan.

At the battle of Fleurus, in 1794, he was chief of the staff under Lefebvre, and there exhibited that admirable coolness and penetration, in the hour of danger, which afterwards made him so conspicuous as a military leader. General Marceau commanded the right of the army, and his division Ardennes was hurled back by a charge of the enemy and thrown into disorder. Marceau, in despair, hurried to Soult, and asked for four battalions to help him restore the combat. But the latter saw that he could not grant his request, without endangering Lefebvre's division, and refused. Marceau, in the agony and confusion of the moment, threatened to shoot himself if he was not aided. Soult told him to be calm and steady. "Rally your men to the charge," said he, "and the four battalions shall come as soon as possible." The words were scarcely out of his mouth, before Prince Coburg was on him like a rolling torrent, and Soult was in a moment in the thickest of the fight. After the battle was over, Marceau sought him out, and generously begged his pardon for his rudeness, and praised him for his valour.

Promoted to General of Brigade this year, he fought bravely at the battles of Altenkirchen, Lahn, and Friedberg. Being detached one day with three battalions and a hundred and fifty cavalry, to cover the left of the army stationed at Herban, he suddenly found himself, in the course of his march, surrounded by four thousand cavalry. His destruction seemed inevitable; but immediately forming his men into squares, he cooley met the shock, while a devouring fire, rolling round the steady ranks, emptied the enemy's saddles with frightful rapidity. But the Austrian commander, thinking this little band must go down before his fierce squadrons, rallied his men at a distance, and again ordered the charge. The trumpets sounded, and these four thousand riders moved to the onset. Advancing first on a plunging trot, they at length broke into a fierce gallop, and with an impetuosity and strength that made the ground thunder and smoke in their passage, burst with a loud shout upon the ranks. The smoke covered both for a moment, and when it lifted, the shattered squadrons were recoiling over the field. Again and again did that splendid body of cavalry re-form and rush to the charge, and as often retire before the steady valour that opposed it. Thus for five hours did Soult stand amid his little band, animating them by his voice and example, till five successive shocks had been repulsed, and then continued his march without having left a single man in the hands of the enemy.

After the peace of Campo Formio, Soult rested for a while; but in 1798, while Bonaparte was in Egypt, he is found again in the field of battle. At the village of Ostrach, with only 6,000 men, composing the advanced guard of the army, he was attacked by 25,000 Austrians under the Archduke Charles. Under the murderous fire of such superior numbers, his comparatively feeble band began to shake. One battalion bent backward, and was on the point of flying, when Soult seized a standard, and rushing to its head, called on the soldiers to follow him, and boldly charged into the very midst of the enemy and thus saved his army from a rout.

The next month he was made General of Division,

and passed through the campaign of Switzerland under Massena. While the latter was winning the battle of Zurich, Soult, stationed between Lake Zurich and Wallenstadt, to prevent the junction of the Austrians and Russians, was equally successful. The enemy was encamped on the farther side of the Linth, in a secure position; but Soult organized a company of a hundred and fifty swimmers, who, with their sabres in their teeth, and holding their muskets in one hand over their heads, boldly dashed into the river at midnight, and swam to the opposite shore. They here made a stand till some grenadiers could be got over, and then attacked the camp of the enemy, putting it to rout, slaying and taking four thousand men. While these brilliant victories by Massena and Soult were sending a few rays of light across the gloom that hung over the French armies, Bonaparte returned from Egypt. Massena was immediately appointed to Genoa; and in assuming the command, he requested that Soult might be attached to him. He had seen his skill and bravery in Switzerland, and he needed him in the desperate undertaking which was now before him. Elevated to the rank of lieutenant-general, Soult passed the Alps; and after fighting bravely, was driven with Massena into Genoa. Here, by his fierce onsets, which completely stunned the enemy, and by his brilliant victories, fighting heroically and victoriously against the most overwhelming numbers, he showed that Massena was not deceived in the spirit he had sought to aid him in this campaign. The last effort that was made, before the French were completely shut up in the city, was the assault on Mount Creto, conducted by Soult. It was a desperate undertaking at the best, and in the midst of the bloody combat a thunder-storm swept over the mountain, and enveloped the two hosts. In the midst of the roar of the artillery, and louder roll of thunder, and flashes of lightning that outshone the girdle of fire that wrapped the enemy, Soult headed a last charge in one more effort to save the day. Pressing boldly on into the midst of the fire, he was struck by a ball, and fell. Supposing he was killed, his men turned and fled. With a broken leg, he was taken prisoner, and soon after sent to Alessandria. Here news was finally brought him that Genoa had capitulated; and immediately after, that Bonaparte was in the plains of Italy, having fallen like an avalanche from the Alps.

Lying on his back, he heard one morning the departure of the Austrian army, as it issued forth over the Bormida to battle. The heavy tread of the marching columns, the rumbling of the artillery, and the thrilling strains of martial music, had scarcely died away on his ear, before the thunder of cannon shook the house in which he lay a helpless captive. All day long, the windows in his room rattled to the jar which the tremendous cannonading on the field of Marengo sent for miles around. Hour after hour, he lay and listened to the fast and fierce explosions which told how deadly the strife was, until at length the retiring tumult declared too well to his practiced ear that France was retreating. Next he heard shouts of victory through the streets, and his eye flashed fire in the eagerness to help stem the tide of battle. All was lost, and he turned uneasily on his couch; when suddenly, towards evening, the battle seemed to open with treble violence. Again he listened; and as the sound drew near, his heart beat quick and anxiously; and as night came on, and through the darkness the fierce uproar approached the city, till the cannon seemed to be playing almost on its very walls—a smile of joy passed over his countenance. The next moment a crowd of fugitives burst through the gates, and the cry of "All is lost," told the wounded chieftain that Italy was won.

Being soon after exchanged for some Austrian officer, he was presented to Napoleon, who had heretofore known little of him, except by report. He asked Massena if he was deserving of the high reputation he had gained The hero of Genoa replied, "for judgment and courage he has few equals." He had fought beside him in three desperate *sorties* from the city, and had seen him charge with a coolness and intrepidity against overwhelming odds that won his admiration and esteem.

In consequence of this high encomium, Soult was appointed chief commander in Piedmont, to quell the brigands, called *Barbets*, and soon after was made Colonel General of the Consular Guard, and given the command of the camp of St. Omar.

When Napoleon meditated his grand descent on England, Soult was placed over the army between Boulogne and Calais. Knowing well what kind of an enemy England was, and the character of her troops, the latter commenced a course of discipline to which French soldiers had never before been subject. With a frame of iron and a will that matched it, he concentrated all his energies to the task before him. From daylight till dark he was seen moving about, now on horseback inspecting his troops, and drilling them to the limit of human endurance, and now passing through their entrenchments and directing their progress. The constant exercise he demanded of the soldiers, caused them to complain to Bonaparte; and the latter finally expostulated with him, saying that he feared the men would sink under it. Soult replied, "Those who cannot endure what I myself do, will remain at home; while those who bear it, will be fit to undertake the conquest of the world." He could not have returned a reply more grateful to Napoleon; and when the latter became Emperor of France, he made him Marshal of the Empire.

He commanded the right wing at Austerlitz; and at Jena assailed the centre of the enemy with desperate energy. At Eylau, he, with Augereau, was first engaged; and, although enveloped in the middle of the field by a snow storm that blotted out every thing from view, while two hundred cannon incessantly played on his staggering column, he was enabled to fall back in good order. At Heilsberg he fought with unrivalled courage; and after the battle of Friedland, marched into Königsberg, after having forced the enemy from the city.

Soon after he was sent into Spain to repair the disasters of King Joseph, whom no experience or instructions could make a great military leader. Ordered to invade Portugal, he carried Oporto by assault with great slaughter; but was compelled finally to retreat before the superior force of Wellesley. To put an end to the rivalry among the various generals in Spain, Napoleon at length appointed him Major General of the French army there; thus showing the high opinion he had of his military abilities. The victory of Ocana soon after justified the confidence placed in him.

For several years Soult carried on this unhappy war in Spain—now pursuing, and now retreating—until the disastrous issue of the Russian campaign, when he was called by Napoleon, in (1813,) to support his falling empire in the north.

After the battles of Lutzen and Bautzen, news reached Napoleon of his losses in the peninsula, and the defeat of his armies at the battle of Vittoria. He immediately looked around among his generals to see who could best repair the follies of his royal brother; and Soult was again selected. But the wife of the obedient Marshal did not wish to return to a country where there was such obstinate fighting with so few laurels, and used all her persuasion, not only with her husband, but with the Emperor, to have him remain. Napoleon repulsed her rudely; and Soult hastened, as fast as horses could carry him, to Paris. Stopping there only a few hours, he pressed on to Spain. Scarcely had he arrived at head-quarters before the army was in motion; and though he did all that human energy could do, he was finally beaten at every point. He, however, fought the last battle—fired the last cannon for Napoleon; and at length, on the news of the abdication, transferred his command to the Duke of Angoulême, and returned to Paris. Confirmed in his ranks and titles by Louis XVIII., he was appointed to the thirteenth military division. He was soon after named Minister of War; and in urging the sequestration of the property of the Bonaparte family, and in bringing General Excelmans before a Council of War, he showed a great deal of gratuitous zeal for his new master.

When Napoleon returned from Elba, Soult published his famous order of the day, in which the Emperor was stigmatized as an adventurer and usurper. Louis, however, suspected him, and took from him his appointment as Minister of War. Soon after Napoleon's arrival in Paris, Soult sought an interview with him, and though it is not known what passed between them, the latter, in a few days, was appointed Major General, and published another order of the day, which shewed a wonderful change he had undergone respecting the "adventurer and usurper." He fought at Fleurus and Waterloo, but not with the energy of his younger days. On the second restoration of the Bourbons he was put on the proscribed list, and fearing he should be brought to trial, published a justification of himself, in which he referred to Napoleon in disparaging terms—an act that must forever be a stain on his character.

Exiled with other French Generals, he retired to Dusseldorf, in Russia, where he remained three years, employed chiefly in preparing his memoirs, which, on his death, will probabaly be given to the world. In 1819, he was permitted to return to Paris, and the next year received again his Marshal's baton. In 1829, Charles X. made him Peer of France, and conferred on him the collar of Saint Esprit. Under Louis Phillippe he became Minister of War, and finally President of the Council. He took an active part in the agitations and struggles of April, 1834. His course, however, not being approved, he retired into private life till 1839, when he again became President of the Council.

Representing the court of France at the Coronation of Queen Victoria, he was everywhere received with the greatest enthusiasm, and the multitude pressed eagerly around him to see one who had been such a prominent actor in the great drama of the French Revolution.

Marshal Soult had less genius but more intellect

than most of the distinguished French Marshals. He had none of that high chivalric feeling which so frequently bore them triumphantly over the battle-field; but he had in its place, a clear, sound judgment, and a fearless heart. It required no thunder of cannon to clear his ideas—his thoughts were always clear, and his hand ever ready to strike. He depended on the conclusions of reason rather than on the inspiration of genius for victory. He calculated the chances beforehand, and when his purpose was taken, it was no ordinary obstacle or danger that could shake it. Such men as Murat, and Lannes, and Augereau, relied very much on the enthusiasm of their soldiers, and the power which intense excitement always imparts; Soult, on the contrary, on the discipline of his troops, and the firmness and steadiness it gives, either in assault or retreat; and hence, when left alone, could be depended on as an able and efficient General. Though impetuous as a storm in the early part of his life, it was the impetuosity of youth, rather than of character; and one familiar with his career, ever thinks of him as the stern and steady Soult. He was more of an Englishman than a Frenchman in his natural character, and succeeded better than most of the other French Generals when opposed to English troops. But though methodical and practical in all his plans he knew the value of a head-long charge, and could make it. Still he does not seem to rise with the danger that surrounds him, but rather meets it with the firmness of one who has settled beforehand that it shall not overcome him. In the tumult and terror of a mighty battle, he moves before us not so much as the genius of the storm itself, as like one who has made up his mind to take its peltings with composure. He stands where the tide of battle flows, like a rock over which the surge beats in vain; and his calm, stern voice, arrests the panic that has begun, and turns the shaking ranks into walls of iron before the foe.

He did not possess that versatility of genius which enabled Bonaparte so frequently to turn his very defeats into victory—he depended rather on the strength and terror of the blow he had planned—and if that failed, it became him to pause before he gave another. Like the lion, he measured his leap before he took it, and if he fell short, measured it over again. But with all this coolness and forethought, his blow was sometimes sudden and deadly as a falling thunderbolt. A more prompt and decisive man in action, was not to be found in the army. As cool amid the falling ranks and fire of three hundred cannon as on a parade, his onset was nevertheless a most terrible thing to meet. He carried such an iron will with him into the battle, and disputed every inch of ground with such tenacity of purpose, that the courage of the boldest gave way before him. Though he performed perhaps fewer *personal* heroic deeds than many others, he also committed fewer faults. After seeing him a few times in battle, one unconsciously gets such an opinion of his invincibility, that he never sees his columns moving to the assault, without expecting sudden victory, or one of the most terrific struggles to which brave men are ever exposed. We do not expect the pomp and splendour of one of Murat's charges of cavalry, nor the majesty of Ney's mighty columns, as he hurls them on the foe, but the firm step, and stern purpose, and resistless onset of one who lets his naked deeds report his power. Soult's eye measured a battle-field with the correctness of Napoleon's, and his judgment was as good upon a drawn battle as upon a victory. Not having those fluctuations of feeling to which more excitable temperments are subject, a defeat produced no discouragement, and hence a victory gave the enemy no moral power over him. It was singular to see in what a matter-of-fact way he took a beating, and how little his confidence in himself was destroyed by the greatest disasters. A man that is not humbled or rendered fearful by defeat, can never be conquered till he is slain.

Soult possessed a strong mind and a great character and in his military life the warrior sinks before the man of intellect, and even British pride condescends to render him homage as an able and great commander.

He has been charged with rapacity while in Spain, and his plunders commented freely on by his enemies, but the charge has never been clearly made out. Still, there is no doubt he did not let the wealth the chances of war flung into his hands, slip through his fingers; and he managed, amid all his tergiversations, and from all the changes he passed through, to acquire large estates, which now enable him to support his rank with splendour.

Soult was not cruel in his disposition, and exhibits none of the ferocity of the warrior in his career. A bold, skilful and inflexible man in the field, he ranks among the first of Napoleon's Marshals.

Napoleon, who, after the battle of Marengo, had asked Massena if Soult really deserved his high reputation, and on being answered in the affirmative, had attached him to his person—gave him command of the army at Boulogne, and afterwards made him Marshal of the Empire—soon after tested his great qualities at the

BATTLE OF AUSTERLITZ.

It was in the latter part of November (1805) that Napoleon, on riding over the country around Austerlitz, determined to make it the battle-field on which he would overthrow the combined armies of Austria and Russia. Rapidly concentrating his forces here, he on the last night of November, found himself at the head of nearly eighty thousand men. His army was drawn up in a plain, with the right resting on Lake Mœnitz, and the left six miles distant on a hill, which was covered with artillery. Two little streams flowed past the army into the lake, bordered with marshes to protect it, while on a high slope was pitched the Emperor's tent, overlooking the whole scene. Opposite the French army was a waving line of heights, the highest of which, Mount Pratzen, a few miles distant, formed the centre of the allied forces, numbering ninety thousand men, commanded by the Emperors of Russia and Austria in person. Under Soult, was placed the finest corps in the army, for the weight of the battle was designed to rest on him, and the heights of Pratzen, forming the enemy's centre, were to be his field of combat.

Napoleon had been on horseback all day long, and after dark was riding along the lines previous to his departure to his tent, when the news of his approach spread like lightning through the whole army. Suddenly the soldiers seized the bundles of straw that had been supplied them for their beds, and lighting them at one end lifted them on poles over their heads, making an illumination as splendid as it was unexpected. All along through the valley those blazing torches lighted the path of the astonished Napoleon—*the first anniversary of his coronation.* Suddenly the enthusiastic shout of Vive l'Empereur, burst around him. The cry was caught by the next and the next battalion as he advanced, and prolonged by those he had left, till the shout of that immense host filled all the valley, and rose like the roar of the sea over the heights, miles away—falling, with an ominous sound, on the camp of the enemy. It was a scene that baffles description. Those myriad torches, blazing and swinging to and fro in the darkness—a broad mass of flame losing itself in the distance—and the shout of that army, rolling in such deafening accents after Napoleon, formed together a far more imposing ceremony than his coronation in the Capital.

Next morning, at four o'clock, Napoleon was on horseback beside his tent. The moon had just gone down—the stars shone pale and tremulous in the sky, and all was silent and tranquil around him. Not a sound broke from the immense host that slumbered below, over which the motionless fog lay like a white covering—or it might be a shroud in anticipation of the thousands that ere night would there lie stark and stiff in their last sleep. But amid this deep hush his quick ear caught a low continuous sound beyond the heights of Pratzen, like the heavy tread of marching columns and rumbling of artillery carriages over the ground. The deep murmur passed steadily from right to left, showing that the allies were gathering their force against his right wing. At length the sun rose slowly above the horizon, tinging with gold the heights of Pratzen, on which were seen moving dense masses of infantry, and poured its glorious light over the sea of mist that slept in the valleys below. It was the "*Sun of Austerlitz.*" The hour, the scene—the immense results at stake, and the sudden bursting of that blazing fire ball on his vision, made a profound impression on Napoleon, which he never forgot.

The allies, intent on outflanking the French, were weakening their centre by drawing off the troops to the left. The Marshals who stood around the Emperor saw the fault of the enemy, and eagerly asked permission to take advantage of it. But he turning to Soult, whose troops were massed in the bottom of the valley near the heights, covered by the fog, asked him how long it would take to reach the summit of Pratzen. "Less than twenty minutes," replied the Marshal. "Wait a little, then," said Napoleon, "when the enemy is making a false movement, it is necessary to be careful not to interrupt him." It was now eight o'clock in the morning, and soon after he gave the impatiently expected signal, and Murat, Lannes, Bernadotte, and Soult, who had stood around him, parted like lightning from his side, and swept in a headlong gallop to their respective corps. Napoleon rode towards the centre, and as he passed through the troops, said, "Soldiers! the enemy has imprudently exposed himself to your strokes. *Finish the campaign by a clap of thunder!*" "*Vive l'Empereur,*" answered him in one long, protracted shout.

In the meantime, Soult emerged, with his strong battalions, from the covering mist, and clothed in the rich sunlight, ascended with an intrepid step, the slopes of Pratzen. It was a magnificent sight, and Napoleon watched with intense anxiety the advance of that splendid array. With banners fluttering in the morning sunlight, and drums and trumpets rending the air, the massive columns streamed upward and onward. In a moment the top of Pratzen was covered with smoke, from whose bosom issued thunder and lightning, as if a volcano was there hurling its fiery fragments in the air. Covered from sight, those two hosts—mixed in mortal combat—struggled for the mastery, while the curtain of smoke that folded them in, waved to and fro, and rent before the heavy artillery, and closed again, and rolled in rapid circles round the hill, telling to the armies below what wild work the stern Soult was making with the foe. At length the fire and smoke, which Pratzen had belched forth for two hours, grew less—the sulphurous cloud lifted in the mid-day sun, and lo, there waved the French standards, while a victorious shout went pealing over the armies struggling in the valley.

Soult, having pierced the enemy's centre, next descended on their left wing. Bessieres was charging fiercely below with the Imperial Guard, and the whole field shook with the shock of cavalry and thunder of cannon; while the entire valley was filled with rolling smoke, in which were moving dark masses of infantry. There was Murat, with his headlong valour, and Lannes, Davoust and Augereau, strewing the fields with the dead. At length, help being sent to Soult—the left of the enemy was borne away, and the allied army routed. Fleeing before the victorious Marshal, Buxhowden bravely attempted to cover the retreat, and forming his men into close column, strove gallantly to direct the reversed tide of battle. But pierced through and trodden under foot, seven thousand fell before the victorious French, while the remainder attempted to escape by crossing a frozen lake near by with the artillery and cavalry. In a moment the white frozen surface was covered with dark masses of infantry, amid which were seen the carefully advancing squadrons of cavalry. Pressed by the enormous weight, the ice could scarcely sustain the multitude, when Soult suddenly ordered his cannon to play upon it. The iron storm crushed through the yielding mass—the whole gave way, and with one terrific yell, that rose over the tumult of battle, more than two thousand men sunk to rise no more. Amid the swimming multitude, the frighted cavalry-horses plunged to and fro, while on the struggling mass the artillery continued to play with deadly precision.

On the left, Bernadotte, Murat and Lannes, were equally successful, and the bloody battle of Austerlitz was won. Nearly thirty thousand bodies strewed the field, and when night again closed over the scene, Napoleon, weakened only by twelve thousand men, saw his menaced throne firmly established. Soult was the hero of the day, and after the battle was over, Napoleon rode up to him and said, in presence of all his staff, "Marshal Soult, I consider you the ablest tactician in my Empire."

Bonaparte never forgot the brilliant conduct of his Marshal on this occasion, and years afterwards, when he was told that the latter was aiming at the throne of Portugal, he made known to him that he had heard the report, but added, "*I remember nothing but Austerlitz.*"

But Soult exhibited his great qualities as a commander in his campaigns in Spain. He showed himself there superior as a tactician to all the other marshals, except Suchet: and was more than a match to any time for the Duke of Wellington. His very first movements convinced Napoleon of his superior ability. Arriving together at Bayonne, the Emperor immediately planned the campaign, and issued his orders. Soult was ordered to supercede Bessières in the command of the second corps, in the path of which Napoleon, with his Imperial Guard, designed to follow. In a few hours after he received his orders, Soult's army was in motion. In fifty hours he travelled from Bayonne to Burgos—took the latter town, gained the battle of Gamonal; and still on the post horse he had mounted at Briviesca, where he took command of the army—pushed on his columns in every direction; and in a few days laid prostrate the whole north of Spain. Following up his successes, he marched against Sir John Moore, and forcing him back, step by step, for a fortnight, across rivers, and through mountains covered with snow, finally drove him into Corunna. There the English commander fortified himself, to await the transports that had been ordered round to receive his army. Soult opened his cannon on the place, and with his weary troops pressed his assaults vigorously, in the hope of forcing the English army to surrender before the arrival of the expected vessels. But Sir John Moore resolved to combat to the last, and prepared for a final battle. In the mean time, to prevent an immense magazine of powder of four thousand barrels from falling into the hands of the French, he ordered it to be blown up. A smaller quantity in a storehouse near it was first fired. The explosion of this was like the discharge of a thousand cannon at once; but when the great magazine took fire and those four thousand barrels exploded at once, the town rocked to and fro as if an earthquake was lift ing its foundations. Rocks were upturned by the shock, the ships in the harbour rose and fell on the sudden billows that swept under them; while a sound like the crash of nature itself, startled the two armies as it rolled away before the blast.

At length the transports arrived, and the embarkation commenced while Soult advanced to the attack. The battle soon became general, and Sir John Moore, while watching the progress of the fight, was struck by a cannon ball on the breast, and hurled from his horse. Rallying his energies, he sat up on the ground, and without a movement or an expression of pain, again fixed his eye on the conflict. Seeing that his men were gaining ground, he allowed himself to be carried to the rear. At the first glance it was plain that the ghastly wound was mortal. "The shoulder was shattered to pieces, the arm was hanging by a piece of the skin, the ribs over the heart were broken, and bared of the flesh, and the muscles of the breast torn into long strips, which were interlaced by their recoil from the dragging of the shot. As the soldiers placed him in a blanket, his sword got entangled, and the hilt entered the wound; Captain Hardinge, a staff officer, who was near, attempted to take it off, but the dying man stopped him saying, '*It is well as it is. I had rather it should go out of the field with me.*'" Thus was the hero borne from the field of battle. He died before night, and was buried in the citadel of Corunna—the thunder of Soult's guns being the mournful salute fired above his grave. Actuated by a noble feeling, the brave Marshal erected a monument to him on the spot where he fell.

The great ability which Soult exhibited in this pursuit, caused Napoleon to rely on him chiefly in those operations removed from his personal observation, and he was ordered to invade Portugal. In the midst of the rainy season, he set out from Corunna, and against the most overwhelming obstacles, steadily and firmly pursued his way, until at length he arrived at Oporto, and sat down before the city.

STORMING OF OPORTO.

A summons to surrender being disregarded, he waited for the morning to carry the place by assault. But, at midnight a terrific thunder-storm arose; the clouds in dark and angry masses swept the heavens; the wind blew with frightful fury, and the alarmed inhabitants, mistaking the roar of the blast for the tread of the advancing armies, set all their bells ringing, while two hundred cannon suddenly opened into the storm, and one fierce fire of musketry swept the whole circuit of the entrenchments. The loud and rapid ringing of so many bells in the midst of the midnight storm—the thunder of cannon replying to the thunders of heaven, as clap after clap broke over the city—the fierce lightning outshining the flash of musketry—the roar of the wind and the confused cries of the inhabitants, as they rushed by thousands through the streets, combined to render it a scene of indescribable sublimity and terror. The French stood to their arms, wondering what this strange uproar meant.

But at length the morning broke serene and clear, and the waving of standards in the air, the beat of drums, and the loud strains of the trumpets told the inhabitants that Soult was finally leading his strong battalions to the assault. After an obstinate struggle, the entrenchments were carried at all points and the victorious army burst with loud shouts into the city. The routed army divided; a part fled towards the fort of St. Jao, the remainder towards the mouth of the Douro, in the hopeless attempt to cross by boats or by swimming. Their general, while expostulating with them on the madness of the effort, was shot by them in presence of the enemy, and the terror-stricken host rushed head-long into the river, and were almost to a man drowned.

But the battle still raged within the city, and the barricades of the streets being forced open, more than four thousand men, women, and children went pouring in one disordered mass, to the single bridge of boats that crossed the river. But, as if the frenzy, and tumult, and carnage were not yet sufficiently great, just then a defeated troop of Portuguese cavalry came in a wild gallop down the street, and with remorseless fury burst through the shrieking multitude, trampling all ages and sexes under their feet. Clearing a bloody pathway for themselves, they rushed on to the bridge, followed by the frantic crowd. The boats sunk, and where they went down, floated a dense mass of human bodies, filling all the space between. The French soldiers as they came up, struck with amazement at the sight, forgot the work of death, and throwing down their muskets, nobly strained every nerve to save the sinking throng. Meanwhile the city rung with fire-arms and shrieks of the dying. Frantic as soldiers ever are in sacking a city, they were made doubly so by a spectacle that met them in one of the public squares. There, fastened upright, were several of their comrades, who had been taken prisoners—their eyes burst asunder, their tongues torn out, and their whole bodies mutilated; in which the breath of life still remained. Fierce cries of revenge now blent with the shouts of victory. The officers lost all control, though they mingled with the soldiers, and by their voice and efforts, strove to stay the carnage and violence. Their efforts were in vain, and even the authority of Soult was, for a while, no more than threads of gossamer, before the maddened passions of the soldiers. *Ten thousand* Portuguese fell in this single assault, and the streets of Oporto ran blood. Only five hundred Frenchmen were slain.

This sanguinary affair being over, Soult immediately established order, and by his vigorous measures, great kindness, and humanity, so won the esteem of the Portuguese, that addresses came pouring in upon him from all quarters, and offers were made him of the throne of Portugal.

But this brilliant opening of his campaign was destined soon to meet with sad reverses. A large English force, unknown to him, had assembled in his vicinity, and was rapidly marching against him. In the mean time, treason in his own camp began to show itself. Many of the French officers had resolved to deliver the army into the hands of the English. This conspiracy extending more or less through the different armies in the peninsula, was set on foot to overthrow Napoleon. It was a long time before Soult could fathom these secret machinations. His own forces—their position and destination, were all known to the English; while he was left in utter uncertainty of *their* strength and plans. But at length his eyes were opened, and he saw at once the appalling dangers which surrounded him. It was then he exhibited the immense energy and strength of character he possessed. An abyss had opened under his feet, but he stood and looked into its impenetrable depths with out a shudder. Not knowing whom to trust—almost enveloped by a superior enemy, he nevertheless took his decision with the calmness of a great mind. Compelled to fall back, he escaped as by a miracle the grasp of the enemy, and once more entered Oporto. Compelled to abandon the city, he continued to fall back, resting his hope on Loison, whom he had ordered to hold Amaronte. But that general had departed, leaving his commander-in-chief to destruction. Soult heard of this new calamity at midnight, just after he had crossed the Souza river. The news spread through the dismayed army, and insubordination broke forth, and voices were heard calling for a capitulation. But Soult rose calmly above the storm, and learning from a Spanish pedlar that there was a by-path across the mountains, instantly resolved to lead his troops over it. The treacherous and discontented were alike paralyzed by his firmness, and saw without a movement of resistance all the artillery and baggage destroyed; and with their muskets on their shoulders started over the mountains, and finally effected a junction with the retreating Loison. Nothing can be more sublime than the bearing of Soult in this retreat. Superior to treason—to complaints and danger, he moved at the head of his distracted army with a firmness and constancy that awed rebellion, and crushed all opposition.

Instead of retreating on the high road, which must have ensured his destruction, he commanded that all the artillery of Loison's corps also should be destroyed in presence of the army. Knowing when to sacrifice, and doing it with an inflexibility of purpose that quelled resistance, he bent his great energies on the salvation of his army. Taking again to the moun tains he gained a day's march on his pursuers. Reorganizing his ill-conditioned army, he took command of the rear-guard himself; and thus kept his stern eye on the enemy, while the mutinous and traitorous were held before him, and in reach of his certain stroke. Thus retreating, the despoiled, starving army at length approached the river Cavado, when word was brought the Marshal, that the peasantry were destroying the only bridge across it. Should they succeed, the last hour of his army had struck; for there it must halt, and by morning the English guns would be thundering on his rear, while he had not a single cannon to answer them. The abyss opened wider beneath him, but over his marble features passed no shadow of fear. Calling Major Dulong to him—the bravest man in his ranks—he told him the enemy were destroying the bridge across the river ahead, and he had chosen him out of the whole army to save it. He ordered him to pick out a hundred grenadiers, and twenty-five horsemen, and surprise the guard, and secure the passage. "If you succeed," said he, "send me word; but *if you fail, send none*—your silence will be sufficient." One would be glad to know what the last desperate resolution of that iron-willed commander was, should silence follow the bold undertaking of the brave Dulong

He departed; while Soult waited with painful anxiety the result. The rain fell in torrents—the wind went howling fiercely by, and midnight blackness wrapped the drenched and staggering army, as they stood barefoot and unsheltered in the storm. After a long and painful suspense, a messenger arrived. "The bridge is won," fell on Soult's ear like hope on the dying. A flash of joy passed over his inflexible features; for he still might escape the pain of a surrender. The bold Dulong, with his strong grenadiers, covered by the darkness, had reached the bridge unseen, and slain the sentinel before he could utter a cry of alarm. But what a sight met their eyes! The swollen river went roaring and foaming by, over which only a narrow strip of mason-work was seen—the wreck of the destroyed bridge. Nothing daunted, Dulong advanced on to the slender fragment, and with twelve grenadiers at his back, began to crawl along his perilous path. One grenadier slipped, and fell with a sudden plunge into the torrent below. But the wind and the waves together drowned his shriek, and the remaining eleven passed in safety, and fell with a shout on the affrighted peasantry, who immediately turned and fled. The bridge was repaired, and by daylight the heads of the column were marching over. Soult had not a moment to spare, for the English cannon had already opened on his rear-guard.

But no sooner was this bridge passed, than another—flying with a single arch over a deep gulf, and called the Saltador, or Leaper—rose before him, defended by several hundred Portuguese. Only three men could move abreast over this lofty arch, and two attempts to carry it were repulsed, when the brave Dulong advanced and swept it with his strong grenadiers, though he himself fell in the assault, dreadfully wounded.

The army was saved and by the courageous energy, skill, and heroism of its commander; and at length entered Orense barefooted, without ammunition, baggage, or a single cannon.

Soult has been blamed for his management at the outset of this retreat, especially for being surprised, as he was, at Oporto; but let one, surrounded by con spirators, and uncertain whom to trust among his officers, do better, or show that any leader has acted more worthily, in similar circumstances, before exceptions are taken.

It would be uninteresting to follow Soult through all his after operations in Spain. Napoleon had gone, and between the quarrelling of the rival chiefs, and the imbecility of Joseph, affairs were not managed with the greatest wisdom. Soult was crippled in all his movements—his sound policy neglected, and his best combinations thwarted by Joseph. The disastrous battle of Talavera was fought in direct opposition to his advice; nevertheless, he soon after had the pleasure of chasing Sir Arthur Wellesley out of Spain. His operations in Andalusia and Estramadura, and the firmness with which he resisted the avarice of Joseph, all exhibited his well-balanced character. In Andalusia he firmly held his ground, although hedged in with hostile armies, and surrounded by an insurgent population, while a wide territory had to be covered with his troops. His vast and skilful combinations, during this period, show the powerful intellect he brought to the task before him. King Joseph could not comprehend the operations of such a mind as Soult's, and constantly impeded his success. When, without ruin to the army, the stubborn Marshal might yield to his commands, he did; but where the King's projects would plunge him into irredeemable errors, he openly and firmly withstood him. The anger and threats of Joseph were alike in vain; the inflexible old soldier professed his willingness to obey, but declared he would not, with his eyes open, commit a great military blunder. King Joseph would despatch loud and vehement complaints to Napoleon, but the

Emperor knew too well the ability of Soult to heed them. Had the latter been on the Spanish throne, instead of Joseph, the country would long before have been subdued, and the French power established.

But it would be impossible, without going into the entire complicated history of the Peninsular war, to give any correct idea of the prodigious efforts he put forth—of his skillful combinations, or of the military genius he exhibited, in his successful career. Yet, arduous as was the duty assigned him, he drove Wellington out of the country; and though fettered by the foolish orders of a foolish king, maintained French power in Spain till he was recalled to steady Napoleon's trembling throne in Germany. Cautious in attack, yet terrible in his onset, and endless in his resources when beaten, no General could have accomplished more than he, and he adopted the only method that could at all be successful in the kind of war he was compelled to wage.

The bloodiest battle during the Peninsular war, was fought by Soult, and lost in the very moment of victory. In May, 1811, he rapidly concentrated his forces, and moving from Seville, advanced on Beresford, occupying the heights before Albuera.

BATTLE OF ALBUERA.

Soult had twenty-one thousand men under him, while the Spanish and English armies together numbered over thirty thousand. The French Marshal, however, relying on the steadiness and bravery of his troops, and not reckoning the Spaniards at more than half their numerical strength, resolved to give battle. The allies were stationed along a ridge, three miles in extent. The action commenced by an attack of French cavalry, but soon Soult's massive columns began to move over the field and ascend, with a firm step, the opposing heights. The artillery opened on the heads of those columns with terrible precision, but their batteries replied with such rapidity, that they seemed moving volcanoes traversing the field of death. Amid the charges of infantry, the shocks of cavalry, and the carnage of the batteries, they continued to press on, while their advancing fire spread like an ascending conflagration up the hill. Every thing went down in their passage. Over infantry, artillery, and cavalry they passed on to the summit of the heights. Beresford, in this crisis of the battle, ordered up the British divisions from the centre. These, too, were overborne and trampled under foot—the heights won—the battle, to all appearance, gained, and Beresford was preparing to retreat.

Suddenly an English officer, Colonel Hardinge, took the responsibility of ordering up a division not yet engaged, and Abercromby with his reserve brigade. These advancing with a firm and intrepid step, in face of the victorious enemy, arrested the disorder, and began to pour a destructive fire on the dense masses of Soult. His columns had penetrated so far into the very heart of the army, that not only their front, but their entire flanks were exposed to a most severe fire. Thus did Macdonald press into the Austrian lines, and taking the cross fire of the enemy's batteries, see his mighty columns dissolve beside him. Soult endeavoured to deploy his men, so as to return a more effectual fire. But the discharges of the enemy were so rapid and close, that every effort was in vain. The steady ranks melted away before the storm, but still refused to yield. Soult saw the crisis this sudden check had brought upon him, and strained every nerve to save the day. His stern voice was heard above the roar of battle, cheering on his men, while he was seen passing to and fro through the ranks, encouraging them by his gestures and example to maintain the fight. Vain valour. That charge was like one of Napoleon's Imperial Guards', and the tide of battle was reversed before it. Those brave British soldiers closed sternly on their foes as in a death struggle. Says Napier, " In vain did Soult, by voice and gesture, animate his Frenchmen—in vain did the hardiest veterans, extricating themselves from the crowded columns, sacrifice their lives to gain time for the mass to open out on such a fair field; in vain did the mass itself bear up, and fiercely striving, fire indiscriminately upon friends and foes, while the horsemen, hovering on the flank, threatened to charge the advancing lines. Nothing could stop that astonishing infantry. No sudden burst of undisciplined valour, no nervous enthusiasm, weakened the stability of their order; their flashing eyes were bent on the dark columns in their front, their measured tread shook the ground, their dreadful volleys swept away the head of every formation, their deafening shouts overpowered the dissonant cries that broke from all parts of the tumultuous crowd, as slowly and with a horrid carnage, it was pushed by the incessant vigour of the attack to the farthest edge of the height. There the French reserves, mixing with the struggling multitude, endeavoured to sustain the fight, but the effort only increased the irremediable confusion; the mighty mass gave way, and like a loosened cliff, went headlong down the steep. The rain flowed after in streams, discoloured with blood, and *fifteen hundred unwounded men, the rem-*

nant of six thousand unconquerable British soldiers, stood triumphant on the hill."

The fight was done, and fifteen thousand men lay piled in mangled heaps along that hill and in the valley. The rain came down in torrents, and night set in, dark and gloomy, over the scene of conflict. But from the dreadful field, groans and cries arose through the long night, as the wounded writhed in their pain. The pitiless storm, and the moaning wind, and the murky night, and heart-breaking cries of the suffering and the dying, combined to render it a scene of unmingled terror. Soult took five hundred prisoners and several stand of colours, while the British had only the bloody field for their trophy. The next day, however, Soult still hung like a thunder cloud on the army of the English. But they, having received reinforcements, on the third day he deemed it prudent to retire. Marmont, however, joining him soon after, he again took the offensive, and drove the English before him, and over the Spanish borders.

It is impossible to follow the Marshal through his chequered career. For five years he struggled manfully against the most harrassing obstacles, and finally when Spain was delivered from the enemy, he hastened, as before remarked, to Napoleon, to help him stem the torrent that was threatening to bear him away. With his departure, victory also departed, and soon the disastrous battle of Vittoria threw Spain again into the hands of the English.

The appointment by Napoleon of Soult to retrieve these losses, showed what his opinion was of the Marshal, as a military leader. Not the complaints and false representations of his own brother, nor the reports of rival generals, could blind his penetrating eye to the great ability of the Duke of Dalmatia. No higher eulogy could be passed on him than this single appointment.

The frontiers of France were threatened through the passes of the Pyrenees, and these Soult was ordered to defend to the last extremity. He found at Bayonne but the fragments of the armies that had battled in Spain, but with his accustomed energy, he set about their organization, and with such untiring perseverance did he work, that in a fortnight he was ready to take the field. Bearing down on Wellington, he poured his strong columns like a resistless torrent through the pass of the Roncesvalles. The gorges and precipices of the Pyrenees rung to the peal of musketry, the roll of the drum, and the roar of cannon, and Soult's conquering troops broke, with the shout of victors into Spain.

It was his design to succour St. Sebastiani, which, with a small garrison, had withstood a long siege, and been most heroically defended. But the energy which he had imparted to his army was only momentary. The soldiers were exhausted and worn down, and could not be held to the contest like fresh troops, and Soult was compelled to retire before superior force. The sudden abyss that had opened under Wellington, closed again, and having repulsed his able antagonist, he sat down anew before St. Sebastiani. Soult had given his word to this brave garrison that if they would hold out a short time longer, he would march to their relief, and he now set about fulfilling his promise, hopeless as the task was, and moved to within eight miles of the place with his army. But the besiegers, in the meantime, had not been idle. The siege was pressed vigorously, and a hundred and eighteen guns were dragged before the doomed town. Before Soult broke so rash and sudden through the Pyrenees, Wellington had made an ineffectual assault on the place, and though the fortifications had been weakened and many of the houses burned, he withdrawing his forces to meet the French Marshal, the garrison had a breathing spell, and made good use of their time to repair their defences.

TERRIBLE ASSAULT OF ST. SEBASTIANI.

Wellington at length placed in battery sixty cannon, some of them sixty-three pounders, and began to play on the walls. The thunder of these heavy guns shook the hills around, and was echoed in sullen shocks on the ear of the distant Soult. For four days did this fierce volcano belch forth its stream of fire against St. Sebastiani, carrying terror and dismay to the hearts of the inhabitants. Nothing could withstand such batteries, and the iron storm smote against the walls till a frightful gap appeared, furnishing foothold for the assaulting companies.

St. Sebastiani stands by the sea, with the river Uremea flowing close under its walls, which in low tide can be forded. On the farther side of this river were the British troops, and on the 31st of August, at half-past ten, the forlorn hope took its station in the trenches, waiting for the ebbing tide to allow them to cross. As this devoted band stood in silence watching the slow settling of the waters, they could see the wall they were to mount lined with shells and fire-barrels, ready to explode at a touch, while bayonet-points gleamed beyond, showing into what destruction they were to move. Soldiers hate tc think, and the suspense which they were now forced to endure, was dreadful. These brave men could rush on death at the sound of the bugle, but to stand and gaze into the very jaws of destruction till the slowly retiring waters would let them enter, was too much for the firmest heart. Minutes seemed lengthened into hours, and in the still terror of that delay, the sternest became almost delirious with excitement. Some laughed outright, not knowing what they did; others shouted and sung; while others prayed aloud. It was a scene at which the heart stands still. The air was hot and sulphureous—dark and lurid thunder-clouds were lifting heavily above the horizon, and the deep hush of that assaulting column was rendered more awful by the hush of nature which betokens the coming tempest.

Noon at length came—the tide was down, and the order to advance was given, and that devoted band moved to the centre of the stream. A tempest of grape-shot and bullets scattered them like autumn leaves over its bosom, but the survivors pressed boldly on, and reaching the opposite shore, mounted the breach and gained the summit. But as they stood amid the wasting fire, they hesitated to descend on the farther side, for they saw they must leap down twelve feet to reach the ground; while the base of the wall bristled with sword blades, and pikes, and pointed weapons of every description, fastened upright in the earth. While they still delayed to precipitate themselves on these steel points, the fire from the inner rampart swept them all away. Still column after column poured across the river and filled up the dreadful gaps made in the ranks of their comrades, and crowded the beach, and still the fierce volleys crushed them down, while the few who passed met the bayonet-point, and fell at the feet of the heroic defenders. After two hours of this murderous strife, the breach was left empty of all but the dead, and the shout of the French was heard in the pause of the storm. In this crisis, the English soldiers were ordered to lie down at the foot of the ramparts, while forty-seven cannon were brought to bear on the high curtain within, from whence the fire swept the breach. The batteries opened, and the balls flying only two feet over the soldiers' heads, crushed with resistless power through the enemy's works. At this moment, an accident completed what the besiegers had begun, and overwhelmed the defenders. A shell, bursting amid the hand grenades, shells, trains of fire-barrels, and all kinds of explosive materials which the garrison had laid along the ramparts for a last defence—the whole took fire. A sheet of flame ran along the walls, and then the mouth of a volcano seemed to open, followed by an explosion that shook the city to its foundations, sending fierce columns of smoke and broken fragments into the air, and strewing the bodies of three hundred French soldiers amid the ruins. As the smoke lifted, the assailants rushed with a deafening shout forward, and though firmly met by the bayonet, their increasing numbers overwhelmed every obstacle, and they poured into the town. Soult, eight miles distant, had just been defeated in attempting to march to the relief of the garrison, and from the heights of Bidissoa, heard that terrific explosion that followed the cannonading, and saw the fiercely ascending columns of smoke that told that St. Sebastiani was won.

At this moment, when the shouts of the conquerors, maddened by every passion that makes man a monster and a fiend, were paralyzing the hearts of the inhabitants with fear, the long gathering thunder storm burst on the town. Sudden darkness wrapped every thing, through which the lightning incessantly streamed, followed by crash after crash of thunder, till the very heavens seemed ready to fall. Amid this storm language of the skies, and war of the elements, and roar of the conflagration that fanned by the tempest, wrapped the dwellings, scenes were transpiring, over which history must draw a veil. Rapine, revenge, drunkenness, lust, and murder, burst forth without restraint, making a wilder hell than man ever dreamed of before. The inhabitants fled from their burning houses, and crowded into a quarter where the flames had not yet come. As men, women and children, stood thus packed together, the brutal soldiery reeled and staggered around them, firing into the shrieking mass, and plunging their bayonets into the old and young alike. Lust, too, was abroad, and the cries of violated women, mingled in with the oaths and blasphemies and shouts of the soldiers. Wives were ravished before the eyes of their husbands, mothers in presence of their daughters, and one girl of seventeen was violated on the corpse of her mother. For three days did the rapine, and murder, and cruelty continue, and scenes were enacted which may not be described, and before which, even fiends would blush. Such is war, and such its horrors.

The Governor retreated to the citadel, and bravely defended himself with a handful of men for several days, still hoping the arrival of Soult. But that Marshal had his hands full to keep Wellington at bay.

At length, compelled to retreat, he yielded the ground step by step, fighting his way as he went. He delivered the bloody battles of Bidissoa, and Neville, disputed the passage of the Nive, and fought at St. Pierre, worthy of a better result. He showed a depth of combination, an energy of character, and a tenacity of purpose, seldom equalled by any General. Had his shock in battle been equal to Ney's, he would have been irresistible. As it was, with half the force brought against him, he baffled every effort of the enemy to overwhelm him, and being driven into France, disputed every inch of his native soil with a heroism and patriotism that have rendered him immortal. Now enforcing discipline, now encouraging his troops in the onset, and now on foot at the head of the charging columns, perilling his life like the meanest soldier; he strained every nerve to resist the advance of his overpowering adversary. He had arrived at Bayonne, and taken command of the disorganized and humbled army in July. Immediately organizing it, he broke like a torrent into Spain, fought seven pitched battles, lost thirty thousand men, and in December was again at Bayonne, showing a firm front to the enemy. For five months he had struggled against the most overwhelming obstacles—fought with troops that would have ruined the cause of a less stern General—struck blows that even against the odds they were directed, well nigh gave him the victory; and amid the complaints of the soldiers and the desertion of his German troops, never once gave way to discouragement. Self-sustained and resolute, his iron will would bend before no reverses, and in that last struggle for Napoleon in Spain and France, and his masterly retreat, he has placed himself among the first military chieftains of the world. It is true, he preferred a less laborious field, and one where constant defeat was not to be expected, and wrote to Napoleon, requesting to be near him. But no one could supply his place, and he was compelled to struggle on. He then submitted a plan for the defence of France to the Emperor, which the latter, it seems, had not time to attend to, and instead of rendering aid to his distressed General, drew away a large force to assist in the defence of Paris. But Soult had served under Massena in Genoa, and knew how to endure. With his army thinned by the demands of Napoleon and constant desertion—in the midst of a murmuring population, he bore up with a constancy that fills the mind with wonder and admiration. To his requests for help, Napoleon at last replied: "*I have given you my confidence, I can do nothing more.*" Never was confidence more worthily bestowed; and though left in such peril, Soult continued to dispute bravely the country over which he retreated from Bayonne, and at Orthez burst on the enemy with such impetuosity that he well nigh gained the victory. Retiring, fighting as he went, he at length entrenched himself at Toulouse, and here, after Napoleon's abdication, though before the news had reached him, fought the famous battle of Toulouse.

Each side claimed the victory; but, according to English historians themselves, Wellington's loss was far greater than Soult's; and the latter was ready the next morning to begin the fight while the former was not. As the two armies thus stood menacing each other the news of Napoleon's abdication arrived. Soult, however, not having received authentic and full information of the terms of the abdication, refused to make any change in his operations, except to grant an armistice till farther reports could be received. Even if Napoleon had abdicated, he did not know that the Bourbons would be reinstated, or that the army should not retain its present hostile attitude. In this uncertain state of affairs, the two leaders again prepared for battle; but the useless waste of blood was spared by orders from the minister of War; and Soult delivered up his command to the Duke of Angoulême. As before remarked, he struck the last blow, and fired the last cannon shot, for Napoleon and the Empire.

His conduct at Waterloo has caused many remarks, and subjected him to some heavy accusations. But the most that can be made of it is, that he did not act with his accustomed vigour. At Waterloo he was not the hero of Austerlitz.

Soult has committed many errors; and it could not well be otherwise. A life passed in such an agitated political sea as his has been, must now and then exhibit some contradictions and inconsistencies. But these minor faults are buried beneath his noble deeds; and his blood so freely shed on so many battle-fields for France —the great talents he has placed at the service of his country—and the glory with which he has covered her armies, will render him dear to her long after his eventful life has closed.

The Duke of Dalmatia is now seventy-seven years of age; and though he has resigned his office of Minister of War, he is still President of the Council, and takes an active part in the political affairs of France.

Nothing shows more plainly the ridiculous self-conceit of English historians in drawing a paral le**i** between Wellington and Bonaparte, merely because the former won the battle of Waterloo, or rather, was Commander-in-Chief when it *was* won—than this long struggle between him and Soult in Spain. The French Marshal showed himself a match for him at any time; nay, beat him oftener and longer than he was beaten. The advantage, if any, was on the side of the French Marshal; for while he possessed equal coolness and prudence, he carried greater force in his onsets. Yet who would think of drawing a parallel between Soult and Napoleon, with the least intention of making them equal. Wellington was no ordinary general; and he receives all the merit he deserves, when put beside Soult as an equal. Pitted against each other for years, they were so nearly balanced, that there seems little to choose between them; but to place either beside Napoleon as his equal, excites a smile in any one but an Englishman.

www.ingramcontent.com/pod-product-compliance
Lightning Source LLC
Chambersburg PA
CBHW031852220426
43663CB00006B/591